HELLFIRE CORNER

Reminiscences of Wartime in South-east England

Roy Humphreys

Compiled by *Ken Flint*

Line illustrations by *Gos Wilson*

ALAN SUTTON PUBLISHING LIMITED

First published in the United Kingdom in 1994
Alan Sutton Publishing Ltd
Phoenix Mill · Far Thrupp · Stroud · Gloucestershire

First published in the United States of America in 1994
Alan Sutton Publishing Inc.
83 Washington Street · Dover · NH 03820

British Library Cataloguing in Publication Data

A catalogue record for this book is available from the British Library.

ISBN 0–7509–0671–5

Library of Congress Cataloging in Publication Data applied for

Typeset in 11/13 Bembo.
Typesetting and origination by
Alan Sutton Publishing Limited.
Printed in Great Britain by
Butler & Tanner, Frome, Somerset.

Contents

Preface   v

Glossary   vi

Acknowledgements   vii

Chapter One
'Fuse all warheads – prepare for war'   1

Chapter Two
'Don't be a bloody fool'   16

Chapter Three
'. . . who's got my eye?'   58

Chapter Four
'We go to change our knickers'   76

Chapter Five
'What – no bleeding bluebirds?'   101

Chapter Six
'Hey – there's some Jenny Wrens here!'   134

Epilogue   179

Index   181

*History with its flickering lamp stumbles along
the trail of the past, trying to reconstruct its
scenes, to revive its echoes, and rekindle with
pale gleams the passion of former years.*

Winston S. Churchill

Preface

Several books exist recording the ordeal of the Dover area during its long years in the country's front line. Some have been written by historians, and some by those who participated in those momentous happenings. But the latter have tended to be persons who served in at least a semi-senior capacity. As far as I am aware Dover's wartime story has never been presented by the lower-deck, the rank and file, the citizens of the area.

So this is an attempt to do just that. Some of the contributions have been solicited, but the majority have been culled from letters written in the course of arranging reunions for all three Services in Dover. But a word of warning might be appropriate. They are essentially memories, mostly taken straight from the mind and rarely from diaries or notes. But because they are treasured memories, or proud recollections of duty ably done, they have no doubt been taken out of store occasionally, dusted off and given a loving polish to restore their wartime lustre.

Apart from the lucky Women's Royal Naval Service (WRNS) and matelots, the daily chore of polishing a brass cap badge will be recalled by all. When first issued, the details of the design and lettering were sharp and clear but with constant vigorous polishing these became blurred at the edge. Quite apart from the extra status this proof of long service gave, this smoothing over of the badge lent an extra sheen to the polished metal. The same holds true for the treasured memories of Dover's wartime garrison. Time has mellowed them, without altering their basic structure, and imparted a wonderful glow.

But the memory can deceive, for nostalgia can often sweeten the past with sentiment. Surprisingly, however, many ex-servicemen and women have a balanced view of the war, without forgetting the pain of prolonged loneliness, separation from their loved ones, nor the personal frustrations during the forced intervals of inaction.

For most of them there was no concept of death or glory as the American films romanticized. In its place was planted a more mature sense of duty and of purpose, where discipline, although not entirely pleasurable, was considered acceptable none the less.

KEN FLINT
White Cliffs Veterans

Glossary

AA	Anti-aircraft	MP	Military Police (red-caps)
ACP	Admiralty Civil Police	MTB	Motor Torpedo Boat
AFS	Auxiliary Fire Service	NAAFI	Navy, Army, and Air Force
AIG	Assistant Instructor Gunnery		Institute
ARP	Air Raid Precautions	NCO	Non-Commissioned Officer
ASR	Air Sea Rescue	NFS	National Fire Service
ATS	Auxiliary Training Service	NSPCC	National Society for Prevention
	(Women)		of Cruelty to Children
BEF	British Expeditionary Force	Oppo	Colleague (slang)
BEM	British Empire Medal	PAC	Parachute and Cable (rocket)
CD	Civil Defence	PC	Pioneer Corps
CMP	Corps of Military Police	PPI	Plan Position Indicator
CO	Commanding Officer		(Radar)
CPFRE	Cinque Ports Fortress Royal	RA	Royal Artillery
	Engineers	RAMC	Royal Army Medical Corps
CPO	Chief Petty Officer (Naval)	RAOC	Royal Army Ordnance Corps
CRS	Casualty Reception Station	RASC	Royal Army Service Corps
Deolali Tap	Mentally deficient (slang)	RE	Royal Engineers (sappers)
DR	Despatch Rider (Royal Signals)	REME	Royal Electrical Mechanical
ENSA	Entertainments National		Engineers
	Services Association	RM	Royal Marines
FANY	First Aid Nursing Yeomanry	RN	Royal Navy
Floaters	Sea Mines	RNPS	Royal Naval Patrol Service
GHQ	General Headquarters	RNR	Royal Naval Reserve
GOC	General Officer Commanding	RNVR	Royal Naval Volunteer
HAA	Heavy Anti-aircraft Artillery		Reserve
HE	High Explosive	RS	Royal Signals
HG	Home Guard	SM	Sergeant-Major
Hispano	Heavy calibre machine gun	Sparks	Wireless Operator (slang)
HQ	Headquarters	TA	Territorial Army
IFF	Identification Friend or Foe	USAAF	United States Army Air Force
LDV	Local Defence Volunteers	V1	Pilotless aircraft (German)
Lt.	Lieutenant	WAAF	Women's Auxiliary Air Force
Lt. Cmdr.	Lieutenant-Commander (Royal	WEC	Women's Executive Council
	Navy)	WLA	Women's Land Army
Luftwaffe	German Air Force	WRNS	Women's Royal Naval Service
Matelot	Sailor (slang)	W/T	Wireless Telegraphy
MGB	Motor Gun Boat	WVS	Women's Voluntary Service
ML	Motor Launch	YMCA	Young Men's Christian
MM	Military Medal		Association

Acknowledgements

The flicker of emotion when re-visiting a wartime venue, whether a naval port, barracks or airfield, almost without exception swiftly conveys the memory back to those formative years where nostalgia lurks in every corner.

We acknowledge with gratitude the help and ready co-operation of the following:

Muriel Golding (née Sidwell); Charles Seyd; Sidney Fisher; H. Clarke; H. Kennedy; Eddy King; P.A. Boys; H.W. Sneller; Len Gower; Ron Somers; Ted Codgell; Robert Sheppard; W. Sandford; William Smith; Peter Spittal; Bernard Harrison; Norman Morris; Fred Tuffey; H. Cossens; Peter Erwood; R.H. Charters; F. Featherbe; Alf Floyd; Jim Elkin; George McIntosh; R.A. Smith; A. Tribe; J. Timberly; Ron Murray; Thomas Cosker; John Payne; Bert French; Lieutenant-Colonel R.W. Swale; Bill Jenkins; Cyril Burden; Cecil Coble; 'Pip' Johnson; Vera Selwood (née Boyce); Arthur Scholes; Harold Michaels; James Smith; H. Burden; Edward Greenstreet; Harold Clay; Jim Harris; Vic Pugh; Harold Firman; Winnie Blackwell (née Middleditch); Stella Ramsey (née Barker); Stanley Saunders; M. Griffiths; Les Wood; Arthur Bridges; Wilfred Ellis; A. Thomas; Richard Shotton; Ruth Stokes (née Buchan); Gwenneth Preece (née Salisbury); Mary Guy (née Evans); William Jacobs; Luke Walsh; W. Cousens; Brenda Hallum (née Sparkman); Donald Smith; Eric Miller; J. Head; William Ellis; Stanley Blacker; Jim Roberts; Tom Stratford; Jean Atkins (née Aitchison); Joyce Spriggs (née Lancaster); William Martin; Ken Nicholson; Gladys Critchell; Olga Kaye; D. Mann; Cliff Durbin; Winifred Crisp (née Lygo); Maurice Gilbraith; Kathleen Higgins (née Cosgrove); Joan Oakley (née Rogers); P. Watling; John P. Dimmer (USA); Paul Alexa (USA); Robert W. Fiske (USA); Alfred Bricker (USA); Carl Hiller (USA); Larry Alcott; Robert Stamp; Charles Hutchings; Basil Carey; Joan Lidiard (née Faulkner); Lorna Dawes (née Hawley); Larry Kettley; Joan Tyson (née Frost); Elsie Curtis (née Mawson) BEM; Warren Rodgers; Mary Holt; John Stoddart; J.W. Ellis; Frank Young; Robert Waugh; Len Hale; A. Olive; Eric Folkson; J. Peglar; S. Rogers; Dick Beardon; C. Tilley; Ron Warren; S. Morgans; Albert Fisher; Brian Kemp;

Jimmie Kay; R. Coyles; Gwen Mackett (née West); R. Derek-Roberts; C. Broom; Jack Pickup; Lillian Stone (née Foster); May Owen (née Pridmore); Fred Griffiths; Edith Ring (née Dossett); Olive Rayner (née Hudson); N. Robb; Mrs Burchell; John Pullen; Douglas Camm; Bill Lucas; John Nicholson; Ernest Hutchinson MBE; A.E. Whittamore; Brian Best; Harry Fewtrey; John Whitehouse; G. Wild; Joe Miller; Norman Glen; John Cheney; H. Batty; Betty Taylor (née Kirby); Alan Styles; John Glover; Fred Sargeant; Rosemary Fellowes (née Keyes); John S. Lucas; Cecil Rowe; Jack Foster; Albert Kingston; H. Shaw; Jim Harris; Ted White; Kathleen May (née Hubbard); L. Pearce; B.K. Pearce; Bill Warbrick; Patrick Churchill; Ted Ashton; Lila Marshall; Robert Murphy; Eunice Mercer; R.G. Crane; Herbert A. Till; Colonel L. McP. Fordyce OBE.

Winston Churchill (outside Dover's town hall), said in a radio broadcast in July 1940, 'This is no war of chieftains, of princes, or dynasties, or national ambitions: it is a war of people and of causes'.

CHAPTER ONE

'Fuse all warheads – prepare for war'

While Britain and France were only just emerging from the state of atrophy caused by the First World War, Adolf Hitler's superhuman will had led the German people swiftly towards war. Pushing relentlessly ahead with a programme of military expansion and modernization, by 1939 he had transformed the Wehrmacht into the most formidable war machine that the world had yet seen

Hitler's ruthless transformation of Germany into a unique power that came eventually to dominate Europe and send tendrils of evil worldwide, gave good reason for Winston Churchill to describe it as 'the greatest tragedy' in the history of mankind.

The endless discussions by politicians over the Munich crisis and the culmination of the policy of appeasement left the British people with few illusions about what to expect if war was declared with Germany. The prospect worsened after Neville Chamberlain's sad voice was heard on the wireless on Sunday 3 September 1939, proclaiming war.

'Peace for our time' rapidly became 'war in our time' as countless civilians promptly signed up to join the armed services. The Territorial Army (TA) units were the first to move on to a war footing, but before long, however, and for the first time in British history, military conscription was imposed.

By then the professional experts in all things military had updated their figures to reveal a most disturbing aspect of unpreparedness. It was a well-known British condition known as complacency, bordering on inactivity, with lax stewardship leading to improvisation.

When the news broke that Britain had finally decided to confront Hitler, the ferry-boats plying between England and Continental Europe were crammed with returning holiday-makers and British Expeditionary Force (BEF) troops. Despite written instructions to 'stay put', many families began to move from the vulnerable areas into the countryside. The wealthier elected to travel overseas, principally to North America, while the less fortunate came under the Government Evacuation Scheme, which was seen initially as voluntary.

Inconceivably naïve was the scheme to send thousands of schoolchildren down to the south-east coastal towns from the heavily populated London areas.

Both Folkestone and Dover were to receive them. In reality – due in part to worried mothers refusing to send them – only a fraction of the estimated 20,000 actually arrived.

There were perhaps people in the British Isles who felt slight twinges of guilt over the invasions of Poland and Czechoslovakia. In the south east of England, however, there was a growing feeling of apprehension, war being the main topic of conversation, largely influenced by the rapid influx of troops and destroyers arriving at Dover.

Kent, the nearest county to Europe, often described in travel brochures as the 'Garden of England', almost overnight became the 'Guardian of England'. The population, both civilian and military, was to endure countless enemy actions in an area which was soon to become known as 'Hellfire Corner'.

Edward Greenstreet had joined the Cinque Ports Fortress (TA) Royal Engineers (CPFRE) in 1938. He was one of the first called up under the Emergency Act, and ten days prior to the declaration of war was posted to the Dover breakwater to assist gunners of 'A' Battery 519 Coast Regiment RA:

I remember I was notified on a Thursday – pay day – at approximately 4.30 p.m. to report to Dover. About fifteen of us arranged to meet. We caught the 7.00 p.m. bus to Dover, all refusing to pay the fare! We eventually arrived at the Lord Warden Hotel on the then Dover bus route. We must have visited all the pubs, arriving at Archcliff Fort at 11.00 p.m. where we were given bread, cheese and a mug of cocoa, and then sent off to the Prince of Wales Pier around midnight.

Kinson's motor boat took us out to the breakwater. After an hour spent cleaning the barrack room (which had been used as an ironmonger's store), we attempted to sleep with only groundsheets and two blankets on the concrete floor. After three weeks of this, palliasses and straw were supplied, and later bed-boards and trestles with sheets, then later still came the hammocks. Comfort at last!

One morning I went sick and the doctor came out by boat and said I had German measles (how unpatriotic!). I was then instructed to pack a small pack with towels etc. and a truck on the pier took me to the Dover Isolation Hospital for a week. Before I left the breakwater I had a wash and shave. About five others used the same shaving water but they didn't manage to catch the measles.

Kinson's boat made three trips daily with rations, shore fatigues, parties for those off duty, taking the sick to the doctor ashore. Also a daily shoe box of fishing worms arrived at a cost of two shillings and sixpence [12½p]. About ten of us split the cost. Whilst unloading the boat one day, in half a gale, we managed to drop half a barrel of beer into the sea. Luckily it was clawed back, though several chaps got wet through in the process. Another boat came out once a week with water for our storage tank; it also brought paraffin and petrol for the engines. This was not a pleasant job, especially

'. . . unloading the boat one day, in half a gale, we managed to drop a half barrel of beer into the sea.'

during the winter months, when paraffin spills soaked the men's overalls. I recall once several chaps were thawing out after unloading gallons of this highly volatile stuff, and someone threw a lighted match on to another's lap. He quickly burst into flames but had the presence of mind to run out and jump into the sea. Twice the engine room had fires as a result of leaks on to red-hot manifolds, but these were usually contained within about twenty minutes.

Police Constable Richard Crane, Folkestone Borough Police, recalls the war situation was accepted by the civilians after the German Army invaded Poland – the reason for Britain declaring war, although matters in Western Europe were fairly quiet:

There were some few incidents which showed the public being conscious of the situation. For example, the manager of a local store caused consternation by pretending to send a message in Morse code to a person in a hotel over-looking the sea.

Inebriated, he created the stir as a prank to fool some soldiers and civilians who had been watching him. He refused to give his name and address, and as the bystanders were quite hostile towards him I took him into custody as being likely to cause a breach of the peace.

The Government was slowly preparing for the real war. Large unoccupied houses in the west end of the town were soon requisitioned and army units moved in. There was a complete blackout operating during the hours of darkness, creating a situation which vandals and petty thieves were not slow to exploit.

A sixteen-year-old alien who had been staying in Wiltshire wandered into the town and became lost in the harbour area. It was a genuine slip on his part, but the interest his presence caused indicated that war fever might emerge, despite the apparent calm on the Continent.

For use on night duty I purchased from Tickers of Northampton a pair of handmade leather boots which had crepe soles, the only footwear at that time to do so. I was able to move about quietly, and if necessary, with speed.

About eleven o'clock at night on one occasion, I was standing at the corner of the High Street and Tontine Street, talking to a colleague, when our conversation was interrupted by the noise of breaking glass. A soldier was eventually arrested but the sergeant refused to accept the charge of wilful damage because the offender was not seen to commit the offence.

The public were inclined to get careless regarding the blackout regulations, but if there was something unusual going on someone would soon report it to the police. A Corporation lavatory cleaner drew my attention to a man in French naval uniform who was taking pictures in the harbour area. He proved to be on leave from the French Navy and was accompanied by an English woman who was said to be the wife of another French naval officer. I was told the photographs were of Folkestone fishermen, but as the officer did not have a permit to take pictures I seized the film.

The police telephone system continuously received messages of alleged suspicious men in motor cars seen in all kinds of prohibited areas. Folkestone was a prohibited area at that time and could only be entered by means of a special permit. There were military check-points on the roads and the police covered the railway stations. At night on the roads adjacent to the seafront soldiers patrolled with fixed bayonets. On frequent occasions on the darkest nights, night duty coppers were often jolted out of their skins while they tested shop doors by the sudden command, 'Halt, who goes there?'. I remember the retort of one policeman who was confronted by two or three soldiers with fixed bayonets held out in front of them. He was so irritated he replied, 'Put that bloody thing away before you kill somebody!'.

Members of the pre-war Territorials, however, had continued to visit their local drill hall where they practised on outdated weaponry to a high pitch of efficiency. Dovorian A. Oliver, one of the enthusiasts in the local TA, was raring to meet the challenge:

I was working at my civvy job of storekeeper at the Elms Vale Building Co. when a despatch rider drove up and said I was to report to the TA drill hall at once. War had not been declared but the Territorials had been called out. I went home, changed into my uniform, and reported. We collected sandbags, hurricane lamps and other kit, and East Kent buses took us up to the Farthingloe gun-sites where we worked in shifts getting everything ready for action.

There were no tents; we slept in the bus or under hedges until they arrived. By the time war actually was declared we were ready – five rounds loaded, and one 'up the spout'.

Alert to the excitement of the possibility of war on his own doorstep, Frank Young exuded boyish enthusiasm:

Just about a month or two before the war started (I lived at 2 Athol Terrace, right on the seafront) they put three or four big dredgers in the harbour, thoroughly dredged it right through, and a week or so before the war began they put a whole load of buoys in there, which we thought was strange.

I had just started work after leaving school at 14 and was working for Bowhills Garage in Snargate Street. I was a petrol pump attendant and in those days it was hand-pumped. I had to be there at 8 o'clock on the Sunday morning to do my morning shift, so got up just after 7 o'clock. My brother and I had the bedroom right at the top of the house facing the sea, and when I looked out of the window the harbour was full of ships. It had just literally filled up overnight with Navy ships and we never heard a thing. I woke my brother up and said, 'Here – have a look at this'. My brother stirred and mumbled, 'Don't wake me up'. But when he eventually looked out he nearly died of shock as well.

Working at the garage I was amazed how many private cars went across to France just before the war started. In those days they had to be emptied of all fuel and oil before being towed down to the Admiralty Pier or the Eastern Docks. I never quite understood the British people going on their holidays when war was imminent. You can guess that we sold a lot of petrol to the locals in the first week of the war, people were coming down to us with bottles and cans to stock up. Petrol rationing was not put on straight away, although it was anticipated.

My old boss, Mr Bowhill, nearly died of shock when war was announced on the wireless. All the cave shelters were still locked up, and when the air raid siren sounded he wanted to get into one. Of course, it was a false alarm. But it was not long afterwards that a ship was towed into harbour after having been badly damaged by a German submarine.

In every generation images of youth have a perennial appeal, recalling for the most part the good times and the sunny days when almost every day brought a new adventure, unhindered by austere newspaper reports of world affairs, suspicion or disillusionment. Muriel Sidwell was helping to assemble civilian gas masks at St James's Boys School in Russell Place, Dover, where her family lived then:

I had left Holy Trinity Girls' School (then known as Pier School) just before war began, and went to work at a small factory on the Lydden Stables site, where we were making horseradish sauce. I then got a job at a cleaners near the Market Square – the owner was said to be of German-Jewish descent. The firm was eventually closed down and the owner interned, but not before we had a works outing in a charabanc to Southend-on-Sea.

We arrived home to a practice blackout. Tin helmeted Air Raid Precautions (ARP) wardens were patrolling the streets, shouting to offenders to 'Put that light out!'. It was eerie to see people trying to find their way around with the help of torches. When war was declared – it was on a Sunday – we had moved to a basement flat in the High Street, where we had fixed our blackout curtains so that we could open the door on to the street without showing any light.

For reasons beyond my comprehension now I remember I wanted to be a heroine like Nurse Edith Cavell of the 1914–18 war. However, soon after the Prime Minister's broadcast the local air raid sirens went off and all the family went out on to the street. ARP wardens were dashing hither and thither, blowing whistles and telling people to 'Get under cover!'. Of course, it was a false alarm.

At that time there were a lot of young soldiers in the town, and mum and dad used to invite some of them to our flat for an evening to share a cup of

'Ordered to carry their tin hats, rifles and gas masks wherever they went; this caused some problems when they attempted to squeeze along between the rows of seats in the local cinemas.'

'. . . I was only fifteen years old then . . . a young cook often gave me suet pudding and custard, "to fatten me up".'

cocoa or Camp coffee with us, making our rations stretch enough to give them home-made cake or toast. There was little for them to do in what spare time they had except walk up and down the streets. Many of the shops in the town centre were already closed. The town was in darkness and they were so fed up.

Soon all the servicemen were ordered to carry their tin hats, rifles and gas masks wherever they went. This caused some problems when they attempted to squeeze along between the rows of seats in the local cinemas. Often the 'Alert' slide would suddenly flash up on the screen and then we would have to leave in a hurry. One film I never did see right through was about American aircraft workers; it was called 'Wings for the Eagle'.

The winter of 1940 was really bad. I was working in a fishmongers and poulterers in Biggin Street, and was once sent out to Green Lane, Buckland, to pick up a chicken. I found out when I got there it was still alive. I had a tremendous job chasing around the pen to catch it. I made regular deliveries to the Officers' Mess and the Sergeants' Mess at the Citadel Barracks. There was always an armed guard at the entrance but I had been given a pass. The kitchens were huge places with enormous long stoves in them. I was always a bit nervous of the soldiers working there. After all, I was only fifteen years old then. In the Sergeants' Mess a young cook often gave me suet pudding and custard, 'to fatten me up', he said. I recall some of them were going over to France with the BEF. By now soldiers were billeted all over the town, even as far as River. I used to deliver fish and sausages to most of them.

As early as 1932 Charles Seyd had joined the Royal Naval Volunteer Reserve (RNVR) in the London Division, and was quite used to being called up by the time war broke out. He had already reported for duty during the Abyssinian trouble, the Spanish Civil War and the Munich Crisis of 1938:

> I served on Admiral Ramsey's staff as a telegraphist RNVR, and recall receiving a signal from the Admiralty on 3 September 1939 to 'Fuse all warheads – prepare for war'. We arrived in Dover just one week before the war actually commenced. Our first enemies were the hordes of bats and rats that lived in the tunnels under the castle. It was known that the latter were big enough to jump up and reach the door handles. I used to double between the wireless office and the telephone switchboard, since I could speak French well enough to understand the operator in Calais.
>
> We had a WRN operator – a coder named Mary Clark. One day Mary brought me a signal which should have read 'HMS *Bulldog* is to proceed to . . . at moderate speed'. In fact the signal read 'HMS *Bulldog* is to proceed to . . . with moderate adultery'. I expressed the opinion that she had decoded the signal wrongly! Some years later (by which time I had become a Lieutenant-Commander) I met her again in Washington where she had just arrived via the French ship *Isle de France*, on which she was the cipher officer. Needless to say we had a joyful reunion, with a minimum of adultery I might add.

HMS *Plover* was a minelaying vessel, designed as such, and launched in 1937. Sidney Fisher joined her in 1939:

> Directly war broke out we loaded with mines and started laying them in the Firth of Forth, off Leith. Our crew was about seventy in total, regular sailors and reservists. A few weeks later we arrived in Dover and with the *Shepperton* and *Hampton* cross-Channel ferries started to lay mines as an anti-submarine barrier in the English Channel.
>
> The mines were set to stay about 90 feet below the sea surface. Inevitably, when we had stormy weather conditions some of them broke loose and became 'floaters', which were highly dangerous to our own shipping. Once we had the unwelcome job of collecting two floaters washed up on the beach at Deal. We towed one back to Dover but the other was so high up on the beach that it had to be loaded on to a Royal Navy (RN) lorry to be taken away. Not a very easy operation.
>
> Then there was the occasion we had collected a mine and strung it up on the port deck. After it was taken away all the ship's metal fittings had to be removed. The mine was one of Jerry's new magnetic ones. Shortly after that the ship was fitted with degaussing gear, miles of thick cable wrapped around the hull. This suppressed the magnetic field of the ship and defeated the magnetic mine threat. But it was a serious threat for a while.

Minelayers were dangerous homes, but we were a happy ship and the people of Dover were good to us and very friendly. We had many good singsongs in the local pubs and plenty of good food: eggs and chips, sausage and chips for only ninepence [4p].

After one good evening, and too much beer, I missed my footing getting into the liberty boat. *Plover* was at anchor and not moored at the time. I fell into the harbour – a sure cure for drunks in winter-time. I saw my cap floating away and, since it would have cost about half a day's pay to replace it, I dived in to rescue it.

Another *Plover* matelot, H. Clarke, recalled the time they were doing a night run in the Dover Strait, loaded with mines, but finished up on the notorious Goodwin Sands just before midnight:

I had the middle watch and was down below. It was clear and moonlight – we thought Jerry must see us and we were scared he would open fire. We waited and sweated it out. Two tugs came out from Dover but could do nothing to help. It was six o'clock the next morning before we floated off the sands. Back in Dover we tied up at the Eastern Arm. We went ashore and walked along the deserted sea front to find a pub open with beer in stock.

'. . . I saw my cap floating away and, since it would have cost about half a day's pay to replace it, I dived in to rescue it.'

Laying mines in the Dover Strait was a serious business. A. Kennedy served on the *Shepperton* ferry, and one of his best memories was of two local girls trying to buy him beer. Although he refused he was unaware that the girls had gathered money to entertain the crew.

Sid Fisher thought the Dover people were really wonderful:

> We had some great nights in the local pubs, in fact, some of the best singsongs I've ever had. 'Run Rabbit Run' and 'We're Going To Hang Out The Washing On The Siegfried Line' were just two of the early war tunes that really caught on. I will always remember the good times, like the snowballing on the dockside with the kids starting it and then everyone joining in. Making safe the mines that washed ashore. On one occasion, civilians watching us passed round the hat. But our warrant officer did not allow us to keep the money. Instead, he sent it to a Navy charity. A local publican, however, left his doors open while the 'bobbies' turned a blind eye. We made the most of a few 'duty free' pints at the publican's expense.

From all walks of life men and women were suddenly thrown together to exert their unused skills and untested abilities. For many their wartime experiences were rich in emotion, a life-style which was totally alien to their humdrum lives in a pre-war social structure of sometimes public indifference. But they soon found new qualities in themselves, expertise that would have remained dormant and totally concealed from their peers in peacetime. They also mixed with other classes and nationalities, the majority of whom they would never otherwise have met.

Almost without exception members of the armed services and civilians alike remember the three cinemas in Dover, the Regent in London Road, the Granada in Castle Street and the Plaza in Biggin Street. The King's Hall in Biggin Street had burned down before the war began. It was almost ready to reopen in September 1939 but the Admiralty decided to use it as a Royal Naval Gunnery School instead. In addition to the cinemas there was the unique Royal Hippodrome in Snargate Street, a particularly fine old theatre seating 580, about which a former patron wrote, 'The bar under the stage had such a unique atmosphere that the finest war artistes of Britain and America, try as they did, could not get it down on paper. It defied English theatrical tradition and allowed artistes to come in wearing stage make-up and costumes to have a drink with the civilians and servicemen from the audience'.

It was one of the few privately owned theatres in the country. It had a stalls and pit area, a circle and four boxes with a gallery above. There was a bar on each level plus public bars with entrances in Snargate Street and Northampton Street. It was in the latter that artistes could meet the public. By over-ordering the theatre managed to keep the bars well stocked, although there was never enough. Quite often the bar takings exceeded the admission fees to the theatre. Dick Whittamore was fourteen in 1939, and had just started work as a page boy at five shillings a week:

I can remember the first air raid warning at eleven o'clock on 3 September, the day war was declared. Everyone dashed for the nearby shelter caves not knowing what to expect. There had been the threat of war a year earlier, air raid shelters had been prepared and gas masks issued. We all hoped we would never need them, especially after Mr Chamberlain's return from Germany, with his famous 'peace in our time' message.

Heavy black paper was used to black out all the windows at the theatre, neon signs were disconnected and the large chandelier hanging in the auditorium was taken down – just in case. The theatre was closed for the first week of the war but reopened on Tuesday 12 September, with a hurriedly put together show, aptly named 'Black Out The Blues', which starred Robin Richmond with his electric organ.

A five piece orchestra accompanied the acts and comprised Charlie Haynes (leader and first violin), Bob Page (pianist), Harry Chandler (trumpet), Bill Delahaye (clarinet), and Mr Cooper (second violin). Unfortunately the drummer left at the outbreak of war and was never replaced. The drum kit remained in situ and another member of the orchestra used to lean across to hit the cymbal or give a drum roll where necessary. Charlie Haynes never missed a performance, despite living out of town at Kennington near Ashford. He arrived each evening in an old car for which he received a petrol ration.

Secondary lighting was supplied by gas, so on the several occasions when the main electricity failed, usherettes and staff were obliged to stand on chairs or be lifted up to light the gas jets in their ornate brackets. There were no mantels so the illumination was quite feeble. There were no Ladies lavatories in the gallery either. I often wondered how the ladies managed during an air raid or a shelling bombardment. Soldiers on low wages were forced to take their girl-friends up to the 'Gods' as it was all they could afford.

The stage manager was Harry Spain, who remained throughout the war, then there was George Sidders the cellarman and stage-hand, Mrs Hanson the elderly cleaning lady who, although she was disabled, never missed a day's work. Nobby Grainger was electrician and spotlight operator, while the usherettes and other staff changed frequently. Occasionally someone would throw a coin or two on the stage to indicate what they thought of a particular act, at other times there were catcalls or disparaging remarks made. In either case most were taken in good part and there were never any fights or vandalism. Strippers were usually told to, 'Get 'em off!' or words to that effect – all good humour in a wartime atmosphere.

Particularly noticeable in the first months of the war was the rising price of sugar from two pence to eight pence per pound (1p to 3½p). Shortages of imported goods were also evident as rationing was introduced. Bananas were not seen for years, ice cream was banned and sweets were eventually rationed. We all carried Identity Cards. There was soon a noticeable shortage of men and we soon began to see conductresses on the buses, known as 'clippies'. Shops routinely closed at lunchtime because of staff shortages and the last buses left the town at nine o'clock. Walking into lamp-posts – although they were ringed with white paint – was not a pleasurable experience and gave a nasty shock and sometimes a bloody nose!

Eddie King, a local man, had joined the 1st Cinque Ports Fortress (TA) Royal Engineers in 1933. He had attended the usual weekends and drill nights at the local drill hall, wearing a uniform that had not changed in style since the First World War:

> My mobilization station was the Knuckle end of the Dover breakwater and I was on the engine-room staff. At that time, and during the early months of the war, the generators were paraffin-operated Crossley engines. They were started on petrol and as soon as the exhaust-heated vaporization box was warm enough they were switched to paraffin. The Crossley engines were also used at Langdon Hole above East Cliff.
>
> The oldest engines were the ones in use at Langdon Barracks. These were Tangyes single-cylinder hot-bowl engines. They were started by using a blow-lamp. It was a slow process getting them started and we used to run them thirty minutes before lighting-up time and continue running them half an hour after sunrise each morning. On a winter night they would use ninety gallons of fuel.
>
> By the outbreak of war, however, the Archcliff Fort engine-room had up-to-date Ruston Hornby diesels and later on the Eastern Arm engine-room had a similar model installed.
>
> Like most TA units we were mobilized as a precaution at the start of the Munich crisis in 1938, and had to man our own stations. This was my first spell of living on the breakwater. Then in the following year we were called up permanently and I served at the Knuckle and at Langdon until the Royal Artillery took over the manning of engine-rooms and searchlights in 1940.
>
> The maintenance of the engine-rooms and searchlights was still left to the RE, and a Royal Engineers Repair Party was formed from the old CPFRE. We were based at the old Garrison Engineers' building at Archcliff Fort. There were about twelve of us electricians and fitters altogether. I was corporal engine-room artificer by then, and Staff Sergeant Hudson was in charge of the party.
>
> At this time coastal artillery was a matter of the highest importance. Generators had to be installed all along the coast. Our task, apart from local duties, was to install the new Lister generators in positions from Winchelsea to Herne Bay. Engine-beds and engine-rooms were built by civilian contractors and then we put in the engines and lights. We witnessed many incidents from Archcliff Fort – the sinking of the destroyer *Codrington*, the damage inflicted on the *War Sepoy*, which was eventually sunk as a blockship in the harbour; we saw the ships returning from Dunkirk with their terrible casualties on board, and numerous dive-bombings of convoys, and the buildings blitzed in Dover.

P.A. Boys was a gunner in the Territorial Kent and Sussex Heavy Brigade, and on 24 August 1939 was called up and sent to Dover. He went to the breakwater while others were sent to Langdon Battery.

It was still peacetime and the ferryboats were running as normal. In those days the trains ran right onto the ferryboats. When war came he was a member of the crew manning two 6-in guns. He wrote:

We also had Lewis and Vickers machine guns and of course one rifle per man. There was also a museum piece of a Vickers gun that fired two-pound shells – when it was not out of action due to frequent jamming. All our food, water and supplies had to be brought out to us by boat as we were, quite literally, out at sea. We watched the men of the British Expeditionary Force going over to France on the ships that had been ferryboats. Little did we suspect that well within a year they would be coming back from Dunkirk in a motley collection of vessels of all types. Nobody who witnessed the return of these men can forget the experience. During this time I saw a destroyer loaded with returning soldiers rammed by another ship leaving harbour from the Prince of Wales Pier. Many were flung into the sea and lost their lives – tragic to be within sight of safety and then be killed. The first boat I saw sunk in the English Channel was in convoy, and it was cut in half by a ship returning from France.

We nearly always got warning that Dover was about to be bombed because German fighters would come over and start to shoot down the barrage balloons, to leave the way clear for their dive-bombers.

Many ships were hit, some sunk and some damaged. Lord Haw Haw boasted in his broadcasts that HMS *Breakwater* had been sunk! Of course it is still there today but minus its weapons and the observation towers. We had a machine gun mounted on one tower, and it was not the best place to be when the Germans fired their cross-Channel guns. We could estimate the arrival time of the shell by counting the seconds after the distant explosion. If they were firing to land in Dover we would hear the shell whistle overhead. It was the ones you did not hear that you said 'That was close!'.

Luck played a big part in it. I have always remembered Major Stiles who, after a bombing raid that was meant to obliterate Dover, paraded every man on the top deck of the breakwater afterwards, and said, 'If any man can stand up and say he wasn't afraid, he is either a fool or a liar – I bloody well was!'.

We were in a wonderful position to make friends with crews of destroyers, and I recall going on board the following, or having their crews visit us: HMS *Codrington*, *Beagle*, *Boreus*, *Boadicea* and *Brilliant*.

Going ashore we went by small boat to the Prince of Wales Pier. Landing back on the breakwater in bad weather was quite a feat and a measure of good luck and exact timing was needed. Once ashore, the first place we made for was the Sailors' Rest in Snargate Street, for a 'cuppa'. From there, half way down on the left, was the 'Sally Ann' where you could get something to eat.

Close by were the air raid shelters that went right under the cliffs. We would occasionally sleep there if we could not get back to the breakwater at night. Across the road was the Hippodrome Theatre where we saw some good shows. In those days a nude on the stage only moved when the lights were dimmed or out. How times have changed! We would also make for the Market Square and the cafe on the corner, run by two girls, or perhaps pay a visit to the pictures. Because of the bombing and shelling there was not a lot to do, so if we came ashore we would either get a bus or else walk to Capel. After living on an area only twenty-five feet wide this was a wonderful change.

On the breakwater we would have been very much on our own. You had to know the ways of the sea or you could quite easily have been washed off. Our first casualty went that way. Sailors used to say they did not want our job. We used to reply that at least we could not be sunk like them! One of the perks of the job, after a shelling, was collecting the stunned fish floating on the water. We would lower a boat and anyone going on leave would have plenty of fish to take home.

'One of the perks of the job, after a shelling, was collecting the stunned fish floating on the water.'

H.W. Sneller joined the 75th Anti-Aircraft (AA) Regiment RA on 24 August 1939:

We had one 3.7-inch gun for practice at the Dover drill hall (formerly a sea-plane hangar, before that a skating rink) but when called up we were issued with two 1916-pattern 3-inch guns with magslip dials for use with the Vickers predictor. These were sited at Frith Farm, Guston. Accommodation was in tents, but huts were rapidly erected. I remember shaving in cold water in the middle of a field, under a running tap that was our water supply before the ablutions were erected. Toilet arrangements were of a similar standard.

A guard was mounted at the drill hall for a while, the small detachment eating at a nearby cafe. With various other gunners I was soon involved with radar training. The first item was to sign the Official Secrets Act with due warning to us about security. As far as I can recollect the first half of our first radar was delivered to the drill hall in late 1939. That was the transmitter, the early radars consisting of separate transmitters and the more complicated receivers. We trainees were sent to a part finished and then abandoned AA site on Chitney Marshes, Iwade, where conditions seemed to us to be somewhat on par with a POW camp! I spent Christmas 1939 there and it was a bitter winter. We were returned to our units after learning very little, then a little while later were sent to Kingshill Camp near Chatham, where life was entirely different, with decent food, good sanitation, warm huts and so on, and we had a radar set that was complete and actually worked! The only problem was the almost total shortage of aircraft to practise on. There were few aircraft flying over Kent in those days.

Len Gower, Royal Artillery, recalled his favourite anecdote while serving on the breakwater:

Part of the daily routine was washing down the walkways. For this task we used to tie a bucket to a piece of rope, throw it into the sea and pull it up full of sea water. Some of the lads were not expert in securing the rope, with the result that one chap lost a bucket. He was charged with the offence of 'Losing Government Property by Neglect'. His ingenious defence was that the charge was wrongly framed as he had not lost the bucket. He knew exactly where it was – but couldn't get to it. Later when things hotted up, any missing buckets were written off as 'Lost Through Enemy Action'.

CHAPTER TWO

'Don't be a bloody fool'

By January 1940 everyone living in the south-east of England acknowledged that war was on their doorstep, despite the opinion of others living further away whose topic of conversation had now changed to more mundane issues. They bitterly complained about the black-out, made jokes about rationing, the evacuees and the air raid wardens. Anyone seen carrying a gas mask north of London was considered 'soft' and thousands of Anderson shelters were left in government store.

Severe weather conditions gripped the whole of Europe from December 1939 until about mid-February 1940. Great Britain had experienced its coldest winter for forty-five years, even the Dover Strait froze between Folkestone and Dungeness. Communications were completely disorganized by heavy snowfalls, bringing down hundreds of miles of telephone wires, and blocking railway tracks.

In the south-east, like other towns and cities throughout the country, large public buildings were faced with hundreds of sandbags to protect them from the devastation of bombs. Slit trenches appeared everywhere and in greater numbers on the coast where, in addition, defence structures brought a new night-time hazard to the civilian population.

The reservists – members of the Territorial Army, Navy and Air Force – were soon joined by women volunteers, suitably re-clothed in either khaki uniforms for the newly formed Auxiliary Territorial Service (ATS), navy-blue for the Women's Royal Naval Service (WRNS), or light-blue for the Women's Auxiliary Air Force (WAAF).

The reservists, male and female, suddenly found themselves dumped in some of the most inhospitable surroundings. But they soon accepted the inevitable and were determined to make the most of it, with a growing sense of resolution and the spirit of camaraderie.

Unity Mitford, the self-proclaimed admirer of Adolf Hitler, arrived at Folkestone harbour with a mysterious bullet wound in her neck. Young soldiers, who had just been issued with a rifle and bayonet, stood guard at the harbour barrier to prevent the journalists getting too close. Her father, Lord Redesdale, was there to whisk her away in an ambulance, away from prying eyes and back to the family seat. Lord Redesdale and his family had been subjected to much persecution as Nazi sympathizers, for he had wished for an Anglo-German understanding.

Unity's arrival reflected the undercurrents that often flowed beneath the surface of an otherwise pacifist climate which had prevailed between the wars. The soldiers on guard duty bore little resemblance to the intelligentsia of professional men and women, journalists, writers and broadcasters, whose propaganda was devoted to bringing about a peaceful revolution. They saw Hitler in a different light and firmly believed that many of the British governing class had more than a little sympathy with the Nazi regime.

The unpreparedness of our forces can be judged by one letter from Ron Somers, who had joined the 74th Field Regiment R.A.:

We moved down to Ash near Sandwich. We were billeted in the grounds of Brook House about half a mile from the village. Some were under canvas and the more fortunate were housed in hop-pickers huts or an oast house. The officers used Brook House itself. Our four 60-pounder guns were positioned by a narrow road at the rear of the house, well set into shallow pits dug into an embankment at the edge of an orchard. The pits were revetted with sand-bags and were carefully camouflaged. The guns' role was to cover Pegwell Bay. They were of First World War vintage and would have been capable of limited effect only, perhaps sustained fire for about half an hour. Small-arms ammunition was in short supply too. Probably we were regarded as expendable!

Ted Cogdell of the 55th Heavy Anti-Aircraft Regiment, wrote the following:

Our regiment consisted of three batteries, Nos 163, 164 and 165. No. 163 was mostly stationed at Dover, with the other two batteries at Rochester, Betteshanger, Folkestone, Canterbury and Whitstable. Once in a while we would be given a break from duty in Dover and would change places with the other batteries in slightly safer locations.

We had just been evacuated from Norway, and after a short leave left Scotland in convoy for an unknown destination. Two days' travelling found us beside the radar station on the white cliffs of Dover. Our Bofors guns were then deployed around the area of St Margaret's Bay, Dover Castle and the entrance to the breakwater – the latter location was only temporary.

Living conditions varied. Some of us lived in Nissen huts while others used tents. Considering the circumstances we were not too badly fed as we certainly had at least one hot meal each day, with of course, plenty of bully beef! One things that stands out in my memory are the mushrooms. I was in Troop HQ in a Nissen hut just down the lane from Swingate Inn, and any one of us gunners could go out early in the morning, and in fifteen minutes could fill a tea bucket (two-gallon stainless steel affairs) with fresh mushrooms. So it was mushrooms with everything. Fried, stewed, on toast, in milk, for breakfast, dinner, tea or supper. Any surplus we would take to the ration-wallah at Battery HQ and swap them for extra bacon or meat. Our cooks did

'. . . any one of us gunners could go out early in the morning, and in fifteen minutes could fill a tea bucket . . . with fresh mushrooms.'

their best, but considering that in Civvy Street they probably couldn't even toast bread, they were open to many suggestions. We had one particular cook who made large pies for dinner. The pastry crust was so hard that the pies were placed outside the hut door and used as a door mat. One of them served very well for about three weeks before it began to crumble!

We soon got used to the air raids, day after day – no respite for the ack-ack gunners. 'Stand-to' was before sunrise and 'Stand-down' was at sunset. But that was not the end of the day. Sirens would sound any time of the night or day and out we would have to tumble.

I was a despatch rider with 'B' Troop, 163 Battery, and when there was an air raid I had to go immediately to the gun-sites in order to collect their Engagement Reports (height of enemy aircraft, number, hits, ammunition etc). So more often than not I would be up on the cliffs looking over Dover and the English Channel. What sights I saw from up there. Perhaps it would be a convoy steaming through the Channel, with its own barrage balloon towed above for protection from enemy dive-bombers. But the Stukas would still come screaming down and try to damage the ships, sometimes with success. While this was going on our Spitfires and Hurricanes were doing their best to knock Jerry out of the sky. Vapour trails, dog-fights, the rat-tat-tat of machine guns, and of course, the black bursts of exploding ack-ack shells. The steady, measured beat of the pom-poms and the flashing trace [sic] of the Bofors shells going skywards remain vivid images never to be forgotten.

Then there were the huge cheers from the gunners when a plane with a swastika on it went screaming down to tumble into the sea. But there was no exultation if it proved to be one of ours. Just a silent and anxious scrutiny to see if the pilot's 'chute had opened.

Later there were the sneak raids – 'hit-and-run' we came to call them contemptuously. An Me 109 or Me 110, would flash hastily in and out, trying to shoot down a barrage balloon. I recall one barrage balloon that broke away from its moorings and went drifting across the town with its trailing steel cable ripping off roof tiles and chimney pots. The maverick balloon was eventually stopped by machine-gun fire.

With our powerful binoculars on a fine day we could see the chimney stacks on houses in Calais from St Margaret's Bay. We could also see enemy aircraft circling over Calais, building up height before crossing the Channel to make their attack. We would sigh with relief when the formation of maybe up to fifty-plus bombers would carry on over Dover to drop their bombs further inland.

Employed by a small firm of accountants in Dover, Fred Sargeant was informed by his boss that the commanding officer (CO) of the Port Security Unit of the Corps of Military Police (CMP) was looking for recruits:

I was 27 at the time so would not normally have been called up then, but I agreed to an interview and was accepted. I passed the medical exam at Canterbury A1 and reported back to the Unit Office on Dover seafront. Expecting to be sent to the local barracks I was surprised when the sergeant-major said I would be billeted in my own home. Next I was to see the Garrison Quartermaster at the castle for a uniform, cap badge and one stripe.

On the following day I was assigned to the Admiralty Pier Marine Station where there was a constant two-way flow of BEF troops arriving and departing. There were also a few refugees and other civilians who had to be segregated to pass through the Immigration Authority's check-point. We worked an eight-hour shift, and apart from a seventy-two hour leave period allotment now and again, this continued for over four years. An alternative tour of duty was patrolling the Eastern Dockyard which was used exclusively by the Royal Navy, under the surveillance of the Admiralty Civil Police (ACP). We used a small wooden hut just inside the dockyard gates, with a coal-burning stove on which to make tea and give us warmth on cold winter nights. The coal was obtained by filling buckets at night-time from the coal trucks in the nearby railway sidings. The ACP of course turned a blind eye to this, as they used the same supply.

This routine was broken on 26 May 1940 when the Dunkirk evacuation began in earnest. As the immigration office at the marine station was too small to cope with the number of refugees disembarking from an assortment of ships the town hall was used. There our job was to assist the immigration

officers by doing body searches for weapons or evidence of origin. Some of
them were soldiers who had lost their uniforms and all means of
identification. Any suspects were taken down to the police cells.

I was patrolling the Eastern Arm of the dockyard one afternoon, opposite
the RN Depot, when I heard approaching aircraft. Glancing up I saw three
Stuka dive-bombers above Langdon Bay and at less than 1,000 feet above the
cliffs. I immediately shouted, 'Take Cover!'. The nearest 'cover' was about
150 yards away in the cliffs behind the oil tanks, and although it meant
running towards the planes and the oil tanks I decided to make the dash. I
had just got into the cave entrance when the first bomb hit a ledge half way
up the cliff face, sending down a shower of chalk and putting the lights out in
the tunnel where excavations were going on. The next bomb sank a
minesweeper and the third just missed the MTB pens. I don't remember
hearing any anti-aircraft guns, they must have been taken by surprise. It was
all over in minutes. After the raid a local fisherman went out in a small boat
to pick up dozens of stunned fish. My share was a 3 lb mullet which helped
out with food rations that week.

The first enemy plane A. Oliver spotted was a Dornier, or 'Flying Pencil' as they
were nicknamed. 'He was flying too high for us to engage – the crafty beggar.'

Then the unit was posted to various sites away from Dover. But I was on
leave in the town one day, having sent my children to Wales, and brought just
my wife with me. We were going down Tower Hamlets Road over the
railway bridge when a Messerschmitt came over with guns blazing. I put my

Nicknamed the 'Flying Pencil', the Dornier 17z was frequently used for shipping strikes in the
Dover Strait in 1940/41.

tin hat on my wife and pushed her down. There are still marks in the fencing at Priory station that were made that day.

Another time my wife and I came back for a week's leave. Jerry came over very low and set fire to many of the barrage balloons. Being so low the ack-ack guns could not catch him until he went over the castle and was caught by the guns at St Margaret's Bay. Meanwhile, the burning balloons were dropping all around Dover. Our pet balloon, the one we used to call 'Lop Ears', came down over our roof and on to a house at the end of the street. I went over to help put out the fire. You could hear the RAF officer in charge shouting, 'A barrel of beer for the crew getting the first balloon back up!'

Both Frank Young and his brother joined the Local Defence Volunteers (LDV), but when they were re-named the Home Guard Frank's brother thought it was becoming too military, so they joined the Civil Defence (CD), Frank as a messenger boy and his brother as a warden at Z1 Post on the seafront:

We used to sleep in double bunk-beds and on a couple of occasions (I suppose we had upset the coppers), about 2 o'clock in the morning a couple of them would come in and put the light on while we were asleep, just to wake us up!

When anything happened it was usually my brother and I who were sent out to investigate. We used bicycles to discover where the incident was and scout around the area then came back and tell them what was wanted. They then passed the message on to HQ to inform them that an ambulance or fire engine was required.

The Sea Scouts used to have the old clock tower on the seafront as their HQ, and when we had time off – usually at weekends – we used to go there, especially when the Dunkirk caper was on. We sat at the windows watching the troops coming down the Prince of Wales Pier. They were in a state and that's a fact. The Sea Scouts had a 32-ft launch called *Stormcock* and we wanted to take her over to France, but the authorities wouldn't let us because we were too young.

I had the letter 'M' on my tin hat, and my brother had 'W' for warden on his. The type of respirator you carried was almost a status symbol. If you had the ordinary civilian type you were just a civilian – ours was not the service type used by the firemen, but if you had this intermediate type you were classed as somebody!

I can tell you the four-minute mile record wasn't broken after the war, but many times during it. Do you know how long it took for a shell to come over from France? I was down in a cave shelter at the back of Athol Terrace on one occasion and when we came out there was an army lorry parked in the road with people crouching behind it. So we asked, 'What are you doing?', and they replied, 'Timing shells'. From the flash of the gun to the shell's arrival took 72 seconds. They checked it quite a few times, and you can go a hell of a long way in 72 seconds, whether you are on your feet or

'Coming down Folkestone Road one time in the pelting rain, we heard a bomb whistling towards us. We skidded into the gutter and laid flat with the water washing along and over our faces.'

your bike! Which reminds me that if you were on your bike and you heard the whistle of a bomb coming down, you didn't get off the bike, you just skidded round and laid it down with it still between your legs. Coming down Folkestone Road one time in the pelting rain, we heard a bomb whistling towards us. We skidded into the gutter and laid flat with the water washing along and over our faces.

My brother and I were going to be ARP despatch riders for Dover. We were given driver's licences and were even shown the motorcycles at a house on Crabble Hill. But we never did become despatch riders. Mind you we could get around very well on our pushbikes. The idea just seemed to peter out somehow.

We knew our own area but on the odd occasion you used to get the opportunity to visit other areas. Like the time we saw a light was showing in someone's window. We took great delight in telling the local warden, 'There's a light in somebody's window'. Often he would reply, 'Well, what are you going to do about it?', to which we would quickly retort, '. . . it's not in our territory!' We would then beat a hasty retreat.

Censorship of national and regional newspapers – 'D' notices – made serious reporting and discussion of the war almost impossible. Newspapers were forbidden to mention the names of individual towns and cities where incidents might have occurred through enemy action, and they could only refer to such places as, 'somewhere in England', or 'in a south-east town'. Such censorship inevitably brought an air of unreality to newspaper accounts of the war.

Refugees fleeing from the Continent before the might of German Panzers caught up with them became a thorn in the side of the BEF who were quickly changing their front line positions in utter bewilderment.

It is not generally known that in the early stages of the war the ferryboats plying between British and French ports were armed. R.H. Charters, of the Royal Army Service Corps (RASC), gives his comprehensive account of his experiences as a gunner on one of them:

We arrived at Dover about 9 o'clock and were shown over the boat we were to go on, the *Monas Queen*. There were four teams altogether, the other three being RA personnel, the arrangements being that two ships started on the English side at Dover at the same time as two ships started from Boulogne on the French side, crossing over halfway in mid-Channel.

We found our quarters very comfortable, and all the guns laid out plus all spare parts for inspection on take over. It took some time to check and divide

Crew members of HMS *Sandown* clean their Lewis machine-gun before embarking on the perilous journey to rescue the BEF from Dunkirk.

all the parts between the guns, and the gun teams were made up of threes – Nos 1, 2 and 3 on each gun, six guns in all on a ship, two on the foredeck, two at the stern and another two amidships.

We first sailed with a boat-load of troops going back to France after having leave. After docking in Boulogne we picked up all the life-jackets, washed down the latrines and washbasins, then cleaned and oiled every gun. A guard was put on duty on the quay day and night on the French side. We continued going back and forth across the Channel, making one crossing each day, always sailing on the high tide from about five in the morning until six or so in the evening.

We were crossing in thick fog one day and going very slowly, and nearly had a head-on collision with another boat. On sighting each other both ships turned the same way. Luckily we managed to end up broadside on to each other. We usually had one or two destroyers escorting us and nearly always an Avro Anson or Blenheim flew over us.

There were times when we were held up by fog and missed a sailing, and once or twice leave was stopped. One time we spent three days in France. I used to go on various walks in France to Wimereux, Ambleteuse, Pont de Bris and other places along the coast and further inland.

Floating mines were plentiful, six or seven would be seen and we would have to steer between them.

Boats of all shapes and sizes were used to evacuate the BEF and Allies from Dunkirk during operation 'Dynamo', May/June 1940.

The war is over for this smiling Stuka pilot, brought down over Dunkirk. Rescued from the sea by the crew of HMS *Sandown*, a paddle steamer, he is here being brought ashore at Dover.

We left the *Monas Queen* on 13 May, having made forty-eight crossings, and joined the *King George V* to sail for an unknown destination. There were several other ships in the group, but as we were the slowest we were left well behind. We steamed up the Channel during the night as far as Scheveningen on the Hague, and rumour got about that we were picking up Dutch troops. In the early hours of the morning we received a signal by flash lamp from a destroyer, and we turned around and steamed back home. We heard later on the news broadcast that the Dutch had capitulated, so it was lucky we didn't go into a harbour there. I had spent the last fifteen hours on the guns without a break.

The scenes we saw in Boulogne were pathetic. Car-loads of refugees were arriving with mattresses on top to save them from enemy air attacks. There were few belongings inside. One car was riddled with bullet holes. Lorries turned up full of families and children, and there were crowds on bicycles.

The harbour was crowded with small boats – ten abreast. I counted more than two hundred, all loaded with families and their relations and what furniture they had saved – perambulators, bicycles, tables and chairs. They all looked so bewildered; it made me see red to think of what they had been through.

When the military HQ was evacuated from Arras, all the luggage and paraphernalia was brought in by goods train and dumped for the night on Boulogne quay. Such a mixture of things: officers valises, typewriters, boxes of small–calibre ammunition. On the following morning some of the officers tried to find their personal luggage and sort out anything of value. They later moved into the Hotel Imperial on the other side of the quay. We had sailed before later learning the hotel had received a direct hit during the night.

We had the chance to fire our guns on one occasion when German planes were sowing magnetic mines outside Boulogne Harbour. There were several of them flying over the harbour and town amidst a deafening noise of gunfire. The sky was a mass of tracer bullets. One plane was seen to come down with its tail shot away.

On 21 May we again went to Boulogne, but this time on the *Biarritz*. We had loaded all the holds and all the deck space and passages with all types of ammunition and shells, and detonators, as well as a large quantity of telephone wire. Owing to a recent broadcast informing all Frenchmen between the ages of 16 and 60 that they were required to join the French Forces, all the dockers had gone. So we proceeded to unload everything ourselves. The crane drivers had also gone, being careful to turn off the main switches before leaving – we could not find them. The quay was crowded with airmen who had been bombed out from one aerodrome to another. They looked very worn and tired. There were also crowds of refugees, still trying to get on to boats. We made a chain and passed boxes of ammunition from one to another, getting rid of it by sliding the boxes down a plank on to the quay and then loading them on to lorries. We even pushed over a wooden latrine on the quay to make more room. We had only unloaded half our dangerous cargo when we had orders to take on board the airmen, who immediately packed in like sardines. Some of their faces looked quite black with grime as they had not washed or rested for days. While they were waiting their turn to come on deck two were shot – one shot off his own thumb and part of his hand, and another was shot in the back by someone else. They all had loaded rifles and pockets of ammunition, which they emptied out for us to use. As soon as we were loaded we returned to Dover. Later that day, when the airmen had gone, I found the complete thumb which had been shot off, lying on the deck. It was a gruesome reminder.

On 22 May both the *Biarritz* and *Monas Queen* left Dover at 4 a.m. for France, carrying not only the half-unloaded cargo of ammunition, but also battalions of the Irish and Welsh Guards. When passing Cap Gris Nez we saw a large ship on fire, and shortly afterwards a German plane was seen flying low down over the sea and close to the shore. In the half-light of dawn our escorting destroyer fired several shots at it but it got away unscathed. Getting closer we saw a tanker had been hit and the sea around it was alight, sending up a huge pall of black smoke.

The Guards battalions were landed with about a dozen anti-tank guns which they managed to wheel down the gangway. They also took with them some bicycles and a few motorcycles and boxes of rations, although they only had time to unload about half of their stores.

For our return journey we took on some Royal Army Medical Corps (RAMC) and a few more airmen, and left Boulogne in a hurry. While running up to Cap Gris Nez our escorting destroyer dropped several depth-charges as two German submarines had been reported in the vicinity. The destroyer kept dashing about all over the place and dropping more depth-charges whenever it heard something with its listening apparatus. The resulting concussions shook the whole ship.

The following day we had orders to stand off Deal in the Downs. It was a lovely day and we slept until a destroyer dashed up to order us back to Boulogne. Our escorting destroyer left us and turned back, and as we got nearer to Boulogne we heard gunfire and noticed all the barrage balloons were down except one. Shells were falling in the basin and near the mole. We manoeuvred to turn round and back in stern first as usual, because we had a bow rudder. Shells began to fly all over the harbour, some rather wild and others very close. One salvo of four landed on either side of our ship – shrapnel splinters pierced my yellow mackintosh and lodged in my overcoat just below my ribs. I was more concerned about the load of ammunition still on board. One lucky shot and that would have been the end of us.

The Port Maritime gave us a signal in Morse code, which I believe our captain was unable to read, either because it was sent too fast or possibly the sender was a German. We heard rifle and machine-gun fire on the hill just south of Boulogne, where the Guards were making a last stand. We had gone over to take them off as they found their position quite impossible. We steamed outside the mole again to be out of range of the shells. Then some French destroyers began to open fire.

Before long a large yellow cargo boat came in and tied up at our stern packed tight with evacuated British troops. There was hardly room to sit down. They were allowed off the boat for a bit, a few dead being carried off on stretchers. The poor chaps were crazy for water and food. So we opened a stopcock on the quay and fitted a pipe to it to fill their water bottles. We also broke open the food cases left behind by the Guards and distributed the tins of food. They were then moved back onto the cargo boat to move over to the Eastern Arm. Before that happened, however, we had spent over three hours carrying water in buckets or large biscuit tins to fill their water bottles and throwing them back to them. Several bottles unfortunately fell into the sea between ship and quay.

On 27 May the *Biarritz*, escorted by a destroyer, left Dover to return to Dunkirk via Calais, running close inshore to avoid the minefields. Calais was burning furiously and we saw one of our planes circling over the shore line, being fired at continuously. It dropped a parachute and supplies to troops. We hadn't got far from Calais along the coast when, without warning, four gun batteries opened fire on us. They were in woods close to the coast and had waited until we were between the two batteries. The firing was very accurate and it wasn't long before they had put five shells into the *Biarritz*. One of them hit the funnel behind which I was sheltering. It blew a big hole in it and sent a shower of glass and metal over me. Another exploded in the Medical Officer's cabin, wrecking everything. Luckily he was not in his cabin at the time. Two shells pierced the ship's side above the water-line, while another exploded in the engine-room, killing one man and bursting a steampipe, twisting thick pieces of metal like thin wire. This shell must have gone out the other side of the hull as it had drilled a neat hole on one side and the other.

The destroyer did some marvellous work – dashing in close, firing all the time, putting up a smoke-screen between us and the shore, and drawing the fire. This action resulted in a shell exploding on her forward gun position, killing and wounding the gunners.

Meanwhile we had turned away from the shore with only one engine working. We limped off through our own minefields back to Dover. We stopped to offer to take any wounded off the destroyer but they said they could manage. One man fell overboard from the destroyer near the English coast, and they lowered a boat to pick him up.

With the *Biarritz* now in dock for repairs, we were moved to the Dunkirk Ferry, a French ship manned by French sailors. The whole move was secret and we were told it was a special mission. A quantity of blankets were put on board in bales together with two wireless vans and some signals personnel – there were about fifty of them who said they had a specially hazardous job to perform. We remained on board all that night, sleeping in all our clothes and getting some peculiar meals. But the trip was called off at breakfast. It was quite a relief. The ship was a death-trap, with its huge deck space and hollow inside. We were sent to a transit camp for a rest.

On 1 June we boarded the *Maid of Orleans*, sister ship to the *Biarritz* and very fast. We took on board three doctors, some RAMC orderlies and a lot of extra stretchers and medical equipment, and one embarkation officer. I was put on a double machine gun on the top of the rear companion-way. We had left Dover by the Western Arm, getting up speed fast, when a destroyer, loaded with troops on deck getting ready to disembark, came in and rammed us just behind our bows, tearing a huge hole large enough to drive several horses and carts through. The destroyer heeled over until we thought she would turn turtle; she shuddered away, her bows buckled in, while about twenty men fell into the water. We went out of the harbour and came back through the other entrance and anchored, dropping by the head but keeping afloat.

In the evening of the following day we were on our way to Folkestone to join the *Ben Mycree*, sister ship to the *Monas Queen*, which had, incidentally, struck a German magnetic mine on 29 May, and been sunk. Six Bluejackets [sailors] had been sent down to augment the crew as well as half a dozen merchant seamen from London. Nearly all the men on board wanted to sign off and leave the ship, except the officers. I had heard of this happening before. They had been over the previous day and seen two other ships sunk very near them by bombs, and were lucky not to have been sunk themselves when a whole stick of bombs fell along the side of their ship.

At first the Bluejackets, with fixed bayonets, guarded the gangway and refused to let them go, but later they were allowed to leave. So we eventually sailed short-handed and with a strange crew. The volume of steam was terrific for about ten miles or so and you couldn't hear your own voice – I thought the boilers would burst any minute! We went along the coast as far as Ramsgate and then over to Dunkirk. We met destroyers stationed at various places en route. Star shells kept being dropped and hanging in the sky. I was in the stern and on nearing Dunkirk we felt a jolt. A small trawler had been hit by us, scraping all down one side, sending sparks flying about like incendiary bullets. She sank soon after we left her. We were not carrying lights.

Reaching the French coast west of Dunkirk we steamed in close under the pall of smoke which was like a wall. Flashes of gunfire could be seen everywhere. We crept up to the mole and were met by a small motor launch with a naval officer on board. He hailed us through a megaphone, asking our name and saying we couldn't get in yet as the harbour was full up and if we couldn't get in by 3.30 we were to go home. His actual words were, '. . . get the hell out of it'.

It was eerie waiting. Star shells lit up the area while occasionally aeroplanes droned overhead. Guns were firing directly into Dunkirk and sheets of flame leapt up into the night sky from the town. It amazed me that the lighthouse still stood towering over the entrance, apparently intact.

We later received a signal to go. So rather disappointed at our fruitless journey, but not sorry to leave before daybreak, we turned back. We were running rather fast, I thought, as it was pitch dark and of course nobody carried lights, when a small trawler suddenly loomed up, crossing our bow. We hit it fair amidships, ramming our bow in and overhanging it, nearly pushing it right under. The trawler slithered to one side and sank immediately. We stopped to lower a boat but luckily a destroyer rushed up so we continued our journey home.

About half way over the captain came down to the guns and ordered all magazines to be taken to the bridge with all cartridges and loaded rifles, and a guard was put on it. I was selected among others, to go below with the captain, with loaded rifles, to arrest six members of the crew, the merchant seamen from London, who were fighting drunk, having broken into the Bond in the first-class saloon. They had been drinking the whisky. We rounded them up and shut them in different cabins with a guard mounted on each one.

Nearing Dover we were told to keep our life-jackets on, as magnetic mines had been sown during the night and the ship was only degaussed on one side. We couldn't get into the harbour right away, so we cruised up and down in front of a minesweeper towing a barge.

On the next day, 3 June, we went on board the *Lady Man*, another Isle of Man boat, and again sailed in the evening for Dunkirk, knowing it was to be the last day of the evacuation. We started before it was dark and on the way up the coast a flight of our planes came over us heading for France. We arrived about 11 p.m. going the same way as the day before, and seemed to be the first big boat in the harbour. There was a northish wind blowing and a bit of a current running. We saw the mole thick with troops waiting to be taken off. The enemy was uncannily quiet. Then all hell broke loose. The town was blazing furiously with shells falling on it, and flames shooting up into the sky. Big naval guns began to fire on the eastern side to keep the Germans back.

Being rather a large boat we offered greater resistance to the wind, so could not get close enough to the mole to tie up. The captain tried and tried, first getting the bow in and then the stern. Two more boats came and took our place. It was made doubly difficult by the many wrecks sunk close to the mole, showing their masts above water. For two and a half hours the captain tried to tie up, at every moment expecting German planes to bomb us.

When we eventually got close in a head rope was thrown to a French soldier. Instead of pulling it in and tying the thicker rope attached to it to a capstan, he tried to tie the thin rope. Nobody could remember the French for 'pull'. After managing eventually to tie up, we slipped the gangway over. Then the stern rope broke, the gangway dropped between the ship and the quay, and smashed to smithereens. We tied up again, and this time the men, all French soldiers, came on – some climbing on hands and knees up the planks of wood we had thrown over.

Fully laden with troops we cut our ropes and backed out of Dunkirk Harbour. Our last trip was not uneventful. We hit the paddle-box of a steamer, banged into a destroyer, and through the noise of destroyers' whistles and hooting steamers, you could still hear the obscene language. I thought all the world would know we were there.

There were dozens of ships wending their way homewards, then as we neared Ramsgate, and the coast, a thick fog came down and we had to stop. We heard one almighty crash in the fog and a lot of shouting. When the fog cleared we moved on, only to find that we, amongst several other boats and destroyers, were on the wrong side of the Goodwin Sands. There was much confusion as everyone had to turn back for over a mile and then come back up on the right side. After we unloaded at Dover we gunners left for the transit camp, where French Army officers and English sailors mixed together in a frenzy of self-congratulation.

Among the first contingent of WRNS to arrive at Dover, and to work closely with Vice-Admiral B.H. Ramsay at the castle, was Rosemary Keyes (Lord Keyes' niece, now Fellowes). She served as a cypher officer from October 1939 until December 1942:

> My memories of Dunkirk are very disjointed and patchy. I missed the start because of illness. On my return to the cypher office night duty had already been established. Before then the WRNS Cypher Officers only worked during the day.
>
> The casemates where Vice-Admiral Dover had his office was a series of tunnels under the castle, a rabbit warren of dark, dreary, damp and airless passages and rooms. We worked all day in electric light and the only time we saw daylight was when we went to the 'heads'. This was a small room with a noisome 'thunder-box', but a beautiful view of Dover Harbour, seen through a window cut out of the cliff face. It was a wonderful place for watching the air raids.
>
> At that time the 'Wrenery' was a small Georgian house, one of a terrace right on the seafront, long since shelled and demolished. Our Chief Officer Miss Currie, was quite tireless during the Dunkirk evacuation period. She took over an empty hotel – the Burlington – borrowed beds and two-tiered bunks, and organized a constant supply of sandwiches and hot drinks. Survivors were brought to the Burlington and in my off-duty hours I worked there serving food and drinks. Most of these men were too tired to care what they were drinking. The majority just fell on to a bed and slept for hours, dead to the world. The ballroom was littered with bodies either sleeping or eating. Clothing was also distributed as most of them were only half dressed. I assumed they had taken everything off when they had to swim for it. Piles of clothing arrived from stores and so we gave out vests, pants, pullovers and socks by the hundreds. I remember feeling a fool for asking them, 'What size are you?' Some tired, bare-footed, bleary-eyed sailor, his hair stiff with engine oil, would stare at me with a blank expression and reply, 'I don't know miss'. They asked for shoes, but of course that was something we hadn't got.
>
> Work in the cypher office during that period was non-stop. It was incredibly exciting and exhilarating, for we knew what was happening before any one else. Signals were de-cyphered, typed and distributed at top speed. Our distribution lists were larger than they had ever been before. Everyone sitting round the enormous table in the Dynamo Room had to have a signal, a process made all the more difficult when the cypher officer had to avoid treading on sleeping bodies. All the staff worked round the clock, and when they couldn't keep awake any longer they just lay down on the floor and slept.
>
> I was on duty with Myrette Ackfield one night when an exhausted, unshaven and quite unknown young naval officer suddenly appeared in the doorway. He said, 'I believe you have an armchair. May I borrow it? My boss

says I can have an hour's sleep'. So of course we said he could but offered our very uncomfortable iron bed. 'No thank you, this is wonderful', he said, slipping into the large leather armchair and falling asleep immediately. I covered him up with a rug. About 4 a.m. the work had stopped temporarily. I lay upon the awful iron bed and went fast asleep. When I awoke I discovered our unknown guest had draped the rug over me without waking me, and had vanished. We never saw him again, nor ever discovered who he was or where he had come from!

Robert Sheppard was barely twenty years of age when he joined the Royal Navy and ended up as a member of the crew on the drifter *Lord Howard*:

I am glad that attention is being paid to Dover and all it had to endure while much of the rest of the country just watched what was going on in newsreels and newspapers. I could talk for hours about the many tragic, exciting, pathetic and laughable (now) things that went on. I sometimes have night-mares about those days, even fifty years later. And the truth about what the authorities did – for instance, getting us to practise cutlass fighting and throw-ing hand-grenades on the beach at Dover while, at the same time, Jerry was dive-bombing the harbour and shelling the town.

Peter Spittal joined the Royal Marines in October 1939 and after his initial training joined the Royal Marine Fortress Unit. He took part in the campaign in Norway, where his ship was sunk, returning up the River Forth on a captured German merchant vessel that was still flying the German flag. He wrote:

I also took part in another piece of little-remembered history. After the capit-ulation of France we made a surprise attack on the French warships lying in Portsmouth Harbour. We took over these ships and the crews were given the choice of being repatriated or joining the Free French Navy.

Then I was posted to Dover. We were billeted with civilian families who treated us very well. We worked on the defence structures right along the coast, putting up gun emplacements and also manning the actual guns. I recall manning a machine gun during the Battle of Britain, on a day when there were many dogfights going on all over the Channel, planes crashing and pilots baling out. We were on parade when one raid developed. A plane was above, and as its bomb doors opened you could feel a sort of swaying as everyone in the ranks looked up. Suddenly, Marines were rushing in all directions looking for cover. Hardly heroic stuff but a sensible precaution!

I remember also installing wooden poles along the coast, to deceive the enemy reconnaissance planes into thinking the area was heavily armed with big guns.

'. . . as its bomb doors opened you could feel a sort of swaying as everyone in the ranks looked up. Suddenly, Marines were rushing in all directions looking for cover.'

It was hardly scientific but ingenuity won the day for Bernard Harrison. He joined a searchlight unit near Guston, Dover, and recalled:

> The Dover years were exciting for us youngsters. We were in action all through the Battle of Britain, with never a dull moment, night or day. There was the occasion when a Dornier 17 bomber, hit by gunfire, was coming down almost over our heads. The German rear gunner fell from his turret and his machine gun fell out with him in our field. We spent all next day rigging up that Spandau machine gun on a makeshift mounting of old gas pipe. It was often in action against enemy aircraft and we obtained our ammunition from other crashed German planes.

Norman Morris had joined the Territorial Army in 1938, and he eventually went into the Cinque Ports Fortress (TA) Royal Engineers Unit, based at the Archcliff Fort. Transferred to the breakwater he witnessed many incidents:

> At the time of Dunkirk I was having a quick whiff of fresh air up on the breakwater deck when I saw a destroyer crossing the harbour towards the Western Dock, with a cargo ship on a collision course. The destroyer was going at a fair speed and was laden with troops on deck. I just knew there

would be a crash. Sure enough, the destroyer ploughed into the other boat, making a huge hole just above the water-line. The destroyer rocked violently from side to side throwing most of the troops overboard. Immediately there were blasts on hooters, and in no time at all small boats were picking up drenched soldiers.

Fred Tuffey, a marine coppersmith at Chatham Dockyard, was employed on detached duties at Dover at the time of Dunkirk. A ship had come into the harbour, holed by enemy action whilst ferrying troops home from the beaches. He was put on the job of welding a patch on to the hull. He was working on a 'cat', a floating platform of timber which was very unstable, to say the least. Things were made more uncomfortable for him, as he slogged on for hours, by the ship's skipper leaning over the rail and goading, swearing at and insulting Fred as he worked.

When the job was finally completed Fred went to his sleeping quarters to get some much needed rest. He was just about to doze off when there was a tap on his door. He was greeted by a solemn-faced apologetic skipper carrying a bottle of rum. The skipper said, 'Sorry I was rude to you, mate. I knew that you were doing your best and as quick as you could. But I saw those poor bloody lads over there being mown down and I just wanted to get back over there and save as many as possible. And that bloody hole was the only thing stopping me.'

During the summer of 1939 H. Cossons was working for the Eagle Steamship Company at Ramsgate Pier Yard. He spent many hours shouting at the visitors 'This way for Calais', 'This way for Boulogne', 'This way for Dunkirk', 'This way for Ostend'. He was then seventeen years of age. He wrote:

Some nine months later I was working for Dr Crawford at Harbour House. I had one of the best possible views of the many vessels returning from Dunkirk packed with troops. I said to the doctor one day that I intended to volunteer to join one of the rescue craft and go across to Dunkirk. His reply was blunt, 'Don't be a bloody fool, Cousins,' (it was always Cousins and never Cossons) '. . . you're far more use to me here.'

As Operation Dynamo reached its closing stages he evacuated his wife, cook and children to Wales, and I was no longer needed. So I volunteered for the Buffs Regiment on Thursday 13 June, and went for a medical at Orange Street, Canterbury. I joined No. 3 Platoon, 'A' Company, 6th Battalion The Buffs, at the drill hall in Shellon Street, Folkestone the same day. It was a wet evening and I felt pretty miserable so I went to a cinema and saw a Mother Riley film.

We spent the next four days at the drill hall, being kitted out and doing basic drill. We spent the nights in slit trenches. On the following Monday we were taken to Lydden Spout by lorry. As we passed through the streets of Folkestone we were cheered by groups of people who thought we were heroes returning from Dunkirk, instead of eighteen-year-old youngsters not long out of school. It was an enjoyable moment – one of the few we ever had.

We spent two weeks at Lydden Spout. The food was good, if a bit rough and ready, and there was no barrack-like atmosphere. The NCOs were a decent lot and we had a NAAFI canteen. We trained hard during the day and spent the evenings on the firing range. When off-duty we would run across the fields and down a steep hill to a pub on the Dover–Folkestone road to enjoy ourselves.

The 75th HAA Regiment RA had two batteries only, one recruited mainly from Dover, the other from Folkestone, and it says much for the isolation of the average ack-ack units in the south-east that in the eighteen months Peter Erwood stayed with the regiment he never made the acquaintance of anyone from the Folkestone battery, which occupied an eight-gun site close to the Swingate radar towers. This was the only Dover gun position that was even half way finished by the outbreak of war. Its field of fire was restricted by the adjacent radar masts, presumably due to the lack of coordination between the RAF and the Army when it was first planned:

The battery to which most of us were posted was No. 233 – the Dover one. It occupied one partly completed four-gun site on the Western Heights, above Shakespeare Cliff, with another two guns positioned just off Guston Road, near the Duke of York's Military School. This site, where half of us, including myself, ended up, was immeasurably the worst of the lot – adrift in a sea of mud reminiscent of Passchendale, without a functioning cookhouse or any washing or sanitary facilities whatsoever. The whole place was supplied by a single standpipe situated out in the middle of a field.

The hut into which some forty of us were dumped in mid-November, was innocent of window glass, lighting, heating or paint. It was also completely bedless, so we made do with straw-filled palliasses and about three feet of space per man. Although the windows were glazed within a couple of days, it was six weeks before the hut was reasonably habitable.

The bath and lavatory accommodation finally came on stream – so to speak – in the following May. Meanwhile, as soldiers do, we put up with it, washed and shaved in tin bowls of cold water, and ate without enjoyment lukewarm food strongly flavoured with soot, cooked in the Crimean-type coal-fired boilers which were the only major item of equipment at the cook's disposal. Natural functions were performed in galvanized buckets, more or less concealed behind flapping hessian screens.

We had to become ack-ack gunners, however, and so there was little time to worry about trifles. Our training started early on the morning after our arrival. Unlike other sites occupied by the regiment, which were equipped with the modern and highly effective 3.7-inch calibre heavy gun, firing a 28 lb shell up to 30,000 feet, we had only two relics left over from the First

World War. They were of 3-inch calibre, firing an 18 lb shell which might have reached 15,000 feet or so with a following wind. The only advantage these 'pop-guns' had was that they could be fired rather faster than the modern 3.7-inch.

We were allocated on a 'take 'em as they come' basis, either guns or instruments, and I found myself learning about the height finder under the tutelage of Bombardier 'Taffy' Cox, in civilian life an immigrant coal miner from South Wales to the Kent Coalfields. One of the minority of NCOs without First World War experience, he was nevertheless an estimable character, whose only awkward feature was a perpetually runny nose. This was often off-putting when one had to follow after him to look through the central twin eyepieces of the Barr & Stroud UB7 height finder. We had another Cox on the gun site, Sergeant 'Bimbo' Cox – also a miner, a fearsome disciplinarian of the old school and a man of stupendous strength though minimal height. His party trick, when we finally graduated to 3.7s, was to pick up a full ammunition box, weighing about 140 lbs, under each arm and then run with them.

We also had a sergeant, 'Taffy' Wakefield, who wore, as did many others, the three First World War medals irreverently called 'Star, News and Standard', or 'Pip, Squeak and Wilfred', and the Long Service and Good Conduct Medal, also known as 'Nineteen Years' Undetected Crime'. He was a great character who unbent remarkably after a few pints of beer. With these, and with the Dover 'mushes', we Londoners with a few Brummies and a group of Sussex boys, welded quickly into a smooth-running unit. We were kept busy all day, and frequently spent half the night 'standing-to' on innumerable false alarms, so we had little time to become bored.

In January 1940 rumours that our long-awaited 3.7s were due to arrive started a flurry of activity, including the movement of the 3-inch relics down to the Dover promenade. Minimum crews were quartered in the regiment's old drill hall on the other side of the road, while the rest started to reconstruct the D3 site to take the four new guns. Filling sandbags and digging a new command post and telephone dugout was all done with pick and shovel, mechanical aids being unavailable, as was reinforced concrete.

In early May I went on seven days' leave. In the small hours of 10 May the 'phoney war' came to a sudden end. When I returned to the unit I found they had moved to a new green-field site near Deal with the two 3-inch guns. A few days later enough of us to man another 3-inch site moved to within a few miles of Ramsgate. It was here that two of the most unbelievable antiques were delivered, which were probably the first ack-ack guns ever made. They were without modern fire-control devices, and had only the so-called 'open' sights. Everything proved to be immovable due to the solid grease in which they had been packed for over twenty years.

To cap it all, we were given the interesting news that there were no other troops between Pegwell Bay and Dover. In the event of an invasion the defence of that line was down to us. With just six rifles and a dozen or so pickaxe helves, the chances of spirited resistance seemed rather on the thin side. Incidentally, none of us had ever fired a rifle, and we had only fifty rounds between us anyway. Our officers instructed us that should paratroops land, we were to rush at them with the pickaxe helves, stun them and grab their guns. How far their tongues were pushed into their cheeks when they delivered those astounding orders, we will never know. Luckily, the situation did not arise, for on 28 May, we were all rushed back to Dover.

Our four brand new 3.7s arrived on the following day, with several lorry-loads of ammunition, having left Woolwich Arsenal in such haste the barrels had not been painted. They were checked over thoroughly and painted, and we were ready for action by the late afternoon. They had arrived in the nick of time, for that night we engaged the enemy for the first time.

It might seem unbelievable, but none of us in the new intake had ever fired an artillery weapon of any sort, not even at practice camp, let alone the real thing. Very few of the others had fired a 3.7-inch which, compared with the old 3-inch, was like comparing a Ferrari with a Mini. We all knew our drill, however, and with the confidence of ignorance, we assumed it would be all right on the night.

In pristine condition this 3.7-in ack-ack gun, only three miles distant from Dover, basks in the hot summer sun while the fledgling crew receive their instruction.

By then I was a telephone operator, and was one of the two on duty in our new command post dugout when the rather bored voice of the control-operator beneath Dover Castle came on the line with, 'Dover guns – alarm'. He had said it so often in the past winter and spring that I suppose he was somewhat blasé. I pressed the alarm bell button and took up my position half way up the steps from the dugout. It was easier to relay messages to the gun position officer (GPO), while my 'oppo' took over the headphones. We duly reported 'D3 ready for action', and as usual waited without expectation for something to happen. But this time it did. We suddenly picked up the sound of an aircraft with an unfamiliar engine note. One or two searchlights, to use an infelicitous phrase, exposed themselves. Low down and to seawards, a Heinkel 115 seaplane minelayer was caught in the beams. Without going into technicalities, this was a very difficult target. It was receding and, more to the point, our UB7 height finder gave progressively less accurate figures the nearer the angle of sight approached the horizontal. To cut a long story short, it was all very chancy even in daylight, but at night virtually impossible.

Despite the range-control card not being in its usual place, the young regular officer from the first course ever to pass out of the famous 'shop' at Woolwich, rose to the occasion, and by inspired guesswork, gave out a likely fuse number to the guns. I remember still the sound of the rounds dropping into the leading trays, the clink of the breech-blocks closing after the rounds

'The earth shook and various constructional defects in our dugout became immediately apparent. A large part of the roof fell on top of my unfortunate co-telephonist.'

'During a brief visit the previous winter he had made his mark by having an all-over wash under our solitary water tap – stark naked, and in several degrees of frost.'

had been rammed, and the crash of the loading trays being pulled clear. There was a moment's silence, then a huge flash and stupendous bang as the four guns fired in perfect salvo.

I had braced myself for some noise but this was something else. The earth shook and various constructional defects in our dugout became immediately apparent. A large part of the roof fell on top of my unfortunate co-telephonist. War is war, however, and I left him to it while I joined in the hunt for the missing card. A second salvo followed, then a third, which was wasted, for *mirabile dictu*, the target disappeared in a huge flash and shower of burning fragments.

This victory was in fact the flukiest of flukes, but it raised our morale to hubris point. 'You put 'em up, we'll knock 'em down', was our battle cry from then on. Two days later, during our usual dawn stand-to, a Junkers 88 was spotted – a perfect target, it was approaching on a steady course at about 10,000 feet. This, we felt, was a pushover. I remember thinking, 'The bastard won't know what hit him', but in the event, we received a pride-tumbling shock of the first magnitude. The first round burst about half a mile from the target, and the remainder were scattered all around the sky like currants in a canteen bun.

It was ludicrously humiliating. One imagined the German pilot lifting up two fingers at us as he made a leisurely turn before flying off quite unscathed. This exhibition was witnessed from afar by several senior officers, and immediate remedial action followed in the formidable person of Sergeant-Major (Assistant Instructor Gunnery) Cullen. During a brief visit the previous winter he had made his mark by having an all-over wash under our solitary water tap – stark naked, and in several degrees of frost. He took us in hand for an utterly exhausting week, after which, considerably chastened, we emerged to become proper gunners.

In total dismay and unbelief, we lived through the next few weeks of Dunkirk and the French surrender. Enemy air sorties increased, the guns taking the brunt of the action. Our shooting was a little better, but still not one hundred per cent effective. The noise we made, however, must have reassured the Dover people that a war was being fought on their behalf.

The real battle started, as far as we were concerned, with the massed bomber formations of the Luftwaffe passing over us to London. We fired into them again and again, thinking we could hardly miss. But they kept formation, and I believe only one dropped out, making smoke from a damaged engine. On their way back, however, it was a different story, for they were less organized and the Dover guns were able to dispatch several of them before they left our shores.

We were now on a permanent 'alarm basis', and the duty crews slept in hastily excavated dugouts close to their guns or instruments. In some cases the excavations had several field drains installed, after a series of nocturnal thunderstorms rapidly produced over three feet of water in the command post dugout.

Life became one long round of firing, carrying shells, washing-out and oiling-up from before dawn until dusk, and although night activity by the Luftwaffe was not comparable with their daylight efforts, we often spent the night on 'stand-to'.

Our shooting improved, and the enemy planes started to give Dover a wide berth. Even so, we were dive-bombed, attacked by fighter-bombers, machine-gunned and later, when the German long-range gun batteries were established in the Pas de Calais, shelled.

While the evacuees were coming to terms with their new and sometimes strange surroundings in the unpronounceable Welsh towns and villages, the seniors – teenagers who had remained behind in the area – were soaking up their wartime experiences like a sponge. Muriel Sidwell recalls:

We had moved to Maxton by the time the first shells came over. There was an explosion behind the Citadel Battery site. We youngsters galloped over, with no thought that other explosions might follow. From the fairly shallow crater we dug out a shell nose cone made of brass with grooves and numbers on it.

It was still warm from the explosion. Much of the shrapnel we collected in those days was warm to the touch, sometimes too hot to handle. But an officer and a sergeant from the battery site saw us with the nose cone and came and took it from us.

In the dead of night on a minesweeper in mid-Channel, F. Featherbe remembers a moment of fear:

It was one of those cold nights with fog and darkness everywhere. We had been sweeping for a week or more to clear the Channel before an incoming convoy arrived, when the lookout shouted that he could hear E-boats in the distance. The noise of the engines was getting louder. We were already shaking in our seaboots. The trouble was we could not see anything beyond our ship. I was manning a twin Lewis machine gun on one wing of the bridge, and there was another on the other side with two more aft. Forward there was a twelve pounder, and around the ship there were boxes of hand-grenades and rifles for those who had no position on deck. But I still didn't feel happy and I was not sure if I was shaking from extreme cold or fear.

The engine noise was so loud I thought the E-boat was going to ram us. We could hear another one close behind. Then all of a sudden our sweep went taut. The sweep, by the way, is kept afloat on the surface of the water by floats, and a copper cable is attached to it because of magnetic mines. The E-boat was caught up in our sweep which had tangled up in its propeller. We shut down the noise of our generators and watched the few feet of cable that was visible in the fog go up and down, until there was one big roar from the E-boat's engines and he was gone.

Alf Floyd wrote that he had been in the Royal Navy with small craft before the war. He thought, generally speaking, that it had been something of an adventure. Then things became serious. The strains of 'Bluebirds over the White Cliffs of Dover' did raise morale and undoubtedly kept his spirits up:

Just after Dunkirk I was a member of the crew of MTB 70. The skipper was Lieutenant Kingchurch. I was a leading stoker then. We arrived in Dover as the nucleus of the 11th MTB Flotilla and were entirely self-sufficient, eating and sleeping on board with trips into the Strait in between. After the harbour was bombed and HMS *Codrington* sunk, we were moved to the Lord Warden Hotel (HMS *Wasp*). There we had the added problems of shelling. We made trips across the water to land agents on stretches of enemy-held coast. Those were the days, or should I say nights, before the exploits of Peter Scott and other small vessel commanders such as Dickens and Hitchens.

During the Battle of Britain period we spent our daylight hours rescuing pilots from their downed planes – pilots of any nationality, until the time we were attacked while trying to pick up a German pilot.

Jim Elkin arrived in Dover with the 15th Battalion of the Queen's Royal Regiment:

'The Fighting Fifteenth' we styled ourselves. We were paraded as a battalion at the castle and our CO informed us that there had been a sentry posted at Dover Castle for over 800 years. Some wag shouted from the ranks that it was about time he was relieved!

I had the job of company clerk. I was responsible for the safekeeping of the secret book containing the plans to be put into action in the event of an invasion. It stated which bridges and so on were mined, and which points were defended by 'fougasses'. (This latter was a device which was concealed at roadsides and when set off would direct a stream of ignited chemicals at any passing vehicles.) We were to fight to the very last round after blowing up all the bridges.

J. Peglar was a gunlayer on the 9.2-in right section gun at the north end of Adisham railway station:

I started my artillery life with 23 Medium Regiment training at Oakhampton but went on to bigger guns at Catterick where we took part in a Gaumont film called 'Britain prepares to meet the invasion'. Our guns fired a broadside of blanks – so effective that the grass underneath the snow caught alight.

Our battery came down to Hythe for a short while but moved on to Grove Ferry where we lived in a pub – an ambition fulfilled.

For many weeks William Smith, with 261 Company Pioneer Corps, worked on the beaches between Sandwich and Deal, erecting fortifications of tubular scaffolding at low tide. At high tide only part of this was visible above water. The whole construction was to prevent German landing craft from reaching the beach in the event of an invasion:

We lost one man at Deal. He was from Oldham and he had stepped on a mine. At one time we were billeted at St Margaret's Bay. I recall the film star George Arliss had a house there.

Attached as a medic to the *Maid of Orleans* during the Dunkirk evacuation period, S. Rogers returned to find himself engaged in setting up a dressing station beneath the officers' mess at the Citadel:

We converted the basement into a complete medical station with an operating theatre. In the circumstances we carried out some remarkable treatment. What with the attacks on convoys and the Battle of Britain going on, plus the shelling, it certainly was 'Hellfire Corner'.

Although Colonel L. McP. Fordyce OBE is not in the category of the 'lower ranks' who make up the majority of the reminiscences in this anthology, he felt he should make some contribution to let people know how searchlights were deployed and operated:

A battery of searchlights was made up of twenty-four sites, spaced about 3 miles apart, covering quite a large area, with an average of twelve men occupying each site. No. 342 Searchlight Battery (1st Surrey Rifles) spread out from Whitstable through to Margate, Ramsgate and Broadstairs towards Dover and a few miles inland. Very briefly, the operational equipment in the early days was a searchlight, a sound locator, a generator for power and two spotters' chairs with high-powered binoculars. The sound locator was made of two large trumpets, 4 feet apart, fixed to a swivel tripod connected by headphones to a listener. A new compact searchlight was later introduced called 'Elsie' which had an effective range of over 30,000 feet.

I took command of the battery in June 1940. My first night in the area was spent in a room above Lucy's the butchers opposite the Red Lion Hotel Wingham, a fourteenth-century inn. Houses were half-timbered and overhung the street. Early in the morning I was awakened by a commotion overhead and putting out my head (half shaved) I saw lots of other heads in the same state looking upwards. It reminded me of a Hogarth print except that the faces were all looking upwards instead of down into the street at a brawl or dogfight. I duly moved into the Red Lion, my new HQ, where we had one half and Mr and Mrs Alexander had the other half, still operating as a very good pub. The townspeople were very friendly to us and took a real interest in our volunteers who came mainly from the London area. This was particularly so when London was being bombed in August and September 1940. Friends whom I call to mind after all this time were the family of Admiral of the Fleet Sir Dudley Pound, who had a house in Wingham and used to ask us to tea, Dr McCrae and his wife, also a doctor who was always on hand if needed, the vicar who allowed me to read the lesson on occasions, and Colonel Newport, Commander of the local Home Guard, who proved most co-operative during the threat of invasion.

In mid-September – I think the 15th – I received the code word which meant 'Invasion expected'. I alerted the officers and all sites and made contact with Colonel Newport who had been sent the same code word. Between us we arranged a method of patrolling the coast in our area and he managed to arm us with small arms, of which he had a good supply. I had a .303 rifle, my service issue 4.5 revolver and such as Colonel Newport could provide. We intended to defend that portion of our heritage to the best of our ability.

Amongst the guns allotted to us was a large leather case containing three gold-mounted Purdeys, double-barrelled sporting guns belonging to the Hambro family. I decided they were too valuable to use on Hitler's rabble and left them in the safe to be handed back at the earliest opportunity.

That night was the strangest and most eerie of any during our stay in Kent. It was a calm night with reasonable visibility except for a slight haze above the sea. Being ready and willing we secretly hoped for something to shoot at. But the night passed without anything happening on our side. About midnight there looked to be a 'Brocks Benefit' across the water which we heard later was the Royal Navy knocking hell out of hundreds of invasion barges on the French coast. So, bleary-eyed, we returned to our duties.

Shortly after I arrived in the area the War Office sent us a batch of recruits termed 'immatures' to be distributed to sites. Before sending them to their stations, Major Edgar Dawes, my Second in Command, and I assembled them on a site near Battalion Headquarters (BHQ) to explain what equipment they would be using. Things were going very well until Dawes whispered to me, 'Look over Dover'. I saw what looked like a cloud of locusts coming in our direction. With our glasses we counted at least twenty German bombers with goodness knows how many fighters weaving above them. I called the immatures together and explained what was approaching and told them to make for the nearest hedges and crouch down, and not look up until the 'planes had passed overhead as their white faces would have been visible from the air. In about twenty minutes or so the lectures were resumed, but inside an hour the bombers, mostly JU88s, were being chased back across the Channel by our Spitfires.

Then there was the occasion when Sergeant Townson, one of our older and much respected detachment commanders and an expert with the Lewis machine gun, was lecturing in the gun pit to his new recruits when he spotted an Me 109 flying in his direction making for France at about 500ft. He clapped a magazine of 27 rounds on his gun and shot down the fighter. It landed nearby, but the lecture went on, much to the admiration of the immatures. I tried to get a 'Mention' for Sergeant Townson for identifying and shooting down the aircraft, but my plea went unanswered.

I used to exchange visits with Major Mills who commanded the Dover Battery with its BHQ at Kearsney Abbey. We used to compare notes as to how our batteries were coping with our portions of the war. Dining at the Abbey could be quite hair-raising at times although it would have been unwise to show it. The place appeared to be a 'Hall of Mirrors' and what with occasional loud bumps and rumbles which Major Mills did not seem to notice I could not help feeling that his BHQ was less healthy than my fourteenth-century pub in Wingham.

At the outbreak of war George McIntosh was stationed at Connaught Barracks, then a training depot for Field Artillery RA. He recalled:

We – the military – were reminded of our responsibilities to be alert at all times. For three weeks we were confined to barracks, with dawn and dusk 'stand-to'. No service personnel were allowed in and out of Dover without permission, and military police patrolled the whole area where buses came and left to check passengers on and off. On one occasion during the Dunkirk evacuation period I was guard commander when two Germans in uniform were brought to the barracks and put in the guardroom. I was instructed that nobody was to approach them. There was a feeling at that time that things were so tense they were not safe from our lads. I was very glad when morning came and they were taken away.

Only eighteen years old and classed in the category of 'immature', R.A. Smith came to Dover with No. 272 HAA Battery RA:

Our troop manned two ancient 3-inch ack-ack guns of 1917 vintage on Marine Parade at the eastern end of the seafront, where the hotels finished and the cliffs started. There were public baths behind us but they were soon demolished by shells, which missed us by a road's width. One of the ironies is that as my mates and I were too young to go to France, we were nearer than any other troops to the anticipated invasion!

Digging slit trenches at Dover for all-round defence kept Dick Beardon busy and gave him plenty of exercise:

Thrown from his crashing Messerschmitt 109 fighter on 23 September 1940, Unteroffizier Dilthey (on stretcher) was rescued by 2nd Lieutenant M.E Jacobs, who swam 200 yards from the shore. Lieutenant Jacobs is walking barefoot wearing a corporal's greatcoat.

I was stationed with the 2/7 Battalion Royal Warwickshire Regiment, and we were part of the main Dover defence, manning trenches along the seafront – some in front gardens. We also had light machine guns on the pier and harbour arms. Sometimes we had the job of taking any shot down German aircrew into custody at our guardroom. They were a cocky and arrogant bunch. When the shelling first started it was taken as warning of an invasion and those not on duty at the time went, armed to the teeth, to the caves to act as reserves.

After short preliminary training with the Royal Engineers C. Tilley suddenly found himself reporting to the guardroom at Shorncliffe Barracks. The next day he was given a real rifle and live ammunition and found himself sharing the responsibilities for the defence of a stretch of the Dover Road:

Our billet was a summer-house at the back of the Valiant Sailor pub at Capel le Ferne. We had a grandstand view of the air battles over the English Channel and saw planes of both sides being shot down. We could also feel the cliffs shake from the effects of gunfire and bombing on the other side in France. We were eventually moved down to Folkestone harbour for guard duties. One of our responsibilities was the maintenance of the demolition explosive charges placed on harbour installations. Our meals were sent from a Pioneer Company cookhouse about a mile away.

A high proportion of the men who endured the rigours and dangers of serving the guns in the Dover and St Margaret's Bay areas were sappers of the Royal Engineers. These men were the specialists manning and supplying the power for searchlights, plus a variety of other skilled and necessary jobs. Someone who served there at the time, Ron Warren, takes issue with points made in some books on the subject. Quite rightly the Royal Artillery have great pride in their guns and served them loyally and efficiently, but as Ron is quick to point out, 'what good are guns unless the target is illuminated and visible?'.

Of course most of the RE, and RE being pre-war 'terriers', we had the great spirit of the Territorial Army behind us and we worked together in the closest co-operation. The first soldier killed in Dover was an RE corporal. In fact he was off duty at the time, asleep in the RE quarters at Langdon Barracks and the hut was peppered with shrapnel. At the time I was on duty at the Eastern Arm, otherwise I might have copped a packet. But it was the old sweats of the Regular Army who cleared up the mess. The officers didn't have the stomach for it and didn't seem to want us to see their weakness. Before then no blood had been spilled. We all learned to see it later on but it was still a nasty sight. Even the doctors could not have avoided being sickened. Often the first to go in and tend the wounded were the nuns who had a priory in Park Avenue near Connaught Park.

During my long years at Dover I acquired the nickname 'The Knuckle Artist'. This was not because I was an expert at fisticuffs or anything like that, but because I decorated the blackout boards at our quarters on the Knuckle section of the breakwater. Incidentally, how many of the present generation appreciate what it was like to have to put up boards at your windows at night? It kept the light from going out but it also prevented fresh air from coming in, and after a few hours being cooped up like that the foul atmosphere was indescribable.

One of the sad things about the early days was that gunners would sometimes fire on our own planes because they failed to recognize them as friendly. Of course it is harder still to recognize one plane from another if it is coming at you head-on. I can recall one instance where the battery commander praised a man for bringing down a plane, and then later had to give him a good roasting when it turned out to be 'one of ours'. But many of us were inexperienced, only kids after all. Firing at static targets was what we had been trained to do.

As an instance of my own inexperience, I confess to having shot a sheep. This came about when I was on guard duty at Langdon Barracks engine-room where the power was generated. The breakwater lookout had reported a flashing light on the clifftops in a remote area. I heard coughing and the rustling of grass so I fired at the noise. The sheep was one which had strayed away from the main flock. For a while my pals called me 'Sheep Shooter', but they should have been there. When you are alone at night you are apt to let your imagination run away with you. Besides when you have a loaded rifle with you it seems natural to be trigger-happy. This was a state of mind that could affect all of us. Of course, in a remote spot like that there should have been two sentries. Even the officers would ring the sentry before visiting!

In late July 1940 airman A. Tribe was sent to Dover, arriving by train and reaching the Priory station at about 10 p.m.

There were about twelve of us and an officer was hanging about on the blacked-out platform. They took us to a hotel in the main street to put us up for the night. In the morning we moved to a hotel on the seafront. There we formed No. 961 Balloon Squadron HQ RAF.

Our barrage balloons arrived from Kidbrook. I stayed in Dover for roughly two years so saw a lot of shelling from France. In fact, they knocked out our hotel so we immediately moved to the caves beneath the castle. Later, we set up our HQ at the Girls' Grammar School, Frith Road, at the back of the town.

Also joining the balloon squadron was J. Timperly:

I recall being annoyed that a Home Guard chap, who visited our site, used to have a Bren gun with him. All we had at the time were Ross rifles and ten rounds of ammunition per man. On one occasion we saw a plane obviously making a forced landing some distance away. We ran across the fields to see what we could do to help. But we were suddenly confronted with an irate farmer armed with a shotgun. We realized we had almost wrecked his crops so beat a hasty retreat leaving someone else to attend the forced landing.

When Ron Murray came down to the area by troop train he was smartly reminded of the battalion briefing they had undergone before leaving: '. . . you are going to an area where anything can happen, so keep your wits about you!' His train was about one mile from Ashford when everyone was obliged to vacate it in a mad scramble – through windows and doors – to tumble down the railway embankments. A German Me 109 fighter began to strafe the train from engine to guard's van:

> There was no great damage or any casualties and we later continued our journey to Dover where army lorries were waiting. They took us back to Sellindge, near Lympne airfield.
>
> As the Battle of Britain started to hot up we came under almost constant air attacks by Stukas. There were a lot of dummy planes positioned around the airfield but Jerry was not deceived for one moment. He just came straight down on the aerodrome, causing a lot of damage and many casualties.
>
> Some time later I was transferred to sound-ranging duties near Shakespeare Cliff, for seventy-two-hour periods. Most of the convoys used to come up the Channel under cover of darkness by then. German searchlights would sweep continuously, looking for them. As soon as they opened fire with their big railway guns we would swing into action with our equipment to try to pin-point their position. We then passed on the information to RAF Bomber Command, who would fly over and give the area a pasting. Air battles were commonplace. We were playing football one evening when a yellow-nosed Me 109 came swooping down out of the clouds. Eventually cornered by two Spitfires, the German pilot was forced to land in a field next to our football pitch. The pilot got out and gave a Nazi salute. Under the impression that German forces had established a landing in the Dover area, he demanded to be taken to the nearest German HQ! He was arrogant, and started to chuck his weight around – that is, until he heard a bullet being put into the breech of a rifle. Realizing that things were not as he imagined he then quietened down.
>
> At this time Monty (General Bernard Montgomery) was then General Officer Commanding (GOC). He was known to be a strict disciplinarian and our officers were somewhat apprehensive when it became known that Monty was to pay us a visit. When he arrived our sentry, briefed beforehand, sprang to attention and gave him a smart salute by presenting arms. But Monty was not impressed and ordered the sentry placed under arrest for failing to check the GOC's identification papers! When Monty visited the cookhouse he

tested the knowledge of the cookhouse staff over purely military matters. He asked questions about the various types of poison gas, but the answers he got were not considered satisfactory so the cooks were packed off on a gas course, while the rest of us received orders to do physical training before breakfast – every day!

Having completed a wireless operators' course at RAF Blackpool and then Yatesbury S. Morgans was eventually posted to Capel le Ferne and billeted in a bungalow called 'Shorncliffe'. The elderly couple who owned it treated him as one of their own. The husband was a retired jeweller who had run a business at Maidstone:

I spent four long winter months at Capel on radio interception work whilst waiting for my recall to complete aircrew training. Together with another 'erk' and a sergeant, I manned a listening post about a quarter of a mile along the cliff road towards Dover. We operated in a building only about ten feet square and that also included our receivers.

Our duty was to listen out for the radio beams used to guide the Luftwaffe bombers to their targets. We had a direct telephone line to our HQ at Radlett who would take reports from posts like ours. Where the radio beams intersected the target could be plotted. The navy had a larger radio building further along the coast where, it was said, most of the staff were linguists. Rumour had it that the Germans carried out commando-style raids on the cliffs immediately below our post. A most unlikely story, perhaps the result of another rumour which alleged that soldiers patrolling the railway at Dymchurch had disappeared suddenly, without trace.

Even so, there were wild winter nights when I would struggle along the cliff road in a gale force wind, my body angled at forty-five degrees against the blast, with nobody about at all. I was a green lad of nineteen and unarmed, and was always glad to gain the sanctuary of the listening post – even if I had then to do an eight-hour stint of duty alone!

Thomas Cosker, posted to Folkestone in 1940, makes his dramatic contribution in an imaginative style:

Usual sirens gone. Watching the enemy planes approaching – fifty from the left, fifty from the right and fifty straight ahead. They'd join up above us and go inland. Not particularly bothered, they won't bother us going in, only dropping their bombs on us on the way back out – if balked. Suddenly an alarming ripple flies past. Behind the enemy formations is the 'BBB' – Big Black Bar. We know only too well what he is coming for. Very low and quite slow he reaches us and starts to fly around in a circle above. If I open up at him with my Lewis gun he gets just above my falling tracer, and round and round he goes, his rear gunner spraying us all the time. He'll do this for half an hour before dropping his bombs on us. We loathed, hated and feared him. One day over the field telephone came the jubilant news that the BBB had been hit. A direct hit over Dungeness. Great joy. Needless to say, next day trailing along behind another bomber formation was a new BBB. Life is very unfair!

One day, very wet and cold with low cloud, I went to the main gate to see if any mail was there for me. On my return, I heard a plane and saw the tail of one going into a cloud. In this weather one of ours, no doubt. A few yards further on I heard a plane diving, and as I looked up it appeared out of the cloud, coming towards me. As I looked bombs fell from it. Down I went, wet puddles and all – crunch, squish, and when I got to my feet and looked around I nearly had a fit. Less than six feet away was a 1,000 lb bomb, and behind me the fin of a 500 lb bomb sticking out of the ground. I quite easily broke the 100-yard sprint world record. This was the occasion when the BBB dropped a delayed-action bomb, which bounced through a basement window of the Royal Pavilion Hotel and buried itself in the cellar.

On a clear day, you could often hear enemy planes droning high in the sky. If you had good eyesight you might eventually spot tiny white dots and begin to count them. Sometimes you could hear dogfights going on above you – the brrrrrr of Spitfire machine guns and the bop bop bop of Jerry firing back – but nothing to be seen.

There was the day when a hell of a racket arose inland seeming to come towards us. We assumed this was a Jerry in trouble, hedge-hopping his way home. Sure enough a yellow-nosed Messerschmitt suddenly appeared over the cliff edge, heading our way and facing the Channel. We all opened fire on him. He eventually turned and forced-landed about 400 yards east of the harbour. My lads, mostly from London, escorted the pilot up the cliffs and it

Junkers 88 medium bombers often made low-level attacks on south-east towns and convoys. Farmers and Land Army girls were machine gunned as they worked in the fields.

Just after 04.00 on 18 November 1940 sleeping residents in Rossendale Road, Folkestone, were buried alive beneath the wreckage of their homes. A German Luftmine exploded within yards of its target, the Junction station, and in seconds the area became a moonscape.

took all my wits to save him from slipping 'accidentally' over the edge. A Spitfire was later credited with shooting the German down. Bang went my chance of an MM!

One bright moonlight night we spotted a parachute coming down. Hurriedly getting some men together, we dashed round to the harbour to capture the parachutist. As we turned a corner a huge blast occurred. It was a landmine which demolished fifty-odd houses including our post and our favourite fish and chip shop. As luck would have it, it exploded on one of the few fully inhabited streets in Folkestone. Gas and water mains were shattered and we had a horrible night digging out pieces of people.

One evening we were ordered to 'stand-to': invasion was a possibility. At dusk RAF planes went scurrying across the Channel; flares went down followed by bombs. German ack-ack shells went up, curving slightly then exploding. Our 'planes kept it up for hours. Later in the week we were told the Germans had tried a dress rehearsal of the invasion, with disastrous results. Weeks, and even months later, I was asked if it was true that we had buried sixty or seventy Germans to a trench in communal graves. I never saw a single body.

Hundreds of shells whistled over one night during an artillery barrage. Shop windows burst with the heavy concussion. It went on for hours and was pretty scary. Imagine our embarrassment – and by now we were no longer 'green troops' – when we found out it was the Royal Navy bombarding the French coast.

When a convoy was passing Folkestone a squadron of planes approached from over the Channel. Our rough and ready way of identifying planes at that time (it improved later) was simply 'pointed wings – ours, square wings – Jerry'. But these were rounded! The planes slowly approached, then made their dive on the ships and dropped bombs. They were almost out of range and I could only fire at the end of their dive. When the smoke and spray had diminished a trawler came out backwards with only one man injured.

Towards the end of November 'they' decided we could have every other night off duty. We went to a large red-brick nunnery above the harbour. I had a vague impression that nuns slept in stone cells with a bit of straw on the floor. But the rooms were beautiful with lovely beds and mattresses. Some of the lads were in a room named 'Holy Innocent', with a card on the door saying, 'Ring the bell for a mistress'.

My second post was on a wooden jetty on the harbour side of the inner harbour; another was a pillbox on the harbour pier adjoining. Between the small pier and our post, which was, incidentally, a submerged barge, there was a gate made of scaffolding festooned with barbed wire. We closed the gate between dusk and dawn.

A very scruffy small boat with an impossible Polish name used to ply constantly between east of Folkestone and the harbour carrying ballast which we shovelled into the barge. It was manned by three men and a fifteen-year-old boy, all of them Dutch. They had one Maxim machine gun loaded with about ten rounds of revolver-type ammunition, and the boy always joined in firing at enemy aircraft when we did. I doubt whether his bullets got half way to the target but he most certainly tried his best.

On the harbour station the buffet remained open. There was the manageress Joan 'Johnnie' Walker, Vera and Eileen Potter. We were always made welcome there. I don't ever remember it closing in the afternoons but, of course, no policemen ever set foot in the harbour to check the licensing laws!

Occasionally it was my job to let the fishing boats out early in the morning when the tide was right. They were only out for a short time and often came back loaded with sprats. As a northerner I had never seen sprats before but I quickly learned to enjoy them. I would lower a bucket over the side to be filled. One day they gave me two large cod. I nipped round to the sergeant cook – one for him and one for me. At teatime I walked past the men queuing for their meal, ignoring the pathetic looks on their faces!

Royal Engineer railway operating sapper John Payne, together with about six other men, was posted to Dover in August 1940, to be attached to the Royal Marine Siege Regiment. Their headquarters was a civilian convalescent home,

Portal House, and a nearby farm was occupied by the Royal Marines. The two long-range guns – Winnie and Pooh – were situated close by. All their mail was censored and stamped 'HM Ships'.

The RE's job was to operate a railway track that had been laid between the village of Martin Mill and St Margaret's Bay. When the track reached St Margaret's Bay it branched off to each gun position, and also to the firing points for the rail-mounted guns. The rail-mounted guns were kept in Guston rail tunnel, between Martin Mill and Dover station. One track had been commandeered by the military, while the civilian trains operated on the other track. When the guns were needed we operated the locos that hauled them to St Margaret's to fire, returning to the tunnel afterwards.

Telephones had been installed along the rail track to act as signal cabins to control the line. One was installed in the base of a large wooden dummy gun, erected in the firing position. Many times I was on duty inside the dummy gun position. Although situated in Hellfire Corner it was the safest place, as the Germans left it alone. After several months in Portal House the REs commandeered another house in Martin Mill, but they still remained under the command of the Royal Marines.

The cordite bins that supplied the guns were built into the railway cuttings and we transported shells and cordite to both the static and also the rail-mounted guns. We used speedy little petrol-driven rail trolleys, that could get us and the Marines to any point very quickly.

Bert French's experiences in the early years of the war took place in the Royal Naval Patrol Service (RNPS) as a crew member of HMT *Lois*, one of the minesweeping trawlers based at Dover:

In September 1940, prior to the first mass raid on London on the 7th, it was a brilliant sunny day. Early in the afternoon the sound of the Dover town air raid warning had just faded away. Looking up into the sky there was a mass of enemy planes that could be numbered in their hundreds, glittering like silver fish high up in the sunlight. It was evident that the distance was too far from the shore-based anti-aircraft guns to be able to touch them but some shells were fired. Within half an hour, however, there were decoy planes that flew low enough to try and draw off any ack-ack defensive measures. The decoys dropped one or two bombs on the town and in the harbour. The force of a bomb exploding in water whilst below deck was my first experience of an underwater explosion. No ships suffered any damage on this occasion.

At one time the minesweeping patrols, in good sea-going weather, were not allowed any shore leave. A few weeks later we learned that our craft had a few loose rivets below the water-line, causing leakage. We were pleased when orders came for *Lois* to be laid up for a couple of days so the shipwrights could work at low tide. Imagine our disappointment, two hours after receiving our repair instructions, to learn that our repairs had been postponed so that we could make way for another trawler which had more urgent work to be done. No shore leave was granted – we just moved to a non-repair quay on the Eastern Arm and automatically we became a Duty Ship.

During an air raid some days later German bombs dropped in the harbour. Whilst we could see smoke rising above the harbour installations, we had no knowledge of any ship being damaged. But within half an hour we learned the trawler which had taken our place in the repair quay had been hit and suffered many casualties. You can never tell when Lady Luck is on your side!

We had the job of escorting a convoy of four vessels – an ammunition barge, a French trawler (captured by the Royal Navy earlier in the year) named *Keriardo*, a large motor cruiser and another trawler – to Newhaven, Sussex. About 3 miles from Newhaven the other trawler skipper asked for permission to take the lead pending the official handover at a pre-arranged point off the Sussex coast. Just 1 mile further on there was a terrific explosion ahead of us – the new leader had struck a mine. There were no survivors. The awful fear that during the night German E-boats had laid some magnetic mines along our coasts was always with us. The order was immediately given for two crew members to use Lewis machine guns and fire from the ship's bows into the water dead ahead to activate any mines in our path. The little convoy was duly handed over to the vessel which came out from Newhaven. We turned round and, following instructions, started our minesweeping duties all the way back to Dover and home.

Liberally laced with cynicism, H.W. Sneller's memoir is a meticulous contribution:

The radar cabins, on trailers, were perched well above ground level and had plywood walls, probably only resistant to air-gun pellets, so we decided to sandbag our sets. We were then at Farthingloe site, and we sweated mightily building the sandbagged walls up to about eight feet high or so. Later it was announced that we were to be issued with a new radar set, and we duly demolished most of the sandbags, put the new set in position, and then put them all back again. Then we were told the set was to be modified to receive an angle of sight and continuous following mode. Down came the sandbags once again and the whole area round the set was levelled. A couple of Royal Army Ordnance Corps (RAOC) bods turned up to fit it. We were given all the bits and pieces to fit the aerial frame, with an inadequate set of tools – of course. We received about ten minutes' instructions on how to use the attachment and then were left to get on with it!

Our plots were fed to the local Plotting Room as well as the site, and they soon became very sarcastic about our height calculations because every approaching aircraft seemed to dive-bomb us. This was reported; various people came, looked at everything and said it was correct, until two civilians turned up with a small balloon and an oscillator which they proceeded to fly from the balloon. In no time at all they found that one aerial connection was the wrong way round and so we had been using the wrong position on our angle of sight equipment.

The only noise in both receiver and transmitter cabins was that of cooling fans inside the sets. When the Mk 2 was produced somebody had a brainstorm. It was decided that perhaps operators could not distinguish right from left. So instead of the noiseless electronic switching, giving two white signals on the displays, they came up with a red and green shutter system that was mechanically driven. The racket from these mechanical shutters was appalling! However, this was soon outmoded by the very efficient American SCR584 radar sets.

One piece of army logic I ran across at Farthingloe gun site concerned the extremely reliable Lister generating sets used for power. Once the Battle of Britain started the coastal radar sets were manned on a twenty-four-hour basis, and consequently it was never really possible to check the oil level in these generators. Although a request for a second generator was made nothing happened. Our Lister began spurting out long flames from its exhaust in the middle of an air raid – and at night!

We had some peculiar 'breaks' and realized that the Germans were putting up barrage balloons after dark, and therefore were able to give warning. Our sets at Farthingloe stood on a ridge that was higher than the cliff edge immediately in front of us, and we found we could pick up targets flying low over the sea, most probably far below most radar coverage.

One night we had picked up a rather slow-moving trace. I reported it to the plotting room for it was only a little way out in the Channel. RAF radar could not find it and presumably somebody thought of the navy. In the greatest confidence we were told that in fact it was a 'blacked-out' destroyer going down the Channel on a very dark night.

Our first plotting of a major enemy formation was, as far as I can recollect, on a beautiful June evening. It was the first convoy raid which was soon to close the Channel to merchant shipping during daylight hours. All available operators, both on duty and off, jammed into the cabins to watch events. The very first trace was an RAF plane which crashed near Hougham after skimming over the gun-site.

During the Battle of Britain period every conceivable aircraft type, including an autogiro, appeared in the Dover area. The autogiro was used for radar calibration. I happened to be off duty one day when we heard an aircraft approaching that was obviously in some kind of trouble. It was, of all things, a biplane, which just managed to lift over the cliff edge in front of us, only to crash on the ridge just to the west of us. All the spare AA personnel rushed over to the crash. It had turned over on impact but the pilot was sufficiently conscious to show us how to unclip his harness in which he was hanging. His first thought was to enquire after his gunner in the rear cockpit. But he was dead. All the time we were there I could hear something dripping on the engine. If it was petrol then we were lucky it did not catch fire.

Not long after the Dunkirk evacuation the ridge in front of us was mined, and from somewhere a soldier suddenly appeared who was convinced he could find his way through the minefield. He was presumably on his way to the Old Folkestone Road. But it was obvious he did not know the way. It took quite a while to find a team of REs and a medical officer with a sack to get through to the remains of the unfortunate, misguided soldier.

During the post-Dunkirk period the Luftwaffe began their night bombing of London; at the same time the RAF were bombing German invasion barges in the French ports. Aircraft were coming and going, all mixed up together. Our form of radar presentation could not cope with such conditions, for AA radar needed to tackle one definite target at a time. The RAF radar with PPI presentation could, with certain limitations, cope with the situation but they too could often get swamped and tell us to cease reporting until further instructions. When that happened we just used to sit, watching, and eating our army-issue supper of bread and dripping.

At the height of the Battle of Britain period at Farthingloe gun-site G. Lewis & Sons were finishing off the static 3.7-in gun pits. All spare gunners were called out to fetch up the ammunition from the reserve magazine. Although the civilian workmen had been sent out of the area when the alarm went, they joined in with their wheelbarrows, and by hand, helped to move the shells into the gun pits during an action.

Half way through her seventeenth year Muriel Sidwell had set her heart on joining the WRNS. Her parents, however, had other ideas and refused to sign the consent form. In those days parents were the 'bosses':

For several months when I was sixteen I worked in the Salvation Army canteen at the Citadel Barracks. We sold cakes known as 'wads', tea and mineral waters to the troops. We also supplied suppers, things like cabbage, sausage and potatoes. Sometimes the soldiers on duty at the gun battery would send over an enamel jug for tea. It was always black from standing on their stove, so we used to scrub it clean before filling it with tea. Once the advanced party of a Canadian unit turned up on motor bikes. One of them asked for a Coke. Although there must have been some on sale in other parts of the country, I had never heard of it. The only coke we had was what we put on the stoves!

At Kearsney there was a sisterhood of nuns. When working at Peakes Stores I would deliver fish and groceries there and be shown through lots of oak-panelled passages to an office where the mother superior (who spoke no English) would pay me. The nuns in the kitchen used to make me a cup of cocoa. We used to converse mainly in sign language and there was always the pungent smell of lovely cooking. Cycling out to Kearsney was all right in fine weather but in the winter months of 1940–41 there was a lot of snow. Once I got as far as Buckland and then had to push my bike the rest of the way. It took me all morning to make the delivery and that afternoon I was so beaten that mum would not let me go back to work. Dad went to the shop to explain, but next day I was back delivering – snow or no snow! At that time my wages were ten shillings [50p] per week.

Mum and I and a friend were blackberrying in the fields behind Farthingloe Farm towards the end of summer 1940. The air raid warning had gone off and all of a sudden there were German 'planes overhead. Then our British fighters appeared, but I am not sure if they were Hurricanes or Spitfires. We were hiding in the thickest brambles we could find, and watched the dogfights. 'Planes were weaving in and out and there was the constant sound of gunfire. It seemed to go on for ages. We saw one 'plane go down between Dover and Folkestone and hoped it was one of theirs. I recall it was a lovely sunny day with not a cloud in the sky.

Later in the war one particular incident sticks out in my mind. A house had received shell damage and had actually collapsed into the centre of the crater. There was a terrible smell of escaping gas everywhere. The ARP rescue squad was just about to tunnel into the wreckage when I arrived. To me everything looked grey, the air, the street, the buildings and even the people. That scene has never left my memory. The smell of damp bricks, plaster and the explosive itself. There was a small body wrapped up in a dirty sheet or nightie. It was covered with a grey dust. It was a little girl of about two years who had been killed. Her mother had been badly injured. One of my pals at the youth club had had his ribs broken in several places. We used to visit him at Buckland Hospital.

I managed to get to see Mr Watkins' house when I had explained to the warden at the road barrier. The front of the house was completely gone. The staircase was half smashed but I could look up the stairs – very gingerly – until I could see into the main bedroom. A large slab of paving stone had smashed the double bed to smithereens. Mr Watkins was on night shift at Snowdown Colliery and his wife and daughters had been evacuated to South Wales. There was nothing I could do to help so I went back home and got ready for work. Mum asked me to meet Mr Watkins at the bus stop when he returned. He was invited back home for breakfast. Nothing could be salvaged from his home.

CHAPTER THREE

'. . . who's got my eye?'

By 1941 over a million men and women had been conscripted into the armed forces; thousands more, rather than be forced to join the Army, had volunteered for the more prestigious Royal Navy or the Royal Air Force. Naturally some of them were eager to leave their onerous family ties and their meaningless daily grind at some thankless job. The majority, however, were whisked away to an uncertain future.

These enforced separations, imposed by conscription, released in some a passion for a home life that was denied them. This resulted in a marriage increase when either sex could claim up to four days' compassionate leave – or what the services called 'passionate leave'.

War Weapons Week in May 1941 was especially aiming at a total of £110,000 to buy two MTBs. No one believed that figure would be met. The final total, however, was £209,105.

On the whole there was a mature sense of obligation as the war progressed in intensity, an almost quiet acceptance for a disagreeable task for which some at least, felt a true sense of patriotism. Even so, during the first tentative months of the war there was not the fierce hatred of the Germans en masse. This came later when the war became more bitter and prolonged, when more and more families were receiving the black-edged telegrams gravely announcing 'missing in action – believed killed'. The true horror of the Nazi regime was not fully realized until the stories gradually filtered back from the theatres of war towards the end of the conflict.

At the outbreak of war B.K. Pearce (née Craig), was a schoolgirl in Dover, and was one of the youngest members of the Women's Voluntary Service (WVS). When the children were evacuated she went to Surrey where her parents lived. Returning to Dover in January 1941, she worked as a telephonist at the GPO exchange in Priory Street, where they received the warning of air raids and sounded the alarm for the town. There was a small emergency switchboard in the basement, manned by one operator all the time so there would be no break in service for priority lines:

I was living in Barton Road then with my aunt and cousin. It was badly damaged by a bomb which fell opposite. We were rather pleased to see the Salvation Army who were the first to call round. As it happened we were all in the Morrison shelter. Had I stayed in bed though, I would have found myself under the dressing table which the blast had thrown on to the bed.

At that time we were not allowed to join the armed services, as GPO telephonists were in a 'reserved occupation', although we carried out part-time ARP duties. Several of us joined the National Fire Service (NFS) as switchboard operators. There was a training exercise one night when an actual shelling bombardment began. No one told me it was for real so every call I received was, as far as I knew, a spoof incident! When the Dover exchange was hit by a shell I was working as relief in Broadstairs. Although we heard a lot of noise that night it came as quite a shock next morning to learn that four men on duty had been killed.

Bill Warbrick, who thought he had been posted to Kent for a rest, was engaged in coast defence:

We had commandeered a Humber Snipe motor car and fitted it with an Army Type No. 11 wireless set. We used it to patrol the beach areas and a sort of observation post for the guns. The brakes on the Humber packed up, but in typical army style we carried on, until one particular night when belting full blast along a beach we spotted a sergeant in the Royal Engineers trying to flag us down. You can imagine it took some time for us to stop, and when we did we had penetrated some distance into a minefield his unit was laying. We spent a very unpleasant night before being extricated.

As a very young Royal Marine recruit Patrick Churchill felt strongly about his responsibilities when on sentry duty on the cliffs above St Margaret's Bay. With almost boyish enthusiasm he imagined himself taking part in a real-life adventure like the stories in the *Boy's Own Paper*.

> There I was on the very point, close to enemy-held territory, gazing at this expanse of water over which an invasion fleet might appear at any time. Just to give my eyes something to focus upon in all that emptiness, I would concentrate on the Goodwin Lightship.
>
> It was at the Deal RM Barracks that I was thrown into the deep end of the swimming pool as a non-swimmer. I was left to splash my own way out as best I could.
>
> Deal was the ultimate in 'bullshine'. We even had to remove our boots before walking over the glass-like burnished barrack-room floors, and even the coal in the bunkers was whitewashed during the summer months. We also had a trained Marine allocated to each recruit barrack-room so that the occupants could be inculcated in the best traditions of the Royal Marines and their discipline.
>
> By contrast at nearby Kingsdown we lived in chalets four to a room. It was relaxing and quite comfortable, but we had a sergeant-major called 'Chalky White' who used to draw a circle around any dirty or dusty parts of our accommodation.

Whisked away to an uncertain future, like thousands of others, William Smith found himself patrolling the quiet country lanes between Deal and Dover:

> In the early days of the invasion scare we had only one Canadian Ross rifle between two men. We also had to be armed when off duty, so we had to go about in pairs. One man had the rifle while his pal carried a bandolier of fifty rounds of ammunition.

Lieutenant-Colonel Swale was Staff Captain of 219 Infantry Brigade based at Dover Castle:

> The battalion at the castle was the 5th Queens, commanded by Lieutenant-Colonel Adams, a most efficient and pleasant officer. The proximity of this unit to the Brigade HQ meant that we saw more of it than the other three battalions. They were as smart as any Guards unit.
>
> The 11th East Surreys occupied the barracks at Western Heights. Their CO, of the famous Drake-Brockman family, was as brave as a lion – and quite potty. My most dangerous moment in Dover was when riding with him in his command Bren-gun Carrier on exercise. Whenever he wanted to stop he would lean forward and bang on the driver's tin hat with a knobbly stick. He drove his officers to distraction by forcing them to dig for anti-personnel

'My most dangerous moment in Dover was when riding with him in his command Bren-gun Carrier. . . . Whenever he wanted to stop he would lean forward and bang on the driver's tin hat with a knobbly stick.'

mines around the area. Apparently the Canadians had planted them but had not kept a record of where they might be. In fact a Royal Engineers officer was killed when he trod on one at the foot of Shakespeare Cliff.

The 10th Battalion Royal Sussex Regiment were at St Margaret's Bay, as near to the front line as anyone. Their CO, Lieutenant-Colonel 'Bolo' Whistler, was a grand chap. Later on he became Brigadier in the Italian campaign and lost an arm there. The remaining battalion was the 4th Buffs – known locally as the 'Bloody Buffs' – who occupied some requisitioned houses along the sea front.

At the Duke of York's School was the 29th Independent Anti-Tank Battery, whose Adjutant was Captain Hamish Wilson. The battery had been raised in Oban, many of the gunners having Gaelic as their first language. They had been one of the few units of the 51st Highland Division to come back from France with all their guns, plus a captured German gun, intact.

I remember the RE Tunnelling Company with much pleasure. They were mostly Welsh miners. They had come from Gibraltar to dig out what later proved to be a hospital but which was also part of 'Fortitude South' deception plan to persuade Hitler that Dover was to be the invasion headquarters. They left tons of excavated chalk spill on the foreshore for the Luftwaffe to spot. Their uniform consisted of a woolly cap, denim trousers and large boots – but no shirts of course.

Dover provided my first experience of women service personnel, Auxiliary Training Service (ATS) and WRNS. The War Office regarded formations like brigades and divisions as 'fighting troops' and therefore quite unsuited for female service. In other words, the Cotswolds might be regarded as dangerous territory but Dover would be regarded as safe for women. I also could not help noticing that the servants at the Constable's Tower Officers' Mess were often ex-gunners with impaired hearing who had been posted on compassionate grounds to places where they would not be exposed to loud bangs!

The presence of so much unexpected female talent was a great joy, not least because the WRNS especially were so punctilious in their salutes to officers whenever we passed or met. The navy had a system of 'Officer Only – Secret' delivery of messages by WRN officers. The rule was that these officers could go singly in the tunnels before 1900 hours but thereafter there had to be two of them. Presumably the Admiralty was not aware that the tunnels were well underground and unaffected by daylight. But the visits were very pleasing. As far as I know none of the WRN officers was ever attacked – at least not in the tunnels, and certainly not by me.

Conditions in the tunnels were not good – cold, damp, dark, poorly ventilated. My own 'office' had inadequate strip lighting and a defective two-bar electric fire whose worn-out elements had to be supplemented by paper clips. We all had bronchial discomforts of one kind or another. I spent three weeks sick due to 'pyrexia of unknown origin' and the MO was worried it might be serious, but fifty years later there is no sign of chest trouble.

'He was very obviously "County" – his immaculate riding boots would have cost a year of my pay. . . . he seemed to epitomize Colonel Blimp.'

I remember Captain Tom Wall MC, of the 16/5th Irish Lancers, who as Garrison Adjutant occupied a suite of rooms in the Constable's Tower. I gathered he was very busy during the days immediately after Dunkirk, but by the time I met him he appeared to be permanently unemployed! He was very obviously 'County' – his immaculate riding boots would have cost a year of my pay. Always in full cavalry uniform and with an enormous white moustache and bulging blue eyes, he seemed to epitomize Colonel Blimp. He was in fact a delightful gentleman.

Brian Kemp was too young to have served in any of the armed forces during the Second World War but he lived in Dover throughout the conflict:

For two years I did not attend school as most of the children had been evacuated to Ebbw Vale in Wales. I remained in Dover, mostly playing on the barrage balloon sites, gun-sites, searchlight sites, and near a mysterious radio station, the purpose of which I still have not discovered. I think the troops allowed us on their sites and played games with us because they were separated from their families and enjoyed our company as much as we enjoyed theirs. Many's the time I have sat on an airman's lap in the winch compartment whilst he hauled down a balloon, or helped retrieve rabbits shot by troops in the fields.

Albert Fisher was posted to Dover with No. 961 Barrage Balloon Squadron from Tangmere in Sussex soon after Dunkirk. They stored their gas cylinders at the local cricket ground:

Three of our balloons were on barges in the harbour and the rest were on the cliffs on either side of the town. We understood our balloons were there to replace ack-ack guns moved to defend London. Our HQ was a large building on the sea front until it was destroyed by shelling. We moved into tunnels under the castle.

We had an observation balloon at St Margaret's Bay near the radar station. Radio messages were transmitted to the French underground from an aerial fixed to it.

Joining 423 Battery in August 1941 H. Shaw and a companion left their kit in the billet and went to the NAAFI. Pooling their resources they just had enough to buy two cups of tea and a packet of Players Weights cigarettes:

The food and billets were only average but the Battery Sergeant-Major was far from popular. The story was told that he would never come back to the battery at night alone just in case a sentry hated him enough to shoot him, and then claim he had not responded to the sentry's challenge. Supper at night was cocoa without sugar and a slice of bread and jam. The BSM used to tip potatoes on the floor each evening and we had to peel them before we got any supper.

I was left with a very red face one day whilst on sentry duty. I had refused to allow a civilian to enter the compound. Then one of our sergeants came on the scene and identified the stranger as Mr Watson-Watt – the inventor of radar!

On one cold and very wet night everyone was turned out. The radar had picked up a couple of strange objects heading our way. Was it the start of the German invasion? It wasn't – and just as well perhaps, because we hadn't any ammunition between us! The objects were two barrage balloons.

We were in a cinema one evening when the alert was flashed on to the screen. I remember two old ladies sitting in front of us who wouldn't budge. 'We've paid for our seats so we'll stop. Hitler knows what he can do with his ruddy aeroplanes.'

Billeted in Sandgate Jim Harris had 'wangled' a weekend pass to go home to Rotherfield, the Sussex side of Tunbridge Wells:

I was due back early Sunday night as I was to start my twenty-four-hour stint as Orderly Sergeant. I was carrying a small brown attaché case in which were socks, my army shirt with three stripes on the arm and a large slice of home-made cake. I got to Sandgate on time and found Lieutenant Jacques waiting for me. 'Hurry up and get changed,' he said, '. . . we have to go into Folkestone urgently to arrest some men caught in a brawl.'

I opened my case – to find a complete nurse's outfit! But I was able to borrow an ill-fitting uniform and went to arrest the men. I later found the nurse's name in the attaché case I had obviously grabbed by mistake on the train. When I rang Ashford Hospital Nurse Taylor said she was shocked to find she owned an oversize army shirt with three stripes on the sleeves – but enjoyed the cake!

In the summer months of 1941 soldiers on the Pier guns and also the breakwater, used to swim naked in Dover Harbour. Then an order was issued: 'This practice will cease forthwith'. Ted White remembers the order came because the WRNS, ATS and WAAFs at the castle had made a complaint. 'It seemed *little* things do not count', he wrote.

One night a ton of coal for our stoves (it was rationed and in very short sup-ply) was silently passed across the railway point and sentry on guard duty until it was equally silently unloaded and the truck returned.

I shared a small room with John Piper who was 'knocking on' and was on the permanent staff caring for our guns. Our Sergeants' Mess was a regular port of call for crews from minesweepers and John would procure such items as leaf tobacco and rum. He demonstrated to me the art of making a 'sprig'. Taking a leaf of tobacco he poured over it dark, strong navy rum, then took another leaf and laid it over the first, adding plenty of rum. When he had about ten leaves rolled up into a sausage shape he bound it tightly with stout cord and hung it on a nail to mature. Some three weeks later he announced it was time to sample the sprig. He cut off a piece about an inch long then filled his pipe and settled down for a long smoke. About an hour later he just fell asleep and did not wake up for over eight hours! Next morning he declared it was the best drop of rum he had ever tasted. In fact, he had actually smoked himself drunk.

The stoicism, courage and sheer 'bloody-mindedness' of the NAAFI girls in Hellfire Corner was never in question, as this fifty-year-old newspaper cutting shows. It was sent in by K. May, who served at Charlton Road, Frith Road and Connaught Barracks:

GIRLS WON'T QUIT BOMB TOWN – When a bomb dropped outside a NAAFI canteen at Dover four NAAFI girls asleep in their quarters were buried under the debris. All were rescued and found to have suffered from shock. During a short leave NAAFI officials arranged for the girls to go to a safer area. But the 'Canteen Commandos' told NAAFI officials, 'Move us away from Dover and we'll give in our notice!'

Private L. Pearce arrived at Dover Castle with the 15th Battalion Queen's Royal Regiment in early 1941. The shoulder flash they wore was a phoenix rising from the flames, and the motto read, 'Be Bloody, Bold, and Resolute.' The motto appeared on fire orders in every pillbox, and at one of them someone had written beneath, 'We're bloody cold and desolate!'

Some of the defence 'armaments' were of a rather haphazard nature, one of which may be of special interest. At the rear of the Keep Wall and to the side of Constable's Tower were the 'Underground Works', and at that time the sides of the passages were lined with 40-pound RAF bombs. Stored elsewhere in the castle were a number of wooden frames approximately 12 feet long, supported on legs which were about 18 inches high. The frames consisted of two solid planks of wood about 6 inches wide, and they were fixed in the legs to form a 'V'-shaped channel rather like a narrow trough. In the event of an invasion they would be strategically placed along the cliff top in front of the Officers' Mess and overlooking the houses at East Cliff. The intention was that the bombs would be placed in the 'V' troughs and directed over the cliff edge towards any invaders at the foot of the cliff. For very obvious reasons these 'weapons' were never tested, and as the threat of invasion gradually diminished, a feeling of intense relief was felt by all those soldiers who had been allotted this rather hazardous role.

Jimmy Kay started off his army career with the 1/7 Battalion Queen's Regiment at the Grand Shaft Barracks, Dover:

An awful place to be stationed. No hot water and no proper lighting. Still they made a good effort to give us an enjoyable Christmas Day. Then we moved to St Margaret's Bay (I wish I had a quid for every time I drove a three-ton lorry up and down those steep bends leading to the bay). I was in the Vickers gun team. Our guns were set to fire on fixed-lines at night. Our billet was the Granville Hotel. Those were indeed memorable days – shells landing on us from the French coast and our guns responding from just behind us.

With a Field Company Royal Engineers R. Coyles was building gun emplacements, camps, moving from place to place and repairing air-raid damaged buildings:

I can recall one damp misty morning when a couple of us were making dummy guns and a German bomber suddenly loomed out of the fog. We just looked up at the pilot, his plane was no more than about a hundred feet up. I have often wondered since who was the most shocked at the confrontation. We only had a hammer to defend ourselves with!

After finishing his training at the shore establishment HMS *Ganges*, Bill Jenkins was drafted to HMS *Lynx* at Dover and joined HMT *Alexandrite* in February 1941:

Another telegraphist who had trained with me also came to Dover but was sent to the *Gulfoss*. Within two weeks he was back home on survivor's leave! The *Gulfoss* had pulled in a mine which exploded. I was on board the *Alexandrite* for well over eighteen months, during which time there were some hair-raising experiences. But the tremendous camaraderie of those times is also memorable.

I can recall being on a rostrum near the coaling dock when Me 109s and Focke-Wulfs bombed and strafed the docks. I reckon I was very lucky to get away unscathed that day. We used to go out minesweeping mostly at night until the danger from German aircraft lessened slightly but I can remember being dive-bombed by Stukas one moonlit night when we had gone ashore for a break.

I especially remember the public houses in Dover which we visited on our rare shore leave: the Rose Hotel, the Crypt and the Grapes, and the pub at the top of the Prince of Wales Pier, where the barmaid was Margaret. Another barmaid was always called 'Dover Lil', and there was a rather matronly lady called 'Dover Flo'. She was particularly fond of our 'Guns' Abbott. Although we as sailors seemed to be her special favourites, the soldiers and airmen shared the dangers of the time and the people of Dover helped all service personnel a great deal. Of course one must never forget the little 'Sally Ann' in Snargate Street. The tea was sometimes a bit stewed but the people who ran it were the salt of the earth.

As a young Royal Marine, Cyril Burden also arrived at Dover and joined HMS
Lynx, when it was situated at Leney's Brewery at the back of Market Square:

> I was a Royal Marine signaller for the Naval Examination Service. I soon
> found out that there was no examination at all and I joined a small detach-
> ment of RM signallers, six of us plus Corporal Jones. Commander Ekyen was
> in command of *Lynx* and he was very proud of his smart Royal Marines
> detachment and wanted us on parade whenever it was possible.
>
> Our signalling duties were performed at the signal station on the Eastern
> Arm of the harbour and on the tugs *Lady Brassey* and sometimes *Lady
> Duncanon*. They were commanded by Lieutenant-Commander Hopgood,
> Lieutenant Holman and Lieutenant Nichols, all of whom were Dover
> Harbour Board employees before the war but had been given naval
> commissions. The rest of the crew were Dover Harbour Board personnel who
> served under T124 Articles and were not in uniform. There was also a radio
> operator, employed by Marconi, attached to the tugs.
>
> The tugs had various duties, standing by to see convoys through, rescuing
> MTBs off the French coast and going to help damaged merchant vessels. The
> officers and some of the crew won high awards – and justly so. We had some
> 'hairy' moments – especially creeping about off the enemy coast in bright
> moonlight to look for damaged MTBs and their crews. Obviously the job I
> and my colleagues did was to send and receive signals to and from the Port
> War Signal Station beneath the castle.

Cecil Coble used to be a fisherman sailing out of Lowestoft. He worked his way
up from cook (in 1926) to deckhand, third hand, mate and finally skipper. But
when the fishing industry was at a low ebb he joined the Tilbury Construction
and Dredging Company which was under an Admiralty contract:

> We were to take out 15 feet of chalk in the Camber, Dover Harbour, with
> another dredger called *Schelt*. This was in early 1939. We worked six days a
> week, twelve hours a day, and sometimes on Sunday for the same money.
>
> As a naval reservist I had to report for duty when war broke out in
> September, and joined a minesweeper bound for Sierra Leone, Africa. On my
> return to the UK for leave and promotion I was eventually sent to
> commission the *Willing Boys*. I remembered her from when she was built as a
> fishing boat in Lowestoft and I had known her owners and captain. So you
> see I was quite at home on her.
>
> At Dover we were an LL sweeper and our job was to sweep from the
> harbour entrance to the outer channels where the convoys went through,
> about two miles out and three-quarters of a mile wide. We would go out at
> 06.30 hours and come back at 23.30 hours – at action stations all the time. I
> was fortunate to have a good crew – always alert. They proved this one day
> while we were carrying out our routine duties. Above the noise of our diesel

engine (which gave the necessary electric current to blow up mines when located) we heard the unmistakable noise of aero-engines. The aircraft – it was a Junkers 88 – dived at us, coming out of the sun, their usual tactics. I gave the order to open fire as soon as we spotted him. Simultaneously we saw the bomb-bay doors open and I immediately gave the order 'hard a-starboard!'. Our gunners hit one of his engines, and it burst into flames. His bombs straddled us, the last one only thirty feet from our starboard side. The explosion lifted us up almost clean out of the water. Luckily nobody was hurt but we had a hell of a mess when we sorted out the shambles back in Dover. We spent three days kitting out again. The incident had been seen by Navy HQ at the castle and the senior minesweeping officer congratulated both me and my crew. He told me to put in a claim for bringing down the Junkers. But two Spitfires from Manston airfield also claimed it, so we did not get the credit after all.

Early one morning, after a heavy gale in the Channel, we found six or seven mines floating in the outer channel. We received instructions by wireless to sink them by gunfire. We managed to get rid of four but our ammunition was getting low so we started back. Then we got word that a mine had been parachuted into the bay near Folkestone. Proceeding there as fast as we could we managed to explode it at our second attempt, just as our ammunition ran out.

Motor launches used to moor alongside us. Most nights about six o'clock they would cross the Strait and send their agents ashore to find out what was going on. They would arrive back before we set out the next morning. We used to loan them our Tommy-guns and ammunition and even our Hotchkiss pom-pom. Luckily they always brought them back otherwise I would have been court-martialled!

Serving as a linesman, 'Pip' Johnson joined the Royal Corps of Signals, 43rd Wessex Division, with their HQ at Canterbury:

We were billeted at Warden House, Upper Deal, laying field cables between Dover Castle and the various camp-sites and gun emplacements along the coast from St Margaret's Bay to Sandwich.

Our vehicle was a three-ton Bedford lorry with the line-laying equipment, such as drums of cable, mounted on the back. One man faced the rear to guide the cable while another sat sideways wearing studded protective gloves so that the cable could be fixed to trees or poles. The poles were 18 feet high with a cross-tree at the top. Sometimes the cable would be laid along the road edge and buried underground at gateways or entrances. There were occasions when instead of burying the cable we would go up and over the gateway using the pole technique. Wooden bobbins were fixed to trees and poles with 6-inch nails – and some of them can still be seen today. That must be a sign of good workmanship!

My father lived in Deal during the war and one night, coming back from the Rose and Crown, he heard a 'swoosh'. He looked over the sea wall and saw a tea chest bumping along with the tide. Reporting a 'strange object' in the sea to the Coastguard, he was told, 'Well, if it's a piece of wood I should take it home'. It was full of tea and free from contamination by seawater because of the tin-foil lining. Tea being rationed, it was a god-send.

When the danger from incendiary bombs was considerable it became the legal duty of those civilians not employed on other essential duties to take their turn at fire watching. This was so that if incendiaries were scattered over a wide area, action could be taken to start extinguishing them before the problem got out of control. The fire watchers used to be posted in most public buildings which would otherwise remain uninhabited at night. Muriel Sidwell recalls:

Our room was at the top of one large building. There were camp beds to rest on with rough army blankets as covers. We slept, or half-slept, fully clothed and ready for any action. I could never rest properly through itching, and a couple of times 'strangers' (fleas, in other words). We used to take our own refreshments, cocoa, milk and sugar, and sandwiches. At seven o'clock we would knock off and go home for a wash, change and have breakfast but it was always too late to get any sleep in a proper bed. Then we were off to work for nine o'clock. War or no war, the manager wanted you there on time and was always on the look-out for late arrivals, checking his watch or looking at the town hall clock. The first day after fire watching was not too bad but the second day it was hard to keep your eyes open.

My mother was given a certificate for working for most of the war years as a cleaner at the Lord Warden Hotel (HMS *Wasp*) and also for being in the first aid team. I can picture my mother now, with three other ladies, waiting at the bus stop. Shells or bombs never stopped them.

Sitting in an observation post on top of the white cliffs Arthur Scholes overlooked the harbour and a wide stretch of the English Channel. His job, primarily, was to locate the German long-range gun batteries on the French coast, passing his observations back to the railway artillery HQ in Eythorne. Using the powerful binoculars issued to every observation post he regularly saw incidents which were never recorded in any official document:

During the Battle of Britain, out in the Channel, there were some large floating buoys, painted a sandy colour with a big red cross on the sides. Any airmen of either side who was shot down could climb into one of these for safety. Each morning there was a race between the British and German high-speed launches to rescue whoever was on board.

One morning MTBs went out and rescued two German airmen. I was watching through the binoculars when the first one appeared on the deck of the buoy. He gave a Nazi salute. A big burly navy matelot whipped an upper-cut to his chin and the German somersaulted backwards into the sea. But, of course, the navy fished him out.

Harold Michaels came to Dover in January 1941, and wrote:

We were quartered in the Grand Shaft Barracks and the town had much to offer by way of recreation considering it was wartime. By the end of our stay, however, it had become almost a 'ghost town'. I played in the dance band of the 5th Battalion Wiltshire Regiment, doing gigs at our barracks and two others, and also for the RAF Balloon Barrage units. When we played at the town hall dances we got paid as well!

What left an indelible imprint on James Smith's memory, when he was serving with 411 Coast Battery RA, was the fact that he could occasionally get away from parades and so on for a spell in the countryside around Deal:

I clearly recall the 5.5-inch naval guns which were placed just below the Dover Patrol obelisk at St Margaret's. They were from HMS *Hood* of First World War days, as were the four others at North Foreland, Broadstairs and

Girl on the town, 1940s-style. Despite the perils and privations of war, there was always a spirit of hope where romance blossomed on the dance floor to tunes like 'Goodnight Sweetheart' and 'We'll Meet Again'.

Royal Artillery gunners 'jump to it' in August 1941, while Lieutenant Tanner takes another shot in the sequence, depicting 412 Battery's 5.5-in guns on the Folkestone Leas.

Folkestone. I used to carry shells to the gun floors just after the civilian contractors had finished their work.

I also remember having to do night guard on the 9.2-inch guns at St Margaret's. There was just a camouflage net draped over them, and it was bitterly cold up on the cliff top.

We had one fatality caused by shelling. The guard at the Dover Patrol Memorial was killed. No sentry was placed there for the rest of that day, but next morning who should be first man to be put there? – myself! The decorative chains round the bottom of the obelisk were broken and the polished stone had been defaced, leaving chips of stone scattered all around. Needless to say I kept to the landward side of the obelisk and watched the shells burst inland. At the same time I was eagerly watching down the road for the chap to relieve me!

No. 681 General Construction Company RE was mainly composed of men from North Wales, and H. Burden spent over eighteen months with them at Dover:

When we arrived we were put into dilapidated wooden huts up near the castle. Wellington Barracks it was called, I think. The huts were probably built before the First World War and then allowed to become run down.

The company's first job was constructing a hospital underneath the castle. We did not get to see the completion of the job as a company of Pioneer Corps men took over. Then we began making gun emplacements on the cliffs; the first of these was for 6-inch guns, capable of firing more than half way across the Straits of Dover, that would have been able to give any invading ships a bloody nose. Our next job was at Capel le Ferne above Folkestone, constructing the 8-inch gun emplacements and all the buildings for the crews and equipment.

But it was not all hard work and no excitement. In fact on more than one occasion it was fright more than excitement that we felt. We once spent a whole day up on the cliffs with shells landing at regular intervals. We began to wonder what we had done to upset Jerry!

We were moved out of the wooden huts and into civilian houses at Stanhope Road, Deal. I think the ATS girls moved into the huts. Anyway, we were very comfortable in Deal until Jerry lobbed some shells across, one of which fell in our road. Hunks of flying shrapnel tore through the house like a great big saw. Of the three people sharing our room I was the only one not injured. One was killed by a shell fragment that went in through his armpit and out through his neck. The other was a sapper who had his leg sliced clean off at the knee. This upset me because, as a sergeant, I had just escorted him back under arrest from Scotland Yard, London. He had tried to sneak a weekend in London, but the red-caps had nabbed him at Euston station. I sometimes wonder if he knew a shell was coming over with his name on it!

At Dover Castle Brigadier Raw RA asked Edward Greenstreet if he would like to transfer from the Royal Engineers to the Royal Artillery. A year later he had been promoted to Warrant Officer Class II in the RA; but remained on the breakwater:

Winter storms and gales at times made the breakwater tremble more than German bombs and shells. During one night of shelling, about four of us in the observation tower were very lucky to have survived a near miss that plopped into the sea behind us. We heard the 'whoosh' and the explosion, and afterwards saw that the second hands had been broken off our watches.

I used to visit the castle to collect the pay and remember getting back to the Prince of Wales Pier just as an air raid started. Looking for shelter, the best I could find was a railway wagon, under which I crawled for about ten minutes. When things quietened down I was crawling out from beneath the wagon when I noticed all the wheels had sticks of dynamite attached in case of an invasion!

During the summer of 1941 we obtained a small boat, but we had the problem of how to get it up on to the breakwater. One of our lieutenants went on the scrounge and came back asking for volunteers. They left the next morning and marched off along the sea front to the Eastern Arm. The lieutenant shouted to the sentry, 'Working Party', and proceeded to 'win' a complete mobile jib and winch. The boat was soon hauled up on to the breakwater and made safe from stormy seas.

When the *War Sepoy* was sunk as a blockship across the Western entrance of the harbour a steel cable was stretched at low level between the Admiralty Pier and the breakwater as protection from torpedoes fired by E-boats. Our little boat went out at low water to salvage a load of useful items, including a steering wheel, four feet across, which was made into a table for the Officers' Mess.

'Who peed on the sergeant-major's teeth?' This was the result of a wild night in the Sergeants' Mess when one particular SM, feeling loaded, went to the edge of the breakwater to relieve himself. He was swearing on his return as he had lost his false teeth as well. The party continued and one after the other chaps went to the same spot for a pee. The following morning a chap gave a shout. He discovered on a small wall, sitting on a 12-inch baulk of timber, the SM's teeth. They were recovered with the reverence afforded the crown jewels.

We also had a sergeant who had lost an eye at some time and which had been replaced with a false one. He always removed it before retiring, popping it into a glass of water. Many times it was either substituted for something else or 'pinched', and he would shout, 'All right, who's got my eye?'

Kinson's boat ceased to operate, and was replaced by a stripped-down RAF launch which didn't last very long. Its demise occurred one dark night on the last trip of the day, when it failed to land about three of us at the breakwater or knuckle. It meant crossing to the Eastern Arm, where it struck the boom defence, was holed and began to sink. We got a ladder and climbed to safety as it sank beneath us.

Someone had some bright ideas at HQ. The first involved about thirty of us going ashore one afternoon to swim along 100 yards in the sea, carrying our full pack and rifle. Another time we landed at night to attack the South Foreland cross-Channel guns – just as an exercise.

Mysterious flashing lights were often reported to HQ. On one occasion a light was seen flashing near the Knuckle Lighthouse, just outside the battery perimeter. Three of us, each with a round up the spout and fixed bayonets, went out quietly into the darkness. It turned out to be a broken lamp fitting, and the glass gave out flickers as it moved in the wind.

High winds and very rough seas one night had everyone under cover. The heavy seas pounded over the top decking. Shells for our guns, weighing 100 lbs each, were heard bumping down the steps from the top to the lower deck. On the top deck was a practice dummy-loader gun of some two tons in weight. Next morning it was gone, washed through the iron railings of the top deck, clearing the bottom deck and railings and falling into the harbour. It was recovered two days later. We later learned that the breakwater battery personnel were regarded as expendable. Had the Germans invaded and captured our guns the big railway guns behind Dover were ready to blast us out!

Rosemary Fellowes (née Keyes) remembers Vice-Admiral Dover being concerned over the safety of all women under his command, especially his splendid WRNS. They had been most upset when their barrage balloon, tethered in the Dover College grounds and christened 'Undulating Ursula', was shot down in flames by a marauding German fighter:

Admiral Ramsey issued strict orders that cypher officers were not to take unnecessary risks when relieving one another during a shelling bombardment. It was bad enough when a small group of German-speaking WRNS, manning the listening post at St Margaret's Bay, were required to run the gauntlet in a local bus whilst delivering their 'top secret' messages to Ramsey's office by 09.00 each morning. Captain Morgan, Chief of Staff to Ramsey, taking a breath of fresh air one evening outside the casemate complex, saw coming towards him two WRNS – Rosemary Keyes and Myrette Ackfield – both completely covered from head to feet in a fine chalk dust. 'What have you been up to?' he enquired. Rosemary replied, 'Those we are relieving have not had any tea or supper, so we thought it time they had'. 'What about the

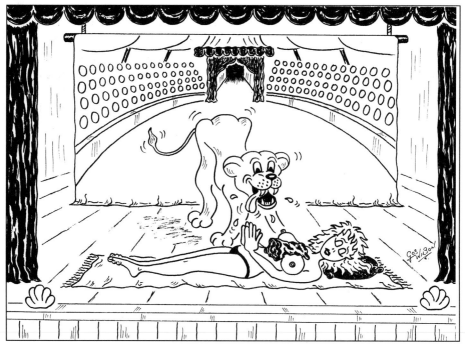

'Eyes tightly closed, the striptease quietly prayed that the cross-Channel guns would not fire a salvo!'

chalk?' Morgan asked, to which Rosemary answered, 'A shell has just struck the cliff face below us – but don't tell the Admiral!'

Then there was the occasion a WRNS driver was waiting at the pierhead when a German fighter-bomber made an attack on the harbour. She got out of the car and crawled under a railway truck. Someone shouted that the truck was full of explosives. She crawled out again absolutely furious, as she was wearing her Number One Suit!

Several animal acts were booked to appear at the Hippodrome during the war and Dick Whittamore soon realized how dangerous it would be if some of them escaped during an air raid or shelling bombardment:

Prince Mercado with his fully grown lioness Lemo came down for a week. The lioness was kept in a large dressing room with a note pinned to the door, 'KEEP OUT'. It used to make the journey from the dressing room, via a small flight of stairs, to the stage twice each evening, and then back again. We assumed it was quite tame as there were never any accidents. The audience was asked to keep still during the performance and especially quiet during the climax of the act, when Lemo was required to take a lump of raw meat from the bare chest of a young stripper. Eyes tightly closed, the striptease quietly prayed that the cross-Channel guns would not fire a salvo!

Arimand Banu and her snakes also appeared several times. The snakes were left in a warm dressing room each night in baskets. We wondered why until rumour had it that one landlady where Arimand had stayed, couldn't find her cat – until she saw a snake with a big lump in its throat!

I wonder how many people remember Cliff Berzac and his mule, Miss Maud? Members of the audience were invited on stage to ride the mule but it always threw them off. He took his mule home with him every night and tethered it in a field. Each evening it had to reach the stage through the theatre's main entrance because the spiral staircase was impossible for it to negotiate.

CHAPTER FOUR

'We go to change our knickers'

On New Year's Day 1942 Winston Churchill, the Prime Minister, was travelling from Ottawa to Washington for a meeting with President Roosevelt. Churchill called his staff and newspaper correspondents to the dining-car of the train. Raising his glass to the assemblage he said, 'Here's to 1942, here's to a year of toil, a year of struggle and peril, and a long step forward towards victory. May we all come through safe and with honour.'

Throughout Occupied Europe the people were still suffering a bitter repression, although those living in Vichy France were indifferent to the privations of their fellow countrymen in the Occupied Zone. They somehow pursued a doctrine of subservience and cooperation with their victors.

In England, however, the people had, by and large, become accustomed and even hardened to the growing demands made on them by the many restrictions of war. In the last months of the previous year the Luftwaffe had ceased their heavy bombing raids, and only thirty-four people had lost their lives in December 1941, the lowest figure since the autumn of 1940.

Civil Defence services were now extremely well organized and some semblance of normality existed among the rank and file of ordinary citizens, whose industrious conduct was – with few exceptions – exemplary.

An exemplary performance in constant demand was that of the WVS, who served meals at the Dover Civic Restaurant, and canteen meals at Victoria Park, and also ran a library at the Information Bureau, Market Square. Gwen Mackett also helped with the mobile canteen van, feeding troops and Civil Defence workers:

> I recall the wonderful drinking chocolate and spam that America sent for us to use on the van. There were dark days and nights in the underground passages that go under Victoria Park after we were bombed and shelled out of our home in Castle Hill Road, but comradeship was so high and everyone was so friendly.

Serving in the RAF Regiment on the radar site at Swingate in 1942 was R. Derek-Roberts, who came under shellfire on numerous occasions. Their site was right alongside the railway that carried the Royal Artillery's big guns up to their firing point:

> On one occasion a fragment of shrapnel finished up on my bed after coming through the roof of the Nissen hut. Luckily, because of an advanced warning, I was in the shelter when that happened.

With the 4th Dorsets stationed at the castle C. Broom and a pal caught impetigo, probably from sharing rough army blankets in the guardroom:

> So we were more or less quarantined in a bungalow. Every day we had to climb the 217 steps to the first aid post at the top for treatment.

Transferred from the Royal Artillery to the Ordnance Corps as a radar mechanic, Ted Ashton was eventually sent to the Dover area to service a highly secret radar set – the X271, mainly used for tracking surface shipping. The new set operated on a wavelength of 10 centimetres, whereas the original Chain Home Low (M1) sets were working on 15 centimetres. He had been told the X271 was superior to anything the Germans had at that time. The new set was located at Lydden Spout, half way between Dover and Capel le Ferne, and right on the edge of the cliff. Housed in a small cabin, it possessed a small antenna that protruded over the cliff but was well concealed:

> Winston Churchill visited the area in 1941 when the weather was good and France clearly visible to the naked eye. 'Ah – the promised land,' Churchill said. Then he was shown the position finder (PF), which was a very power-ful telescope swinging in an arc over a large map marked with grid squares and bearings. Focusing the telescope on a position gave its bearings and range at once. Churchill took off his gloves and chucked them to Admiral of the Fleet Sir Robert Keyes with a brusque, 'Here, hold these', and pro-ceeded to bend down to focus the PF on Calais town clock. Straightening up he said, with a grin, 'No wonder they missed the boat, their clock's five minutes slow!'
>
> When radar jamming first started to become a problem with the CHL sets I was called to a meeting with the 'boffins' – Dr Varley, our own radar officer Lieutenant D. MacDonald, and an RAF pilot who went under the alias of 'Mr Smith'. Whenever jamming occurred I was instructed to take a quick bearing and then telephone a Folkestone number and ask for Mr Smith. If he was not available then I was to leave a message saying, 'I have some nuts and bolts for him.' I assumed he (Mr Smith) was stationed at RAF Hawkinge. If he replied he always asked, 'How many nuts and bolts?' and was particularly concerned where they were coming from. Usually the signals were from the Wissant area, between Calais and Cap Gris Nez. My impression was that he would take similar information from other radar sets, then take off in an

aircraft especially equipped to 'fix' the source of the interference. This
inevitably sent Bomber Command to plaster the whole area with bombs.

About 23.00 hours on the night of 12 February 1942 the three German
warships, *Scharnhorst*, *Gneisenau* and *Prince Eugen*, slipped stealthily out of
Brest Harbour to make their daring dash through the English Channel; and
there was jamming of the M1 radar. I followed the usual procedure and rang
Mr Smith. A female voice answered and told me he was not available. So I left
the 'nuts and bolts' message.

At 07.00 hours the following day I was roused and told the X271 had got a
fault and was off the air. It was over an hour before I got the set working. I
had to re-calibrate by using the usual Permanent Echo Points – Dungeness,
the Varne Buoy and Cap Gris Nez. As I traversed the antenna I picked up
echoes which I took to be E-boats near Blanc Nez. Soon other echoes
appeared, setting out from the French coast in places between Boulogne and
Calais. I anxiously rang the ops room to know if any enemy forces were being
plotted and was astounded when they said 'No'. I insisted that something
unusual was afoot and was informed reconnaissance aircraft would be sent
out. The German warships at that time were either out of my range or else
head-on to my antenna.

Events began to happen rapidly from then on. Three large echoes were
detected off Boulogne but we could not appreciate their actual size until they
rounded Cap Gris Nez, by which time the echoes nearly swamped the X271
screen. The rest is now well known in the annals of history.

Some months later I needed to telephone Mr Smith. I asked him where he
had been on 12 February. He told me he had been shot down over France. I
enquired how he had managed to get back. 'Ways and means, old boy!' he
replied.

The Fleet Minesweeper HMS *Wedgeport* received a new captain in 1942:
weighing in at around twenty stone he was immediately nicknamed 'Guts',
among other less complimentary names, although he was competent enough in
ship handling and all other duties. But whatever he was given to eat, recalls
Robert Murphy, it was never enough:

He drove us junior officers wild with his gross appetite. As the wardroom
dues were shared out equally it came hard on us trying to keep him fed. But
one day the supply officer was bribed to supply extra rations. A big serving
dish was found and this was laden with chips, fried bread, tomatoes, beans,
bacon, spaghetti and eggs. It was a perfect mountain of food, and we thought
he might be shamed into more reasonable behaviour. The steward carried in
the dish, lifted the lid to uncover this steaming pile of food. But the skipper
did not bat an eyelid. He simply prodded the food and bellowed, 'Steward,
where's the bloody sausages?'. After eating the whole plateful he beamed at us
and remarked, 'Now, that was a decent meal!'.

Robert Waugh was with 1st Battery, 1st Searchlight Regiment behind Dover Castle. They moved around from site to site until the 'Thousand Bomber' raids began in May 1942:

We were at Frith Farm then on a disused playing field living in some old tarred huts that were an improvement over tents we had been used to. We had Canadians attached to us working their Ground Location Radar system, while we operated our searchlight radar. The Canadians' sense of discipline was quite different from ours. We were still there when the first of the Thousand Bomber raids on Germany started. Watching them go over on the radar was like looking at grass cuttings on the screen. It made operating our radar quite impossible.

We moved to Troop HQ at Whitfield, living in Nissen huts which were a vast improvement over the previous tarred huts. Our job there was to act as beacons for the bombers returning from their raids over the Continent. We were allowed only half a minute to get the searchlight beam in operation and pointing at a designated aerodrome. I would be woken up at all hours of the night and would have to get my gumboots on and start up the generator.

On one particularly cold night, when you could hear the frost crackling in the air, I had been woken up and rushed out in tin hat, gumboots and just a shirt. I stood at my post for two hours in the freezing cold because the duty attendant had not been roused!

We had a visit from a brigadier on one occasion who was not happy that I had given orders to spread newspapers over our recently scrubbed floor. Although far from good, our living conditions had improved. The cooking stove was not as clean as he would have liked and our stores were not up to regulation standard. He warned me that if things did not improve I would lose my stripes. I complained to the troop officer about the brigadier's unfairness, but he wanted to let the whole thing drop. But I insisted that I wanted to go ahead, as King's Rules and Regulations stipulated that no inspection should be made after five o'clock, and the brigadier had come much later than that. Eventually a letter was received which conceded that the inspection was out of order.

Another move, this time to West Studdal, might have resulted from my 'brush' with the Brigadier. Our little cookhouse was in fact a former toilet, and for a toilet we had just a canvas screen in one corner of a field. Eventually, however, timber and other materials were delivered and we erected our own huts. No glass was supplied so we used old sacking to drape over the windows.

Although we were doing a technical job in very difficult conditions the army still wanted to impose petty discipline. I almost came to blows with one unreasonable officer which cost me my third stripe, and I found myself reduced to bombardier once again!

Among the many Canadian units stationed in England during the Second World War was the 1st Canadian Radio Location Unit, whose members were trained radar operators and were loaned in teams of five to British anti-aircraft regiments, primarily in the Dover area. Cecil Rowe was one of the first five to arrive at the Farthingloe gun-site in July 1942:

Our team at Farthingloe Farm, just above the Hare and Hounds were Cecil Rowe, Dick Hunter, George Lumsden, Leo Robbins and Cecil Owens. The British soldiers seemed to give us a wide berth, they didn't speak much to us, until one day in the mess hall I was talking to one of them, who said, 'When we heard the Canadians were coming we were a little apprehensive as we heard they were on the wild side and always looking for a fight. You chaps are all right'.

Growing on the surrounding hills were a lot of big blackberries so we asked the cook if we picked them would he make us pies. He agreed. We picked a large pailful and he was as good as his word.

We used to go to the Hare and Hounds fairly often for a drink, and there were two young girls there, Doris and Gladys. Leo Robbins got quite friendly with Doris and it soon became apparent to the rest of us that this association could be turned to our advantage at closing time. Leo and the rest of us were often invited into the back room for another couple of hours of free drinks! One night on our return from the pub a bunch of us were singing and making one hell of a racket, when we told Dick Hunter he couldn't climb a telegraph pole. Dick was about half way up when a friendly policeman arrived on the scene. 'All right chaps, down from the pole – and on your way', he said.

I married an English girl and had arranged for a room with a lady named Kathy. She once – and only once – asked me if I had any washing that needed doing. It so happened that I never washed my socks but kept buying extra pairs from the QM stores. A vast accumulation of dirty socks was crammed into my kit bag so I gave them to her to wash. The next day when I arrived it was quite a sight to see a whole line of clean socks swinging in the breeze. But I was never asked for laundry again!

We eventually moved to another gun-site just above the gasworks to join another bunch of Canadians. One night when the guns were firing there was a premature muzzle explosion. One of the British gunners was killed, and the shrapnel struck our Nissen hut, piercing it in several places and severing a clothes line hanging about head height. Those off duty were lying down on their bunks in the hut, which almost certainly saved their lives or prevented serious injury.

The number of radar operators increased until there were between fifteen and twenty on each site. Our team was moved back again to Farthingloe Farm. When we arrived the hut was stone cold and a dozen or so Britishers were already there. We asked them why the fire was not alight. They replied,

'Not until four o'clock'. So Dick Hunter and I went out to the wooden bunks and removed all the single headboards. We soon had a fire going. But it wouldn't last forever. That night, at about midnight, Dick and I took off with two sacks and made for the cookhouse compound, which was surrounded by a fence and topped with barbed wire. Dick stood against the fence and I went up using his cupped hands, shoulders and his head. I had already filled one sack with coal and had started on the second one, keeping a wary eye on the cook working in the kitchen, when I heard an officer's car returning to the gun-site. To cap it all we were in the officers' parking area. I hollered to Dick, threw the sacks over the fence and we ran back to the hut, with them over our shoulders. As we burst through the door the others asked what was wrong. Quick as a wink Dick replied, 'The guilty flee when no man pursueth!'

The power plant for the radar sets was a three-cylinder diesel, very reliable but it had to be hand-cranked at a fair speed to get it started. A new Cummins arrived with an electric starter, and we were all given instruction on the proper starting procedure. This involved pushing a button to start and when the motor was going, push another button very close to a whirling fan-blade, to transfer the power to the radar set. It was about 02.00 one morning when the sirens went. Darrell Holmes and myself ran to the Cummins, but the voice of our sergeant hollered that he would start it. His name was McKenzie, and he was a miserable type. We made for the radar set and heard the motor start. Almost immediately we heard a scream and loud cussing. We returned and there was McKenzie with his fingers sliced off. He evidently had not used the correct procedure. We picked up the fingers the following day whilst explaining the incident to our officer. Sergeant McKenzie went in to hospital and we never saw him again. We supposed he was sent back to Canada.

On the occasion we visited an experimental site in a nearby valley, we were asked by the British troops to play a game of football. They were sorry they had asked. We bulled right through them knocking everyone out of our way. They complained we were too rough. They were better players and had more finesse but we had a good rapport with them – despite our lack of field decorum.

Eventually we moved to a gun-site near St Margaret's Bay, and we were there when Canterbury was attacked by fighter-bombers. During the day Focke-Wulfe 190s came over the site to shoot up everything in sight. They were so low the 3.7-in anti-aircraft guns could not get a low enough trajectory to open fire. An officer was hollering for small ammunition, but the aircraft flew over so fast with their cannon spraying that he never did get it. Ironically, the only building to suffer damage was the Officers' Mess!

Serving in the WRNS from August 1941, Vera Boyce (now Selwood) spent eighteen happy months at Dover:

I lived at Dover College and did some duty at the switchboard below Dover
Castle, but most of the time was in the supply depot, known as the
Champagne Caves. Our boss was Paymaster Commander Peary. I recall all the
people I worked for as if it all happened yesterday. I remember the Crypt
Restaurant, the Shalimar Hotel and especially the two old ladies who kept it,
and then there was the Creamery Cafe.

We held a garden party in the college grounds, a thing I find hard to
convince people happened in the middle of a war, but we really did. Admiral
Pridham-Wippel judged the ankle competition and Captain Curtis-Wilson
brought a team who gave a PT display.

The base supply depot was at the old brewery behind the Market Square.
There was a supply office and clothing store in the caves, past the Granville
Docks, where we had boat clothing, seaboots and oilskins. We often had to
work late at night to kit out sailors from the Motor Torpedo Boats when they
had been sunk in the Channel. We issued dry clothes, cigarettes and tots of
rum.

An invasion exercise was held on one occasion in the Citadel, and we had
to sleep in the dungeons for one night. I was given the task of labelling any
corpses that might come ashore. Thank goodness that never happened. I

'We held a garden party in
the college grounds, a thing
I find hard to convince
people happened in the
middle of a war, but we
really did.'

served for five years, ending up at Portland Bill as a Petty Officer, but Dover holds my happiest memories.

As a Royal Marine recruit at Deal Jack Pickup has never forgotten the square bashing and the spit and polish. Nevertheless, he liked the town on the few occasions he was allowed out of barracks:

> Messerschmitt fighters used to make low-level hit and run raids in 1942. There was never any warning. They would often machine gun across the parade square yet by the time you had got to a shelter it was all over. I was just twenty years of age and away from home for the first time. It was pretty scary but then we were all in the same boat – so to speak.

Lilian Stone (née Foster), serving in the NAAFI, was stationed at Connaught Barracks, the Citadel and many other locations for various periods:

> As was the case with many of the girls who worked with me, the strain took its toll on my health, and I had to leave.

Minesweeping operations in the Dover Strait could safely be done during the daylight hours in 1942 while the year before it was carried out during the night. A telegraphist on HMT *Alexandrite*, Bill Jenkins took great delight in firing a .303 rifle at the mines as they were cut and bobbed to the surface:

> I had a hammock and trying to 'sling' it in the confined crews quarters of a trawler was sometimes hilarious. I managed to spread it out on the floor of the W/T cabin, but unfortunately, my first night's sleep was disturbed when one of the crew, having been ashore on a night out, decided to urinate over me!
>
> My first trip in the *Alexandrite* was memorable too as we were recalled because of exceptionally heavy weather. I can still remember coming back to harbour at the Eastern Arm entrance with the *Androdite* following astern. At times she was momentarily clear out of the water and you could glimpse daylight beneath her. I was seasick for a couple of days afterwards but never again was I troubled by it.
>
> As an easygoing type just twenty-one years old, I was soon accepted by the rest of the crew. I was lucky in having been an employee of the General Post Office as my navy pay was made up to my civilian pay. I had spare cash when many others were 'skint'. With the usual wartime spirit of share and share alike we could sometimes wander up to the pub at the end of the Prince of Wales Pier to enjoy a pint or two on my extra cash.
>
> We enjoyed many nights ashore in Dover of course – visits to the pubs and the town hall for the dances. I remember one night when Willie Nichol and John Porteus and I went to a dance at the town hall after consuming a lot of

cider and whisky, and found ourselves walking on the roof of the building. Fortunately we didn't fall through. We also had trips to Deal, Folkestone and Canterbury, with various amorous adventures! Invariably we missed the last train back to Dover and usually slept on a bench in the station waiting room until the first train the next morning.

Seaman Sanders and Leading Hand Jimmy Morrison, were sent ashore on one occasion to collect our rum ration as we had run out. But suddenly we were ordered to sea. The two rum collectors had not come back. When we finally got back into harbour on the following morning there were the two of them – with empty jars. No official action was taken and the loss of the rum was put down to 'breakages'.

The cook was considered an important member of the crew. When I joined, the cook had been a bricklayer in civvy street. The galley of the *Alex* was always infested with cockroaches, although I cannot recall them being on the menu! Messing was on a do-it-yourself system: a crewman was appointed to buy supplies out of the monthly allowance and at the end of the month we either had a profit or a loss. If it was a loss the 'messman' usually got the sack and a new one was appointed. As 'sparks' I was absolved from this rather dubious duty. Instead I got the postman's job collecting the mail from a basement office at a house at the end of the pier.

The anti-aircraft rockets mounted on the pier are never to be forgotten. They frightened us more than Jerry. Once a stoker was climbing down the

'The two rum collectors had not come back. When we finally got back into harbour . . . there were the two of them – with empty jars. . . . the loss was put down to "breakages".'

Winston Churchill's famous words, 'This was their finest hour', usually attributed to the Battle of Britain fighter pilots, can be equally attributed to the gallant men of the Coastal Forces, who fought in the narrow seas for four years.

stairway to the mess deck with his dinner plate when one of the rockets went off just above us. Poor old Fitzpatrick ended up at the foot of the stairs with his dinner spread all over his face!

Within four months of arriving with Motor Gun Boat 331 at Dover Harold Clay was lying wounded in Buckland Hospital. Six months later he joined the 5th MTB Flotilla at Dover on MTBs 25 and 354:

Looking back, a lot was crammed into the two and a half years I spent there. We attacked enemy convoys, did escort duty for our minelaying MLs in the German shipping lanes, escorted the minesweepers, and took part in clandestine operations, such as landing commandos on the French coast. Leave was minimal and time ashore in Dover restricted, so by the time the Allies had captured northern France and our flotilla had gone to Dartmouth to begin paying-off, I felt somewhat older than my twenty-odd years. Losing shipmates and burying them in the Priory cemetery was a saddening experience.

    The Dover people were quite wonderful, they accepted me into their homes and shared their meagre food rations with me. It was Dr Gertrude Toland who operated on my leg in August 1942 and I am quite sure that she saved it from amputation. In Castle Street, just off the much battered Market

Square, there was a seafood shop run by Mr Vickery and his two daughters selling cockles, whelks and oysters. They used to visit me when I was in Buckland Hospital. When I was eventually transferred to hospitals in Chatham and Dartford, they invited me to spend weekends with them because I was not allowed to travel very far. Considering that I was, after all, just one of their customers, and anyway sailors were not supposed to have the best of reputations where young girls were concerned, it was grand not only to be accepted but to be welcomed into their home. They were lovely people.

On 17 May 1942, the day when Christchurch, Folkestone, was bombed by Focke-Wulf 190s, Jim Harris was among a company of soldiers attending church parade – compulsory in those days:

We had just left Sandgate High Street and were marching up the hill to Folkestone when the air raid siren went. There were sounds of aircraft and, without being ordered, we naturally flattened ourselves against either side of the road, taking what cover we could from the steep banks. There was an almighty explosion not too far away. The 'raiders passed' signal was sounded so we marched to church again. But when we got there the church had been hit. It was virtually demolished except for the tower. Five minutes earlier and we would have been done for.

Our particular infantry unit had quite a few men of Italian and German extraction who had been transferred from the non-combatant Pioneer Corps. They wanted a more active role in the fighting but not where there was any chance of them coming face to face with their own countrymen. Although there was little chance of Italian troops coming ashore, the threat of a German invasion was real. How our comrades of German extraction would have acted if that threat had materialized is anyone's guess.

The barrage balloons provided Lieutenant-Colonel Swale – and the Luftwaffe – with endless amusement. One snowy night in September 1942 he was duty officer at Brigade HQ when one of them broke away and disappeared:

The 4th Battalion Somerset Light Infantry found it bouncing about on the Deal road and rang up to ask me what should be done with it. I rang No. 961 Squadron RAF and they said that the Somersets should either provide a lot of soldiers to hang on to it, or else find something firm to tether it to!

Amusement came in many guises. At St Margaret's Bay was the 10th Battalion Royal Sussex Regiment and they had a keen subaltern called Shippam, a member of the famous Chichester potted meat family. Each morning he took his platoon on to a scrap of turf near the cliff edge for PT. The men always took the long way there, through a gate, but young Shippam used to vault a spiked fence to be there first. But one morning he slipped and

'I rang No. 961 Squadron RAF and they said that the Somersets should either provide a lot of soldiers to hang on to it, or else find something firm to tether it to!'

hung from the iron railings with a spike through his calf. It meant several weeks in hospital for him. The usual accident report went up from his battalion through brigade and divisional HQs and eventually South-East Command HQ. Command wanted to know if this officer had been ordered to vault the fence. This started a chain of memos which shuttled back and forth for weeks, until the brigadier took a red ink pen and wrote 'This keen young officer was *on active service* within sight of the enemy in occupied France!'.

As an Engine-Room Artificer (ERA) Vic Pugh arrived at Dover with the first Motor Gun Boat of 2 Flotilla; the rest came as they were made operationally ready:

Our arrival coincided with a greeting from Jerry by way of cross-Channel shelling. Not thirty minutes before a great many windows in the Lord Warden Hotel [HMS *Wasp*] had been broken by the blast of near misses.

Our very first trip out of the harbour was eventful. Soon after arriving we left for an exercise and I went along to do some engine adjustments. Almost an hour later, having completed the task, I climbed up to see what needed doing on the bridge and wheelhouse. We had been travelling at great speed. I had no idea of bearings so could be forgiven for assuming that the coastline ahead and only a couple of miles away was England.

I asked the skipper if we were going back to Dover and he said he would have to turn the boat around. He proceeded to do just that when shells began to fall around us and then six enemy planes came in low with their machine guns blazing. I went back to the engine room so saw little of the subsequent action, learning later that we had downed one aircraft and damaged another. On inspection our boat had suffered very little bullet damage.

We remained based at Dover for a couple of months whilst the remaining MGBs joined us, then we transferred to Ramsgate to make up the complete flotilla. At Ramsgate we were billeted in the 'Merry England' fun centre, actually in the lounge bar. The stokers and ordinary seamen had to make do with the public bar. The base was known as HMS *Fervant* and was really equipped as a signals base. Our stores and workshops were under the arches on the inner harbour and the Officers' Quarters were at the Yacht Club. We used to go to sea and take part in actions but eventually this was stopped as Engine-Room Artificers were highly trained and in short supply.

The dash through the Channel by the three German warships has always puzzled me. I maintain that the Germans should not have been able to surprise us as it was known almost to the day that the ships were going to attempt the break-out. I had taken a boat to Shoreham for repair work but had been so suddenly and urgently recalled that the Base Engineer Officer met me at the railway station to ensure no time was wasted. When I asked what all the panic was about he informed me that in five days the German ships would be coming through. We had a mad working schedule getting everything ready. But the first we knew of the action was on a Thursday lunchtime when six Swordfish aircraft flew over the harbour. Our boats soon left, returning later undamaged by enemy action but having taken a bashing in the choppy sea. They had brought back a few of the Swordfish pilots and crews.

Arriving at Dover on High Speed Launch No. 171 from the RAF Air Sea Rescue base at Newhaven, Sussex, Harold Firman thought they were just going on loan for a few days as a replacement for a boat lost – probably HSL 120. They stayed for three years!

Our billet was in the Southern Railway annex opposite the Lord Warden Hotel and the official address was 'HMS *Wasp* c/o GPO London'. The accommodation was meagre: eight beds in one room with a communal wash-basin and toilet. Headquarters of 27 Air Sea Rescue (ASR) Motor Craft Unit (MCU) was at Ferry House across the square, also our mess room. We had two lady civilian cleaners who came in every day.

Our boats were berthed in Ferry Dock on the port side, with the Royal Navy MTBs and MGBs, and sometimes MLs, on the starboard side. During

In August 1941 Stanley Baron, a *News Chronicle* reporter, was invited to accompany the crew of an ASR launch on a rescue trip. He later wrote, 'Out from the cliffs of Dover go the RAF launches – turret machine guns ready to deal with any stray Messerschmitt'.

good weather the duty boats moved out to the extension pier. At night each duty boat had to provide someone to stand in a little telephone box situated under the bridge mechanism to await sailing orders.

Because of our liability to be instantly recalled to duty, despite being stood down, Squadron-Leader Coates allowed us a little leeway in our mode of dress, which did not go down very well with officers of No. 961 Balloon Squadron. They took umbrage at being saluted by men wearing just gumboots, seaboot stockings and white sweaters, instead of the traditional uniform of white collar and tie and highly polished black shoes. Deep down, however, I believe they realized the dangers we faced and that we were doing our duty no matter what state our dress.

All our boats were the 'whaleback' type, and some numbers I can recall were 138, 140, 147 and 122. At night, if there was a shelling warning, all duty boats sailed round to the submarine pens, lowering their masts as they went. If you were still in the pens at the next high tide your mast and radio aerials would hit the top of the pens.

We were recalled to Newhaven on one occasion, not long after we had arrived at Dover. What a trip! There was a heavy but short sea running and I was convinced we were going to nosedive down like a submarine. As we rounded Beachy Head a huge wave seemed to pick us up as if by an unseen hand. The bow was pointing downwards and our propellers were clean out of the water, racing away like mad. We came back on an even keel with a huge surge of sea which swept all our deck gear away.

Just as we limped into Newhaven and berthed in the river, a pair of Messerschmitt Bf 109s flew over at mast height. We could not open fire because other vessels were close by. The following day our boat was hoisted out of the water and it was discovered the Napier Sealion engines had been damaged by the heavy weather conditions off Beachy Head. Two days later we were back in Dover with HSL 186. About this time a number of boats were allocated to Ramsgate, and all three stations – Ramsgate, Dover and Newhaven – were preparing for the Dieppe raid in August.

Most of our time was spent at sea, waiting at a rendezvous such as North or South Foreland, Dungeness or the Goodwin Sands, waiting for a crash call. When that happened we would complete a square search, centred on the position given to us by W/T from Naval HQ, Dover.

When the Germans started to flout the Geneva Convention by ignoring our yellow-painted decks, it became a common occurrence to be attacked. The more we were attacked the more our defensive armament increased. We had arrived at Dover with just one Lewis gun in each turret. These were eventually replaced by the more powerful twin Vickers and a further replacement brought in the gas-operated Brownings. Half a dozen of these heavily armed HSLs left Dover for rescue work during the ill-fated Dieppe raid. Our vessel was attacked just after stopping engines in order to lower a crash mat to pick up a Spitfire pilot – Sergeant Tyrell. It was getting on for 16.00 hours and we were only about 500 yards off Dieppe. Sergeant Tyrell had been sitting in his little dinghy since about 02.00 hours and we were convinced he had been used as a decoy so our boat could be lured into a trap.

That day I lost many colleagues on other launches, either killed or taken prisoner. We saw a launch burning on our port side, that could have been HSL 122. Two vessels were lying close to her and suddenly sped away towards us. We hurriedly got under way with Focke-Wulf 190s still attacking us, and pursued by E-boats. Our engineers took off the flame traps on each engine and our skipper, Flight-Lieutenant Hasty, showed great courage whilst weaving and dodging the E-boats' fire. They gave up chasing us in mid-Channel.

We eventually tied up in Wellington Dock, Dover, to off-load our four casualties and Sergeant Tyrell. I was twenty years old at the time. When Squadron-Leader Coates shouted, 'get your wounded ashore and get back to Ferry Dock – you are duty boat', all my pent-up emotions – bottled up until then – bubbled up. One of my best pals was, at that moment, being stretchered off. For about an hour or more I really hated Coates! What I didn't know then was that our vessel was the only ASR boat to return from Dieppe.

It seems quite unbelievable now but on one occasion we actually took the widow and mourners of a cross-Channel skipper, who had recently died, to scatter his ashes on an appropriate spot where the ferry-boats used to pass.

But it was not all doom and gloom. Another unusual trip occurred when we were unexpectedly called out whilst eating lunch at Ferry House. I noticed as we cast off there was a Surgeon Lieutenant-Commander RN on board. He was chatting to our RAF nursing orderly and as we cleared the outer harbour I could see them preparing blankets and hot-water bottles. We followed the harbour wall around until we came upon a young WRN in a bathing costume, perched on an indentation in the wall, sobbing her heart out. She had been swimming with another WRN off the beach, had got out of her depth and panicked. But she had managed to scramble on to the ledge while her companion swam ashore to raise the alarm. She was kept in the naval sick bay which, not surprisingly, received a procession of RAF visitors that night.

Whenever we rescued airmen we usually painted an RAF roundel on the wheelhouse. A swastika was painted on for any German aircrew picked up and later, when we rescued American aircrews, we painted a white star of the USAAF. We asked the WRN what we should paint to record her rescue. She settled for a naval anchor with her name beneath it.

'We followed the harbour wall around until we came upon a young WRN in a bathing costume, perched on an indentation in the wall, sobbing her heart out.'

A more unpleasant memory is doing a square search off the Goodwin
Sands area with another launch at two in the morning in pitch darkness.
Normally in an operation of this kind you did not see the other vessel until
the search was completed or a rescue was reported by W/T in code from
Admiralty Dover. This night our look-outs kept sighting what they thought
was another HSL but as we were under wireless silence there was no
communication between vessels. At the debriefing it was realized that we had
been tailed by a German E-boat!

Some of our trips were dull, boring, routine ones. We had to check
regularly that the life-raft was correctly anchored off Dungeness. We did our
own cooking if at sea for any length of time and were allowed to do our own
provisioning from RN stores. There were many occasions when we just
drifted with the tides off Dungeness waiting patiently for a distress call.
Receiving a signal to return to Dover we sometimes, quite unofficially,
wandered slowly inshore near Dymchurch or Hythe to get among the local
fishing boats. From our stock of food we would hand out tins of corned beef,
butter, sugar, self-heating soups, spam and pork sausages. In return we would
get fresh fish which often meant fish and chips for tea. Any surplus was
usually given to the three local pubs we used and any civilians we regarded as
friends.

On more than one occasion the Walrus seaplane, also on air sea rescue
duties and based at RAF Hawkinge, would taxi almost all the way across the
Channel, in very choppy seas, with a 'ditched' pilot on board, unable to take
off. Another time we actually saw a pilot bale out of his aircraft and picked
him up almost before he got wet! We rescued the crew of an American Flying
Fortress and they were so grateful we were presented with their leather flying
jackets. When we disembarked the very wet and hungry crew of a German
E-boat they still possessed an air of arrogance. And then there was the rescue
of a Polish pilot, who had sustained a shattered shoulder during a dogfight. As
he was unable to swim, our coxswain tied a line around his waist and swam
half a mile in a heavy sea to reach him.

There were sorrowful times too: a seaman rescued but found to be dead; a
pilot rescued and landed safely only to die some days later. But I also
remember the cheerfulness of a WAAF nurse in the station sick bay of
No. 961 Balloon Squadron at Dover when I was very ill, and the ARP
warden who insisted on dragging me into a cave shelter near Shakespeare
Cliff when I was set on going to my boat during a shell attack.

Once we had an open day in Wellington Dock and with pride I showed
civilians my wireless cabin. Close by was the stage-door bar of the
Hippodrome theatre where we rubbed elbows with the current stars of the
stage. In the Market Square was one of Dover's characters who had a snack
bar on wheels – but it never moved. I believe his name was Bill. He was
always good for a bacon sandwich and a chat when things were quiet. In the
Cinque Ports Arms there was a large steel-topped table on the same principle

'. . . I cannot forget the overwhelming satisfaction of finding aircrew floating helplessly and so forlornly in the water . . .' wrote Squadron-Leader 'Wally' Wallens DFC, a pilot with No. 277 (ASR) Squadron, based at RAF Hawkinge.

as a Morrison shelter, where many a brave airman, sailor or WRN would dive for cover during shelling or an air raid.

The crew of trawler HMM *Fyldea*, including Albert Kingston, would always remember that awful 'gut' feeling which grips body and soul when one fears the worst has happened:

It was about September 1942 when *Fyldea* was duty ship to operate Asdic Patrol in mid-Channel. We cast off, left the harbour and steamed for the start point. After some hours of nothing to report we suddenly picked up the noise of high-speed engines. The asdic operator thought it was a German E-boat going at half speed. We closed to about a thousand yards and brought our twelve-pounder to bear. We then fired off a few star shells for illumination and then followed with some high explosive shells. A hit was observed on an unknown craft and we all cheered like mad. We closed in to pick up any survivors but discovered it was one of our own MTBs. Can you imagine our feelings? One of the survivors, however, told us that they had struck a mine and our shells had not hit them. The sigh of relief which went round the ship was indescribable.

HMS *Brock* was short of a gunlayer and signalman, Jack Foster and the 'bunts' from HMS *Kingscourt* were 'deputized':

> We could hardly see the vessel ahead for thick fog. Then the fog lifted in a flash and Calais stood out as clear as a bell. It was 'Sweeps in' and 'Hard about'. The opposition fired a few rounds just to scare us but I never knew a trawler could move so fast.

Winnie Blackwell (née Middleditch) enlisted in the ATS at Southend in February 1942, arriving in Dover as a telephonist:

> We worked on a three-shift system, had good food, clean, dry working conditions with reasonably good accommodation. Some girls in the Forces were not so lucky. When our little band of ATS girls arrived we were informed there was a dance on that very evening. We all went. There seemed to be hundreds of handsome young soldiers there and I was lucky enough to meet my future husband there, and luckier still that he came home after the war.
>
> Most of our entertainment was dances at the town hall or going to the cinemas. On one occasion the alert sounded and we were obliged to leave the dance sharpish. As we went out someone said we could return some other night if we could show our ticket. There was a mad scramble over the floor to find discarded tickets.

ATS girl Stella Barker was with the signals section of the 71st AA Brigade, billeted in a requisitioned house at 71 Castle Street:

> If we were in the house at night when a shelling warning sounded we had orders to dress, don our steel helmets and run for the nearest shelter in the nearby park. An hour had to pass without a shell landing before the 'all clear' was given. Sometimes we would be waiting more than an hour, then just getting into bed when another salvo arrived. Off duty on a Saturday evening we used to hitch-hike to Folkestone to dance at the Leas Cliff Hall. We used to go to the tea dance, pop out for fish and chips, and go back for the evening session. After dancing at the Dover Town Hall we would often scrounge a sandwich from the refreshment ladies to take back for our fire watcher on duty at our billet.

Between 1941 and November 1943 Stanley Saunders served in the area as a Senior Class 1 nurse with the RAMC:

> In our static role we were used as a Casualty Reception Station (CRS) and in the field role as a Field Ambulance or Field Dressing Station. I helped man a CRS at the Metropole Hotel, Folkestone, the Citadel at Dover and the castle.

One of the things that caused a great deal of dissatisfaction, especially amongst the inhabitants of Dover and Folkestone, was the fact that there seemed no point to the shelling duels taking place every day. The enemy would send over a certain number of shells so it seemed we would have to retaliate with a similar number. In fact we now know that our guns never made any attempt to start a duel but would only open fire at German shipping passing along the French coast. Sometimes we would leave the CRS at the castle to lay on the cliff top just outside the entrance, watching for the flash on the far side and then waiting for the explosion this side. I remember clearly being advised never to use the public convenience in the Market Square in Dover, because it was a favourite aiming point for the German long-range gunners. The square, that is, not the loo!

I shall never forget the time when we received over a dozen soldiers who were burnt in a very tender place. A mustard gas training exercise had gone wrong and they had gone to the lavatory with mustard gas still on their fingers and hands. Their private parts were red and sore and blistered. What I learned from nursing them made me very grateful that no mustard gas was ever used in anger during the last war.

As you crossed over the bridge to the castle entrance there was a guardroom – the original gate-house – with a room which had iron bars at the windows. One night three German prisoners, who had survived a mid-

'I remember a very prim and proper ATS girl going up to the barred window, turning round and lifting up her skirt. She then bent over, saying "That to you lot!".'

Channel battle with one of our Motor Gun Boats were put in the guardroom, (wearing cooks' 'whites' as replacements for their own uniforms). I remember a very prim and proper ATS girl going up to the barred window, turning round and lifting up her skirt. She then bent over, saying 'That to you lot'.

At the castle there was a gang of us RAMC lads, ATS and WAAFs. We often would go out together as one crowd. One of our favourite places was the cinema at the bottom of Castle Street. As soon as we got there the girls would always go to the lavatory – and for quite a while. The boys used to get quite niggled waiting for them to return so everyone could settle down to see the film. So I asked my partner why the girls didn't all go to the loo before leaving the castle, as we did. She replied, 'We don't go there to pee – we go to change our knickers. We are not going to sit here all evening in those regulation bloomers with metal fasteners at the waist and leg'. I replied that surely they should not come out in regulation knickers if they were that uncomfortable. She whispered, 'But we have an underwear inspection before we can leave. You know the highly polished metal plate set in the ground outside the guardroom window? Well, we have to stand over it while the WAAF sergeant looks at the reflection!' The polished plate had been installed by a regiment of the Black Watch, long before the war, so that men in kilts could be checked to make sure they were properly *undressed*.

'She whispered, "But we have an underwear inspection before we can leave. . . . the WAAF sergeant looks at the reflection!".'

'. . . there used to be a daily patrol over the Channel by two Spitfires. Everyone nicknamed them "Gert & Daisy". To me they were a comforting sight,' wrote Mrs M. Griffiths of Deal.

Living in Deal for most of the war years Mrs M. Griffiths thought the bombing was just about bearable but the shelling was very unpleasant:

Once a week I went on a YMCA tea van round to most of the gun-sites on the Dover cliffs. We were based at Nonington, as the Dover YMCA Depot had been shelled out. On more than one occasion we found the gun-site we happened to be visiting had been wiped out by shells the previous night. Our round took us near the Duke of York's School on to the hush-hush radar pylons, to the barrage balloon site in the dip, and then to the ack-ack sites on the cliffs.

My lasting impression is of the cheerfulness, wit and stoicism of the soldiers and of how delighted they were to see us with our stewed tea and tiny ration of five cigarettes. They used to say it was such a change to see a couple of female members of the human race after staring at grass and sea all day long.

For three nights each week I helped at the YMCA canteen. The menu was simply sausage and chips, or sausage and mash, but we were always well patronized with queues from the counter to the door – soldiers, sailors, airmen and Marines. They were all marvellous and helpful and so well behaved. During shelling later they would be turned out of the three cinemas that Deal had then and as the only other entertainment was the pubs, they would swarm to our canteen. A good job it never received a direct hit or there would have been a massacre.

In the spring of 1942 there used to be a daily patrol over the Channel by two Spitfires that everyone nicknamed 'Gert and Daisy'. To me they were a comforting sight. But one fine morning I happened to lean out of my bedroom window to see this reassuring sight, only to be blown back on to my bed. It wasn't one of our Spits but a German plane on a 'hit and run' raid. The bomb he dropped made a bit of a mess of a house only six doors away. It was, fortunately, like so many others in the area, quite unoccupied.

Stationed in Walmer with the 5th Battalion The Dorsetshire Regiment, Les Wood recalls some of his experiences:

We had a platoon officer, a keen chap fresh from battle school, who built an assault course where each day before breakfast we were required to run the gauntlet. He used to fire his revolver – and not always in the air! Eventually, the CO had to call a halt to this assault course. Fractured arms, wrists and ankles – it was causing more casualties than the enemy!

'He used to fire his revolver – and not always in the air! Eventually, the CO had to call a halt to this assault course. Fractured arms, wrists and ankles – it was causing more casualties than the enemy!'

Heinkel 111 bombers sometimes released their bombs over the Dover area on their way back to their French bases.

On occasions we would get instructions to open all the windows to prevent blast damage when our long-range guns opened fire. We did a lot of Bren-gun Carrier training at Oxley Bottom and once or twice acted as the 'enemy' on combined exercises with the Home Guard.

The regiment suffered its first fatal casualty through enemy action. Some of the lads had spent the evening in Dover and were waiting near a bus stop for the liberty truck to bring them back to camp when a shell exploded close by. Two of our carrier platoon mates were killed with several others from the battalion.

I remember Walmer as having very few civilians about. With the shortage of civilian manpower we would be called upon to help out at harvest time. We helped the Women's Land Army girls in jobs like potato picking, threshing corn with a steam engine, picking fruit and sprouts on a bitterly cold morning. We earned an extra sixpence per day [2½p], but this could only be drawn when going on leave.

May Owen (née Pridmore) was one of the longest-serving members of the ATS at Dover, having joined the 42nd Platoon of the Kent Company ATS before the war started:

I began army life at Langdon Barracks in the armament office where we saw lots of action when the German planes dropped bombs on the harbour and town. We became accustomed to air raids and shelling. It became a way of life. Later I was moved to the headquarters office of 519 Coast Regiment RA. Eventually I ended up in the operations room under the castle, which proved quite an interesting and exciting experience. There were fifteen of us ATS girls divided into three groups of A, B and C watches. The ops room was manned day and night, always with a duty officer. We kept in contact with the coastal artillery regiments by telephone through the switchboard room. The regiments would use their radar to locate the enemy shipping in the English Channel and would telephone the range and bearing to the ops room. This information was then plotted on wall charts and on a plotting table.

Fred Griffiths was the cable sergeant for the 43rd Divisional Signals unit, detached from their Ashford HQ to provide telephone communications between many units in the Dover area:

> We were based at the castle but not down in the tunnels. We came under 129 Brigade for pay and so on, their HQ being at Ripple. Many's the time I was blown off my Norton motor cycle when the radar masts were being attacked. But I came through it unscathed. They seemed to kill more sheep than humans! The mining families near Deal often invited us into their homes and made us feel very welcome. We even used the pit-head baths at Betteshanger Colliery. Memories are a little hazy after all these years but I will never forget the Salvation Army Club van which used to visit us with 'char and wads'. The theatre and cinemas served us well, often keeping going during an alert just as the Windmill boasted it did in London.

Ex-Sparker (wireless operator) John Stoddart, of HMML 138 Coastal Force, was in and out of Dover and has distinct memories of the submarine pens and the Prince Louis public house in Snargate Street – a favourite haunt of naval personnel before it was demolished by a German shell:

> We did seventy-two-hour patrols between Newhaven (HMS *Aggressive*) and Dover. When the weather was too rough and in excess of force seven we would shelter in Dungeness Bay, but when it became too severe we entered Dover, courtesy of V.A.D. (Vice Admiral Dover) whose call-sign was 'Monkey Tommy Uncle' in Morse code. The phonetic call-sign changed to 'Mike Tango Uniform' at 00.01 hours the day after the Yanks came into the conflict. Poor old 'Monkey Tommy Uncle' disappeared for ever more.
>
> Fitted with kites and otters for sweeping mines we were, on one occasion, shelled from Cap Gris Nez whilst hanging around like sitting ducks manually hauling in our sweeps and praying for the order, 'Cut sweeps' from V.A.D. But he never relented from his safe haven in the castle.
>
> On another occasion we scrambled out of harbour with the RAF rescue launches and the Norwegian MLs when an air battle resulted in several crew members landing in the 'drink'. We picked up one member of the Luftwaffe just off South Foreland in a force seven gale. When we put out the net we nearly drowned our crew and Jerry, who disappeared under several feet of water. We had to cut our 'friend's' soaked, tight-fitting black leather jacket off with a jack-knife, and then covered him with a blanket. Back in harbour the castle sent transport down to the dock. We witnessed another enemy survivor climbing the iron rungs of a ladder from a Norwegian boat stark naked! Who could blame the Norwegians? They did well to bring him back alive.

CHAPTER FIVE

'What – no bleeding bluebirds?'

At the back of everyone's mind as the door to 1943 opened was an appreciation of the responsibilities that lay ahead. Few people – civilian or the rank and file in the armed services, based anywhere in the south-east of England – required a visual incentive. It was so easy to find amidst the many ruins and drab dilapidation of 'ghost' towns on the very edges of the English Channel. Always present, reminders of the need for urgency, were still the black-out and the incessant drone of the sirens.

In October and November of the previous year a combined operation was launched to oust Field-Marshal Rommel from Africa. In retaliation, on Armistice Day the Germans took over, lock, stock and barrel, Occupied France – until then known as Vichy. Also in November the great Russian campaign was launched in the Stalingrad area. On the other side of the world American and Australian Forces were beginning to rout the Imperial Japanese Forces.

In January 1943 Bomber Command was increasing its offensive against Germany, joined by the USAAF heavy bombers who made their first raid upon the Third Reich.

At the Casablanca Conference in January, the Combined Chiefs of Staff resolved to begin the detailed planning of Operation 'Overlord' – the proposed Allied invasion across the English Channel.

There were times in 1943 when the lists of code-names for umpteen military exercises not only confused the Germans who were listening in to our radio signals, but also confused everyone else. Not least was the Dieppe raid of August 1942, code-named Operation 'Jubilee'. Even the hardened generals on both sides of the conflict seemed duped by this expensive exercise. However, the Pas de Calais opposite Dover loomed ever larger in the sights of German consciousness as the point of assault for the Allied invasion to come.

By now, of course, almost every man, woman and child in England was affected by the war. Planning became a question of how little or how much their lives were to be interfered with when the assault took place. One of the priorities considered was the possibility that any extensive military movement in the south-east might attract an increase in Luftwaffe activity. While contingency plans were put in place to minimize the effects of German air assault upon the local civilians, on the other side of the coin there was the necessity to allow troops movement unimpeded by any civilian activity. The equation was further compounded by the need for absolute secrecy in these sensitive areas.

It was not until mid-1943 that the planners realized the full implications of the daily requirements of the civilian population, especially in the south-east, such as food, coal, water and electricity. Much of this was acquired from 'coastwise' shipping, the system of small-tonnage vessels plying between harbours along the coasts of Kent and Sussex. The immediate stoppage of these coastal convoys became another priority, not least because the vessels were destined to be requisitioned for military purposes.

It was equally important in 1943 that not everyone should be aware that the military and naval exercises now being planned were merely a feint and not the real thing. The rope of security was drawn ever tighter around the poor, suffering civilians, but the local newspapers, still restricted under the 'D' Notice, were allowed to use the phrase 'Second Front'. ARP services were overhauled, the Fire Services were strengthened, stocks of food and fuel were increased and the military scoured the countryside looking for suitable buildings to be requisitioned.

The first of these exercises, 'Starkey', took place on 8 September 1943. It was a clear sunny day and by late afternoon General Sir Bernard Paget (Commander-in-Chief, Home Forces), and Lieutenant-General Frederick Morgan (Head of Combined Chiefs of Staff), with American Generals Jacob Devers, Cliff Lee and Idwal Edwards of European Theatre HQ, were standing on the beaches around Folkestone and Hythe.

Gunners of the Coastal Batteries, many of whom had never fired a shell in anger throughout their period of service, had been stood-to since dawn. The rank and file were quite unaware of the implications when they suddenly observed, in full view of both coasts, an impressive convoy of merchantmen. In the sky there were formations of American and British fighters. By late evening the whole cast of Operation 'Starkey' had miraculously disappeared from the Straits of Dover. The deception was complete. The gunners were stood down, totally bemused by the whole affair. They stared across the becalmed water at the luminescent wavelets and wondered when the German long-range guns would open fire.

Edith Ring (née Dossett) was with No. 961 Balloon Squadron, and was extremely grateful for civilian hospitality:

Molly Cook was another WAAF serving with me, who was engaged to a Norwegian sailor whose boat was sadly hit by a mine. We used to go away together for a weekend to the lovely Walker family who farmed at Westenhanger. We had to go away every four weeks or so in order to get a couple of nights' undisturbed sleep. The Walker's son, Hector, used to make apple-pie beds. But they were really super hosts and made us WAAF girls feel very welcome.

Olive Rayner (née Hudson) served in the WRNS but her posting to Dover caused ill-feeling among the matelots:

> We were billeted at 14 East Cliff. Many nights we had to get out of our warm bunks and go into the damp caves which were virtually at the bottom of the garden. I think '14' was joined to '16' by knocking the wall through. I was the first supply rating posted to the victualling office at HMS *Wasp* and the male staff were none too happy about it because it meant they would be going to sea when WRNS replaced them.

N. Robb served as cox'n on board the minesweeper HMMS 87:

> When she was on the grid next to the 'Hotel de Paree', as we called it, a shell struck us, killing the leading hand. Both myself and a gunner were injured.

Mrs Burchell wrote:

> My father, Ted Hobby, was a sergeant in the Royal Artillery. My dad and his friends used to catch fish on the breakwater, put them in sacks and send them home to Lewes by train, for their families. My mother was a WAAF stationed at Manchester. When she married my father in 1943 she was transferred to Dover, so that they would at least see one another sometimes. My mother was

HMS *Taipo*'s 'tiddly-suited' crew, seen here at Admiralty Pier, Dover, belie the fact they were in constant danger from unannounced German long-range shelling.

a telephonist and my father used to phone her when the barrage balloon
'Bunty' was shot down. My mother was a corporal, I think, with No. 961
Balloon Squadron. She left in 1945 to have me – the only way to get out of
the WAAF!

Posted from Plymouth to 418 Battery RA in early 1943, John Pullen ended up
with the 'Knuckle Battery' at the eastern end of the breakwater:

By then the very cryptic two-colour tiny arm 'flashes' on our uniform were
being replaced by the full unit insignia. We were the Three Trees, oak, ash
and elm, of 12 Corps. They said General Montgomery was at the 'Elm'. I
actually saw him once when I was guard commander up at the Western
Heights. He swept up in his Humber staff car, stopped for the sentry briefing
and then went through and away out of sight.

We had three Battery Commanders in my time. The first was a little too
fond of whisky. He was later removed. Captain Peel was a gentleman. After
him we had Torin Thatcher, the distinguished film actor, who kept going off
to make films.

In the draft of a dozen newly qualified radio operators was eighteen-year-old
Arthur Bridges, sent to Dover with the 2nd War Office Signals:

We travelled down by train in Field Service Marching Order (FMSO) plus
our kitbags. It was quite a feat to get in and out of railway carriages in all that
clobber. Big pack on your back, small pack bouncing against one buttock and
a full water bottle bouncing against the other, gas mask (officially known as
'respirator, anti-gas') on the chest, ammunition pouches held up by shoulder
straps and belt. We were ordered out of the train at Kearsney Halt although
we had been told our destination was Dover. We struggled into our webbing
gear outside the station and just stood there, wondering whether we were
within the shelling area, or what life held for us now that we were in the 'real'
Army and not just under training. Most importantly we also wondered what
the grub would be like.

We were taken off to our billets in the village of Temple Ewell. I remember
'Wee' George unbuckling his belt and letting his accoutrements slide on to
the floor. He plonked himself down on the bunk of his choice and said, in his
best Max Miller impression, 'What – no bleeding bluebirds?'.

Days later we moved into billets at Crabble Avenue and went through the
same moving-in procedure of filling a mattress cover with straw, filling in
forms and reading all sorts of standing orders. The other wireless operators
already there were mostly older men who had been kept in signals for some
time but had not actually been on active service. They kept just a little aloof
from us new sprogs, which made me feel I had a lot to learn about radio
techniques. But we were soon joined by blokes who had been with the

8th Army in the desert and really knew their stuff. Most had been pre-war regulars and had been trained for many months longer than those of us who attended a wartime shortened course. But they were friendly. Back at Catterick anyone with a stripe on his arm was supposed to be treated as a sort of shining tin God. Stand to attention and say, 'No, Corporal; yes, Corporal; three bags full, Corporal'. But these chaps from the desert all wore stripes, yet they were very matey. Of course, on parade we had to treat them as NCOs, but off parade we could be on Christian name terms, providing we were not too cocky. We were at last serving with real soldiers and we became quite a close-knit mob. If the Cricketers pub on the corner of the avenue had beer, and if we had enough money left after sending some home, paying for the usual 'Wad and char' and for things like soap, razor blades and metal polish, we would sometimes gather there in the evenings.

We worked in shifts, doing one night duty in four and one evening duty. Time off was time off – unless there were fatigues to be done or guard duty. We sometimes were required to stop in our billets on PAD [Passive Air Defence] similar to ARP duties or fire watch duties. I soon settled down and was quite content with my lot, serving in the front line of the country (as the newspapers put it), and able to go home on leave once in a blue moon. Probably due to the somewhat primitive living conditions of unheated

'Someone started to sing a carol. So we gave a recital all the way down Castle Hill, through the town and out along the London Road.'

houses, I contracted pleurisy and had to go into hospital. On discharge from hospital they sent me to Portsmouth, but I jolly soon perked up when I was sent back to good old Dover. I was welcomed back with open arms.

Two things stand out in my mind from my Dover days. The first is coming off duty on Christmas Eve from the underground HQ at the castle and climbing wearily into the personnel truck with the rest of the shift, including the ATS girls who shared our transport. Someone started to sing a carol. So we gave a recital all the way down Castle Hill, through the town and out along the London Road. The ATS had by then organized a concert party complete with choir so they gave our singing the real musical touch. Often we had belted-out raucous Army songs or popular ballads as we went back and forth from billet to castle. But this was a quality rendition – *par excellence*.

The other is a picture of our section drawn up on parade in Crabble Avenue the day we left Dover. The radio trucks and trailers were all in line. Then a few of the people came out of their houses to see us lined up in separate crews. Sergeant Neves ordered 'Mount Up!', and we got into our vehicles, then moved off in convoy, guessing (and we were right), that our destination would eventually be Normandy.

In 1943 the RAF, having sent too many wireless mechanics to the Middle East, called for volunteers to man wireless stations in the south-east of England. Douglas Camm volunteered and was sent to Eastbourne. Further personnel were required to man 'Oboe', a piece of equipment so secret that there were only four such stations in operation. One of them was at Walmer near Deal:

A little wangling and a judicious pound note to the corporal in charge of the orderly room and I found myself billeted with my aunt and uncle at Gladstone Street, Deal, where I used to spend my summer holidays. I was given the front bedroom as my aunt and uncle could not stand reveille sounding every morning at the Royal Marine barracks, just a few houses away. They even provided a bicycle for me to get to Hawkshill Down where there were three other stations.

The cinema on Deal seafront had so many shrapnel holes in the roof that we had to wear tin hats when it rained. Try necking in the back row with a tin hat on! There wasn't a NAAFI in Deal so we used to gather in a little cafe on the seafront called the Golden Hind. On the ceiling in one pub was a huge drawing of a nude woman.

Bill Lucas was a driver with 124 Command Mixed Transport RASC:

We were a kind of dogsbody unit who did the fetching and carrying for all the units in that neck of the wood. One of our regular runs was to take building materials for the gun emplacement for Winnie – the big gun at St Margaret's at Cliff. I also used to bring shells from the ammunition dump at

Tonbridge. Three shells was a full load for my Canadian Chevrolet. Very vividly I recall a test-firing of Winnie one summer afternoon. I was having a kip in the cab of my truck after dinner when there was one almighty bang. I thought we had been bombed. A corner of the church tower fell alongside me. It gave me a real fright.

Later I used to take the Home Guard to the Eastern Arm at Dover to fire the 6-in guns for target practice. The target was towed behind a launch and they were supposed to fire close to it but not hit it. But they used to aim at it because the sooner it was sunk the sooner they could get to the pub. What a way to win a war! We also took scrap cars and lorries to Sandwich golf course where Spitfires could practise shooting them up.

Early in 1943 Ken Flint left Catterick to join the 2nd War Office Signals at Dover. Not until he was on the train out of London was the destination of his little party of newly trained wireless operators made known. Whether this was a security precaution, or simply the Army's attitude of treating 'other ranks' merely as pawns in the game of war he cannot remember:

Actually we were keyed up and raring to go, intent on trying out our operating skills on 'live' radio circuits. Unfortunately this was not to be. First we spent some few days cleaning out billets for ATS girls to occupy at Temple Ewell. When we finally moved closer to Dover, Crabble Avenue, we found the same task awaited us.

Still, we found our requisitioned houses a great improvement on the accommodation Catterick Camp had accustomed us to endure. There we slept on 'biscuit' mattresses on the floor, thirty-two men in a room designed under the Hore Belisha programme for eight. I made a bee-line for the bottom position of a two-tiered bunk, and was to regret that for a very long time. Our mattresses were straw-filled palliasses, and whenever the chap on the top bunk turned over I was showered with chaff and dust. Having served our apprenticeship as sweepers, 'spud bashers' and general beasts-of-burden, eventually we were introduced to our place of duty, a large headquarters and signals centre deep beneath Dover Castle. To reach this entailed a ten minute walk. At the entrance to the complex of tunnels a military policeman was stationed – not the red-capped authoritarian 'monster' we had been conditioned to fear during our early months in the Army, but a blue-capped soldier of rather more mature years, thus less intimidating.

First we walked along rough-hewn greeny-grey chalk passageways cut out of solid chalk. Occasionally the steady drip of water not only permeated the ceilings but also our forage caps. The tunnels rambled gently downwards until we were at the top of a very steep flight of concrete steps, fortunately well lit and provided with a handrail. At the bottom was a maze of passages with fluorescent lights, festooned with pipes, cables and nozzles blowing out tangy salt air.

For a week the Senior Service took us in hand, and we operated wireless sets in the Royal Navy radio bay until we were deemed sufficiently proficient to be let loose on Army communications. But the keen edge of our recent training was soon dulled. We youngsters had been inculcated with the latest security radio techniques and were very conscious that the least little slip in correct procedures might attract the attention of the German monitoring service, and do untold harm to our cause, not to mention the trouble it might cause the poor operator deviating from the straight and narrow. But the 'old hands', the experienced operators, the men we had been led to believe could send and receive Morse and read a newspaper at the same time, still used all the little mannerisms, the personal trademarks, the irregular procedures we had been taught to avoid. After a short while we too relaxed some of our strict adherence to 'the book', at least until we found our ranks being increased by older soldiers recently returned from the victorious campaign in the desert. These experienced operators, men like 'Hoppy' Hopkinson and 'Bill' Williams, taught us that the enemy intercept stations had capitalized on the quite unnecessary procedural slips our wireless 'nets' had made before El Alamein, and gleaned much information from that. It seems that when we captured German positions some of this carelessly 'leaked' information had been discovered.

I remember that our stock of military slang was enriched by these men, all of whom wore the Africa Star medal ribbon and tiny metal figure '8', denoting they had served with the 8th Army. We learned to call bread 'rooti', to talk of 'bints' where we would once talk of 'tarts' (this was not necessarily a derogatory expression as it was derived from 'sweetheart'; in fact I was proud that I had a pretty 'tart' living along the avenue from our billets). So you would hear such words as 'charbash' (well done), 'ackers' (money) and 'Susti wallah' (lazybones) being bandied about by lads who had never been further than a day trip to the Isle of Wight!

At the end of 1943 I was on night duty in the radio bay deep under the castle. It was in the small hours of early morning and I had been sitting with headphones on in front of a receiver (our transmitters were up on the cliffs in the Langdon area, worked by remote control from our Morse keys in the radio bay), concentrating on accurately recording the umpteenth of a never-ending stream of five-letter cipher 'groups'. The door was flung open dramatically and three or four face-blackened and tommy-gun-armed commandos burst in. Their officer waved a pistol at us and ordered us to 'Switch off and stop sending any more gen'. We were slow to obey – partly because to us in the Royal Signals the proper slang word for information was 'griff' and never 'gen'. Also we were conditioned to obey officers we knew. Anyway, at that hour in the morning, with one's brain addled with radio atmospherics and interference, one's speed of reaction was slow. Perhaps I can best describe the officer's own reaction as 'Basil Fawlty-like'. Eventually he had his way and we sat back in our chairs obediently. The raiding party then left us in peace and went, as I understand it, rampaging through the whole of the combined headquarters. Had they but known it the Army cipher room was at the end of our bay, and boasting of having captured that would have been worth while. Quite naturally, there was never any publicity of this mock raid executed by, I am sure, the Royal Marines at Deal. But rumour said that they had climbed the cliff face and entered the tunnels by the back door – quite literally. There was a ledge on the cliff face with a small NAAFI canteen supplying tea and coffee to duty personnel. The top brass had never arranged for any defence of this back door, taking the view I suppose, that the Germans would never attempt entry by such difficult means. I have often wondered what my reaction would have been if those commandos had been wearing field-grey uniforms!

In the gunnery office deep in the bowels of the earth beneath Dover Castle, was Wilfred Ellis. He now recalls '. . . a certain amount of nostalgia when people arrive at our age':

> I well remember a lovely girl in the First Aid Nursing Yeomanry (FANY) who was based at Folkestone but used to come out to Canterbury and thence to Dover Castle, where she would chauffeur me on my frequent visits to various gun batteries. I first met her when I was on a shoot at the Lydden Spout Battery. She probably had ferried one of the officers from the castle. We chatted for some time and got on well but when I came to put my uniform tunic on she quickly noticed I was only a Warrant Officer Second Class and so things never were quite the same afterwards, although she continued to drive me about 'on business'.
>
> Lydden Spout was quite a spectacular spot, the cliffs dropping straight down to the sea. During the war I used to run down the path leading to the searchlights and then run back up again. Not that long ago I went back there and just looking down the path gave me vertigo. I remember that in summer the gorse was lovely, and we could go out picking bilberries and mushrooms.

With an ack-ack unit that had been through the blitz on Liverpool, A. Thomas shared the trials and tribulations with the people of Thanet:

> In the spring of 1943 we arrived in the Margate area to help in the defence of the German 'hit and run' fighter-bomber attacks. For billets we were placed in requisitioned guest houses near the seashore. We arrived in the very early hours. A fellow sergeant and I were making our way down the promenade to find a postbox to send letters home. Just as we turned to go back to the billets all hell broke loose!
>
> We had heard the sound of planes coming in off the sea but it had not registered that they might be hostile – after all, we were new to the area. There had been no warning siren or any indication of impending danger. Suddenly bullets ricocheted and splashed about the road and seaside properties. We sought the only shelter available at such short notice, which

was the kerbside. The racket from the aero-engines, machine guns, bombs and collapsing buildings was indescribable. Afterwards there was a deathly quiet; although it seemed like ages it was most probably only a few minutes.

Our immediate concern was to check on the safety of the men in their new and unfamiliar billets. Our 'B' Troop had had a miraculous escape but our mates in their billet near the tennis courts had received a direct hit. We were on the spot within minutes and it was a tragic sight, one that is still fresh in my mind in spite of the things I saw in Normandy on D-Day, and then during the Rhine Crossing.

RAF radio operator Richard Shotton served in Gibraltar before being sent back to England, in connection with jamming the Luftwaffe radio beams guiding their bombers to their targets:

Our site was on the cliff top quite near Shakespeare Cliff. We had all sorts of code-names for the various wavelengths, such as Aspirin, Bromide and Meacon. This was after the German *Knickebein* system of radio guidance had been abandoned. This system had consisted of two beams converging on the pre-selected target. The bombers flew along the centre of the two beams by keeping the volume of the streams of dots and dashes constant in their ear-phones. When the dots and dashes merged they had reached their target.

I was billeted at one of the miners' cottages near the Priory Station, Dover. On my very first night I was woken up by what I thought was a big fire across the road, with flames shooting across the sky accompanied by cannon fire, bells ringing and much crashing and banging. I leaped out of bed and rushed to the window. It proved to be an air raid-cum-dogfight with aircraft diving all over the sky – fighters and bombers all mixed up and tracers streaking everywhere. I saw one plane falling to earth in flames and the whole scene was lit up when it crashed. Fire engines and police and rescue vehicles whizzed by at great speed. Then the family I was billeted with rushed into my room and dragged me down to the shelter.

I later changed my billet to a house in Folkestone Road, further out of town and nearer to the radio site. It was certainly safer. Later on the shelling during the daytime seemed continuous. The look-out over the harbour, an area which was out of bounds to us, used to sound the alarm. People sheltering behind the main street went into the caves and if we had gone to a cinema there was a door near the screen that led directly into one cave.

Ruth Stokes (née Buchan) was one of a small group of ATS girls who took over duties from the men in the RA operations room beneath Dover Castle in 1943:

There was one particular chap on duty in a room adjacent to ours who was very handy. For a small payment he would trim our hair. He would often bring with him lumps of chalk from the cliffs, carve them into toby jugs in Churchill's

'. . . the door opened and in came Winston Churchill. . . . I was concerned that the Churchill toby jugs might be visible to the great man.'

image, paint them and then sell them for a modest charge. In June 1943 we were told to expect a visit from someone important. On the actual day cigarettes and ashtrays quickly disappeared like magic. Our morning mail was put away and the room made generally spick and span. Then the door opened and in came Winston Churchill, followed by Mrs Churchill, John Wynant, the American Ambassador, and the US Secretary of State for War, H.L. Stimson. Mr Churchill went straight to the major in charge, but the others just milled around asking awkward questions. I was concerned that the Churchill toby jugs might be visible to the great man. I need not have worried for the carver had got the message and everything was cleared away out of sight – well almost.

After just two weeks' basic training at Mill Hill, Gwenneth Preece (née Salisbury) was posted to the WRNS at HMS *Wasp*, arriving on Christmas Eve 1942 and feeling very homesick:

Nobody appeared to be expecting me and there was no bed available so I spent my first night sleeping on a board placed over a bath! The following day I was sent to 14 East Cliff. When a shelling warning sounded at night we went to the cave shelters by crossing the road immediately behind our billet. There were bunk beds there and we were sometimes given an orange – an absolute luxury in those days.

My mother was allowed to visit me on one occasion, having obtained special permission from our captain. She stayed at the Hotel de Paris where the beds were so high off the floor there were steps to climb into them. It was a new experience for her when we took a trip to Folkestone and we had to show our passes.

I can still recall the effort it took to climb the steps from the casemates beneath the castle, after a gruelling night-long watch. We would arrive blinking into daylight. Ultra-violet treatment was provided to keep us fit. For relaxation we would occasionally walk to a farmhouse where we could get tea with new laid eggs (one each) and home-made cakes. Once I volunteered to help the war effort by lending a hand to harvest potatoes – 'Digging for Victory' was a way of life then.

The only hotel I can recall being open in Dover was the Shalimar along the seafront. For entertainment there was the Leas Cliff Hall ballroom in Folkestone, and we had numerous invitations to dances at the various barracks and the Royal Marine Depot at Deal. There were some very exciting days at Dover and everyone had their lucky escape story to tell. Mine was getting off a bus at the Market Square where moments later a shell exploded on the exact spot!

'My appearance caused hoots of laughter, wolf-whistles, and good-natured, if somewhat uncomplimentary, advice,' wrote Mary Twyman, one of over four thousand Land Army girls, seen here on the Maidstone cricket ground, Moat Park, in 1945.

'Sometimes we would be lucky and get lifts on army transport such as jeeps and lorries, and once I arrived home in a Bren-gun Carrier.'

In the spring of 1943 Mary Evans (now Guy) joined the Women's Land Army and most of her service was spent in and around the Dover area:

I lived at Walmer and our HQ was at Reach Court Farm, owned by Gilbert Mitchell, who was area manager of the Kent Agricultural Executive Committee. Many of the farmers in Hellfire Corner had moved away and their land had been taken over by the Women's Executive Council (WEC) so that food production could be maintained.

At first there were only three of us but in the end our numbers built up to fourteen. We had pushbikes to get around on, marked with the KWAEC yellow flash. When the weather was bad we used buses but these did not run when there was shelling. Sometimes we would be lucky and get lifts on army transport such as jeeps and lorries, and once I arrived home in a Bren-gun Carrier. The light railway running through to St Margaret's at Cliff carrying the shells for the long-range guns often gave WLA girls a lift!

We often used to get our midday meal at a nice restaurant in Dover, Igglesden & Graves, and would usually have tea or lunch breaks in St Margaret's Bay at a cafe run by the Crannis family. We saw plenty of action, dogfights overhead with parachuted descents, and sheep killed by bombs and shells.

Like a service number – never forgotten – Bill 'Jacko' Jacobs recalls his time with the Royal Navy:

My ship was the Motor Launch ML140, a craft made entirely of wood with twin Packard engines. Armament was one Oerlikon aft and another amid-ships, a two-pounder forward with a Lewis machine gun on the bridge and four depth-charges on the aft decking. I joined the ML140 at Newhaven as she was being fitted out. We belonged to the 5th Flotilla, about six or seven of us, numbered I think, 137 to 143. We then sailed for Dover and took part in minesweeping operations to keep the Channel open for our food convoys. Sometimes we would be working in misty conditions and when the mist would suddenly lift we often found ourselves under fire from German shore batteries. An axe was always kept handy to chop through the cable to make a quick getaway, setting a zigzag course back to Dover.

Also on Motor Launch ML140 Luke Walsh recalls the several occasions when they rescued airmen in the English Channel:

Our largest 'catch' was the crew of a Flying Fortress which had ditched. The amusing thing was that the crew at first took us for the enemy. We were so intent on the actual business of fishing them out of the water that very little was said. When they realized we were British they were so delighted they gave us their French currency that they always carried in case of a forced landing in France and the need to escape. Those francs came in really handy when we eventually landed in Normandy after D-Day 1944. Two or three times we helped one particular Walrus pilot who had been sent out to pick up ditched airmen, and towed his flying boat back to Dover.

As a lieutenant troop commander in charge of 'Dog 1' at Shakespeare Cliff and later of 'Dog 8' at Langdon, Ernest Hutchinson MBE arrived at Dover from Northern Ireland in the spring of 1943, and stayed until September 1944, '. . . when the doodlebugs had been seen off':

We brought various pets with us from Belfast, mostly cats and dogs. The first time our guns fired the dogs fled and never came back. The cats tore around the gun pits like mad, but they didn't leave us. They stayed in our mess (half a Nissen hut), which had four British and four Polish officers. We kept a black tom cat there whom we called 'Stinker' – for obvious reasons. He would turn up for meals and a rest about every three days, and attended to his latest wounds. At 'Dog 1' our accommodation was more commodious. Battery HQ was there also, and there was a Canadian radio unit attached. One of the Polish officers married a Dover WRN and later became a naturalized Briton.

    The battery I was most involved with was 416 of 173 Regiment RA. We had a fair amount of Cockneys and in the doodlebug days any doodlebug that carried on towards London made them come out with the strongest language imaginable, so direct at times that I thought it was directed at me personally for letting the doodlebugs through. But my parents *were* married and I was the fourth son!

After the doodlebug campaign we stayed on for a while to clear up some of the temporary gun-sites between Dover and Rye. We had a few ATS in the regiment, mostly drivers. They were always well respected and most welcome when they came bringing messages and so on.

When posted to the Western Heights from Staffordshire in 1943 John Nicholson thought he was a little older than most in 90 HAA Regiment RA:

In those days the war seemed set to drag on for decades and I dreaded the thought of being sent to North Africa. At Dover I got a lot of practice driving our heavy trucks and also a lot of practice scrubbing floors on my hands and knees, as a punishment for failing to do it 'at the double' when ordered. But what I remember most is the night I went to a concert in the town. All of a sudden bombs were falling. The lights went out. To keep our spirits up we had a sing-along. I found out afterwards that a power cable had been severed and our officers' quarters damaged. On the whole the lads were a grand crowd, but the comradeship we knew and shared could never be carried into civilian life – more's the pity!

In 1943 the Germans were becoming desperate to put up some sort of retaliation in response to Bomber Command's heavy raids on German cities. They sent over small bomber sorties, coming in over the Wash to reach London,

Through binoculars he observed four Focke-Wulf 190s heading towards the town. Within seconds, the grey-camouflaged, red-nosed fighter-bombers were pulling up to clear the East Cliff.

then heading for the English Channel where, above Calais, a steady searchlight beam set up vertically gave them a visual point to aim at. Robert Waugh recalls:

From London Jerry would stick his nose down in a shallow dive and head for Calais like the clappers. By the time he got over Dover he was usually very low. We picked one up one night and Wally Johnson, our machine gunner, let fly at him but it was too low and Wally had every chance of hitting us instead. Wally stopped firing and waited for it to pass before firing again. We watched his tracers hitting the aircraft which zoomed flat out for Calais. Not long afterwards a JU 88 bomber did the same thing, but this time we saw the engine cowling knocked off by Wally's shooting.

On another occasion a plane came over and everything fired at it. It sent out the correct coloured signal flares for the day so we took it for a friendly aircraft and everyone ceased firing. But we had a new and very conscientious middle-aged chap on radar and he kept tracking the plane repeating, 'The cock's not crowing', meaning the Cockerell device installed on our aircraft to indicate friendly was not operating. So we decided it was an enemy plane and got it in the searchlight beam again. All my lads started blazing away with all they had. The aircraft crashed into the sea. We are still waiting for our barrel of beer – the prize offered for 'downing' an enemy plane!

Even today W. Cousens remains convinced that the role of the Women's Services in the front line areas has never received the attention it deserved:

Often the girls shared exactly the same dangers, performed perhaps identical duties and almost always had to put up with living conditions that were austere to say the least. And they were often only eighteen or nineteen years old. I know the female species is supposed to mature quicker than the male, but how would you like to find yourself away from home and in the middle of a war at that tender age? You must also bear in mind that the Women's Forces were paid substantially less than their male counterparts.

So my memories are of a depressing Dover, with ruined buildings, closed down shops and businesses, but enlivened by the smartly turned out women; WRNS in trim navy blue uniform and caps setting off their white shirts, ATS in khaki and WAAF in light blue with gleaming buttons. They also seemed to be the leading lights in the do-it-yourself entertainment that was so necessary for our morale. If there was a concert or some kind of show being organized in Dover, you could bet your bottom dollar the girls would play a great part in it.

Similar austere living conditions are recalled by F.B. Hallum, who served in the ATS from 1943 to 1945, attached to HQ of No. 455 Regiment RA:

Our billets were old wooden huts at the top of Castle Hill. The rumour was that in the Great War they had been married quarters but had been condemned as unfit to live in. They really were dreadful and, of course, being exposed to the elements up there we really suffered. After much effort we could sometimes get the boiler going to warm up water for a bath. But we preferred to make a weekly trip to the YMCA in the town and bathe in comfort. During the last war the YMCA, and of course the good old Salvation Army, were very good to the Forces.

I had a pal whose boyfriend was billeted out near River somewhere. His unit was in requisitioned houses and they used to march in a squad, towels and clean underwear under their arms, all the way to the Civil Defence HQ behind the town hall. These were showers originally put in to decontaminate people who had been exposed to mustard gas or any other chemicals – had they been used.

It was always a treat and a great pleasure to sit down only a few to a table instead of in a long line in the messroom, and be served spam and chips by two old ladies who ran a local cafe.

Serving with the 2nd War Office Signals at Dover Castle as a Despatch Rider (DR), Don Smith shared the same messroom and billets as the radio operators:

Our unit did not mix well with the operators. For one thing we had different places of duty and also different hours of duty. The operators, teleprinter and radio, worked underground, which we thought was a cushy job. We, on the other hand, were on the surface in all weathers and naturally always likely to be shelled or bombed, and a motor bike gives little protection from either. We despatch riders looked upon ourselves as the cream of the Royal Signals – daredevils almost. And being in Dover *and* a DR gave us that certain *esprit de corps* that we felt put us above the operators. In any case, we thought most radio operators were a bit 'Deolali Tap' with all their weird jargon. If we were sitting in the little shop along the end of Crabble Avenue having a cup of tea and a scone where the Beards family ran a refreshment bar, the radio operators would sometimes show off by 'da-di-dahing' at each other so that we DRs were left out of things. It was a kind of class distinction if you like but I don't think you could say it had to do with actual class. I guess we were conditioned to think in terms of various trades or occupations as belonging to a certain type of person.

Of course it was a lot safer on the roads in those wartime days. Apart from the danger of coming face to face with a tank, the chances of having an accident were no more than being copped by a shell or bomb. Unless of course, we got mixed up with a long army convoy, then it could be dodgy weaving in and out between the vehicles.

Once I had stopped for a quiet Woodbine up on the cliffs. Stretched out on the grass in the warm sun, the war seemed a million miles away. Then, without any warning, the 15-inch long-range guns opened fire near Langdon. I felt the 'crrrump' more than heard it. It took a second or two to realize it was our guns and not a Jerry shell!

'Apart from the danger of coming face to face with a tank, the chances of having an accident were no more than being copped by a shell or bomb.'

After completing his six weeks' army training in his home county of Yorkshire Eric Miller became bored with the monotony of Catterick Camp. He longed to get into some sort of field unit and into the mainstream of the war:

> Attending church parades on Sundays, kit inspections, polishing brasses, elaborate parades every morning on drill before we could get on with the day's training hardly seemed likely to win a war.
>
> There was much speculation where we would be posted when we finally passed our trade tests as wireless operators. We knew that drafts were going overseas but that many troops were being kept in the UK for the eventual invasion of Occupied Europe. We were also aware that some personnel were being sent off to oblivion to the Shetlands and Orkneys on monotonous garrison duty. This was not an enticing prospect, so when we found our little group was off to front line Dover there was some relief, mixed perhaps with apprehension. We already knew the area was known as 'Hellfire Corner' – so that was not appealing. On the other hand at least we would be in the UK and so be able to go home on leave occasionally.
>
> I had been prepared to arrive at a town battered and quite dilapidated by the effects of being so close to the enemy, so that was no shock. Still, I had expected the few civilians remaining there to be slightly cowed and resigned to their fate. Somehow I had this mental picture of them cowering in air raid

shelters all the time, or scurrying from place to place with their ears cocked for shells arriving. But nothing could have been further from the truth.

We had moved into requisitioned houses where a very high proportion of the rest of the street was occupied by the civilians. They welcomed us almost as if we were new neighbours moving in, which I suppose we were. They were certainly not in any way unduly worried about the possibility of enemy attacks. With rationing so tight, there was not a lot they could do about offering much hospitality. But cups of tea were offered and there were offers to mend clothes and darn socks, things we had been taught to do since enlisting, but not very skilfully. And of course, soon some of us managed to 'get our feet under the table' – in other words, form an attachment with a family. Sometimes this was on a purely neighbourly basis but sometimes there was a romantic attachment. That meant an occasional meal eaten off a properly set table with a cloth, and not off a bare scrubbed wooden trestle.

Life settled into a routine. Duty in the radio room under the castle, guard duties and fatigues, occasional evenings at the pub on the corner and visits to the cinema. We even managed to arrange some concerts at the messrooms at Crabble Paper Mill.

But there was more than the frequent shelling warnings to remind us there was a war on. We went out into the Kent countryside on long wireless exercises. Once we were ordered to parade in full battle order with steel helmets and rifles and had to tramp for hours in infantry formation across

'Once we were ordered to parade in full battle order with steel helmets and rifles and had to tramp for hours in infantry formation across ditches, along hedges and through woods in the hot sun.'

ditches, along hedges and through woods in the hot sun. I remember thinking that if this was what the jungles of Burma were like, then I would prefer the desert or the Shetlands!

But when our time came it was Normandy we were sent to. As our little convoy of radio trucks formed up at Crabble, quite a few housewives and kids gathered to wave us 'bon voyage' and Joe, the landlord of the pub, went round to each truck distributing free cigarettes. That is one of my dearest memories of the hospitality of the Dover people.

Towards the end of 1943 the danger of invasion was considerably reduced although it was still a possibility. Regular Army commitments meant that they were stretched, but now the Home Guard was considered sufficiently trained to take some of the strain in the sphere of coast defence.

Aged only sixteen, J. Head joined the then Local Defence Volunteers, later re-named the Home Guard. This was in October 1940 and he served throughout the war until the HG was ordered to stand down in November 1944. Accordingly, twenty-seven men of a Sandwich platoon were picked to take over 338 Battery RA from the Regulars at Sandwich Bay:

It is summer, and the lone Home Guard turns out for his stint on the white cliffs. He looks over the English Channel to the coast of France and wonders . . .

We were given some training in gunnery. I remember Captains Elston and Parsley, and Lieutenants Leroy and Minney were the instructors, with Sergeant-Major Rose and Bombardier Whatmore instructing on searchlights.

In April 1943 we were considered efficient enough to take over the 6-inch guns and we had our first practice shoot at a 'Hong Kong' target towed behind a small vessel. I had become Lieutenant in Command of the unit by then and the following month was made up to Captain and sent to Plymouth for an intensive gunnery course.

On my return I was called before Lieutenant-Colonel Newport, the Home Guard Battalion Commander, and reprimanded for telling the Regular Royal Artillery officer who was teaching us parrot fashion, that we knew the first part of the Gunnery Manual by heart but as our training time was limited we should concentrate on gun control fire orders and practice on the simulator. Soon after this the Regular Army officers were posted away leaving me in sole charge with the sergeant-major and bombardier as permanent staff, with the rest of the gun crew being part timers like myself.

The battery observation post was built on to a green-tiled sea front house owned by the Slazenger family. It was demolished after the war. My junior officers were Lieutenants Ken Thomas and John Wadbrook, both Home Guard men. The Officers' Mess was in one of the coastguard cottages at the rear of the old Guildford Hotel.

During one of our practice shoots the officer supervising, a lieutenant-colonel of the Royal Artillery, gave the order 'Stop Loading'. According to the manual this meant that guns already loaded should be fired and not loaded again. In fact the order given should really have been 'Stop Firing'. What happened was that the two loaded guns sent a shell apiece towards three minesweepers making for Ramsgate Harbour. Luckily they missed. The lieutenant-colonel apologized to the trawler skippers – but much to my annoyance, I got the blame for the incident.

William Ellis remembers the towing launches in the Dover area:

The War Department target-towing launches were the *Sulva*, the *Struma* and the *Flying Fox*; the latter was diesel powered while the other two had petrol engines. There was also the *Queen Gull* launch, a remote-controlled boat operated from the clifftops at which the guns could shoot. I recall one particular shoot of the three 8-inch guns at Capel le Ferne being memorable in that we almost hit the towing launch itself. Obviously the crew took a very poor view of this, although they would have been even more dismayed if an 8-inch shell had bored through the decking under their feet! I was instructed to find out what had gone wrong and to help allay any fears that this might happen again. We were using an up-to-date system of plotting bearings, a magnetic synchronous apparatus which was quick, easy and virtually foolproof. There were two dials to give the bearing, one was the coarse dial and the other gave a fine reading. One division out on the fine dial would not produce too much error, but on the coarse dial it could produce a serious error.

When the Royal Marine Division was disbanded in 1943 so that the RM commando units could be set up, Stan Blacker was told he was too young to be a commando. He was sent instead to the RM Siege Regiment at St Margaret's-at-Cliff:

We arrived at Dover Priory station where lorries were waiting to take Royal Artillery and other units' personnel to their billets. No such luck for the Royal Marines. We marched in full marching order (64 pounds of kit and an 8-pound rifle) through Dover via Martin Mill and on to St Margaret's-at-Cliff. At least we were not burdened by our kitbags – they were taken by lorry. Our destination was Townsend Farm – 'A' Battery HQ, and also Lydden where 'B' Battery was located. Our billets were Nissen huts. Most of the men already there were RM reservists and a lot older than us.

At 08.00 hours the next morning we were paraded and formed into sections, which meant a twenty-four hour stint on the guns, twenty-four hours on fatigues and various other duties, with twenty-four hours on guard duty. There were two 14-inch guns, fitted with 18-inch turrets to increase operating room. They had been named Winnie and Pooh. There was also an experimental gun called Bruce. We were assigned to Winnie, with Corporal Gant as our instructor. The normal naval gunnery training course was sixteen weeks but we just received training on the gun itself.

A gun crew consisted of twenty-five men of all ranks but the number on each gun-site was higher because a firing control room was manned and also the pom-pom guns, multi-barrelled ack-ack guns for defence against low flying enemy aircraft, had to be crewed.

Behind the 14-inch guns were the shell and cordite magazines, small buildings protected by a layer of earth. Closer was a small shelter built of railway sleepers also covered with earth. This was where the crew sheltered when the gun was actually fired. The complete area was covered with camouflage netting. A railway track ran right up close to each gun-site so that shells and cordite could be unloaded. The underground control and firing centre was immediately behind the guns, together with billets for the duty gun crew, toilets and kitchen range on which meals for the twenty-four-hour periods were cooked. Viewed from behind all one could see was six inches of smoking stovepipe protruding from the ground. These billets would have to be spotless when we finished our tour of duty and there were fatigue parties constantly wandering about the whole camp area keeping it shipshape and Bristol-fashion – in the best traditions of the RM.

The entire area was surrounded by anti-personnel mines, the road leading to the gun compounds was covered by machine guns set up on fixed-lines. All a sentry had to do was squeeze the trigger and the whole road was sprayed with bullets.

Winnie and Pooh's maximum range was twenty-eight miles, their shells weighed nearly three-quarters of a ton each and needed almost a quarter of a ton of cordite charge to send them on their way. At the highest point in mid-Channel the shell would be nine miles above sea level. After about 150 rounds had been fired the barrels would have to be changed by a firm called Stothert & Pitts of Bath.

We trained on Winnie, bringing up shells on a small trolley and winching it up by hand to the loading tray. An electric rammer on 'full charge' rammed the shell down the chamber followed by four rolls of cordite encased in pure silk, so that no smouldering remnants were left after firing. The Marine in charge of the rammer had to make sure the final roll of cordite went in with the red detonator patch the right way round and the rammer was switched to 'half power', otherwise the whole gun would have blown sky high – and us with it! The breech was closed electrically and a tube inserted into the mechanism. A wire went from the tube to a static pistol firing device in the control room. At any time we were required to man either the pom-poms or the experimental gun.

Bruce, the experimental gun, had a 16-inch barrel fitted with a liner to reduce the calibre to 8 inches, but the chamber was enlarged to take a 13.5-inch cordite charge which sent the shell seventy miles. The wear on the barrel was so tremendous it had to be changed after twenty-eight rounds were fired. Bruce was always kept pointing east towards the North Sea where the fall of shot could be plotted. It was never fired at the enemy!

When we were fully proficient on all the guns another duty was found for us – patrolling the village and cliffs. We had our own little canteen across the road from Townsend Farm, where we could purchase tea and cakes and limited bottled beer. Most of our off duty time was spent playing Tombola – known nowadays as Bingo. Some of the unlucky ones used to finish up owing three weeks' pay, but any debts were quickly settled.

Loading the guns at night was precarious. We would often be sweating with fear as we rolled shells out of the magazine with only a small shielded light to ensure that we did not touch the black detonator on the nose cap which would have exploded instantly.

One of the most remarkable scenes I have ever witnessed was when, as well as having planes spotting for us, we had also, on occasions, a barrage balloon with two airmen in a basket slung underneath. The balloon would go up to about three hundred feet or so. Nine times out of ten this was done in broad daylight and the Germans near Cap Gris Nez – brilliant gunners – would air-bracket the balloon, putting airbursts all around it. If you were right under the balloon you could hear the RAF men shouting at the tops of their voices to be brought down. The airmen below would then reel it down with the winch lorry, and the wire cable would become smoking hot with the speed of the descent. Out would leap the two spotters from the basket – even before it reached the ground – and run like blazes. They would shout, 'Bugger that

'. . . in broad daylight . . . the Germans near Cap Gris Nez – brilliant gunners – would air-bracket the balloon, putting airbursts all around it.'

for a lark', but a couple of days later would be prepared to go up again!

Most of the houses in St Margaret's village had been left exactly as they were when the occupants were advised to leave hurriedly in 1940 because of the invasion threat. There were clocks still on mantlepieces, pictures on the walls and even a tablecloth quite undisturbed. The whole nine months that I was there our discipline was such that no houses were ever entered.

Shore leave, trips to Dover, was a bind. We had to walk to Martin Mill station and then take a train to Dover. The shelling warning always seemed to go off just as we settled down in a cinema or had ordered a pint in a pub. Off we had to troop to the nearest shelter. It was due to this problem that our CO decided we could have a seventy-two-hour pass to travel home once a month.

The farmyard was used for those awarded pack drill for 'crime'. Wearing full marching order the defaulters marched around for an hour each evening. If the Provost Sergeant gave the order 'Enemy in sight in large numbers', the defaulters continued jogging but at the same time had to raise and lower their rifles above their head.

We did plenty of sport, football matches, tug-o'-war competitions against the Royal Artillery, RAF and the South Wales Borderers, and just about every unit in the area. It helped our morale and kept us fit.

Once we were proficient on our own guns we used to train with the railway gun crews at Lydden. Conditions were far from ideal for we lived out of our kitbags which made it difficult to maintain the smart appearance expected of Royal Marines. But there was a war on and so it was accepted, although there were plenty of moans. There was a tiny stove to heat the living area in a wagon but nevertheless the draughts were annoying. We also had a long walk to the ablutions where the water was usually freezing cold. But its advantages compensated as we were further from the danger zone and so could relax, although sentries were still posted, and we were still in danger of being bombed or shelled. However, we were closer to the general community and could see and talk to civilians.

The railway guns weighed about 250 tons each and were a most impressive sight. Each shell weighed over half a ton. To avoid observation by enemy reconnaissance aircraft the railway guns were hidden in tunnels during the daylight hours but for training purposes the Royal Engineers would bring one of them out close to our camp at Lydden station. Information on suitable targets came from the plotting room at the castle, and whenever a new target was found engineers would lay a new spur line at right angles to the main line. One of the main differences in handling the railway guns was that they were loaded entirely by hand. The crew numbered as many as thirty, which included ammunition and cordite parties.

'Loading the guns at night was precarious. We would often be sweating with fear as we rolled out shells from the magazine.' Above: Winston Churchill pays a visit to the railway guns.

A complete detachment for a 13.5-inch gun was an engine, the gun itself, a wagon for cordite and shell, a galley (cookhouse) wagon and accommodation wagons. Once on the move to their various positions these detachments must have been an impressive sight and something that will never be seen on Kent's railways ever again.

Travelling up to the firing positions the loading crew sat twelve-a-side with their backs against railings on a long metal platform. The gun was loaded by hand-winching a shell from the ammunition wagon to the loading tray. Then the twenty-four gunners would take hold of a huge wooden rammer and place it against the rear of the shell. When the order 'Load' was given these men would run as fast as possible along the metal platform and the shell would be pushed into the chamber. The cordite charge was similarly dealt with. With the loaders crammed against railings, the gun portion of the train was uncoupled and pulled forward away from the ammunition wagons. The crew then hurriedly dismounted to form up some distance away. The officer would then fire the gun using an electrical device. At this stage we would pray that the brakesman had applied the brakes on the gun wagon as the recoil would have sent it down the track at about 60mph! There was one occasion when the railings gave way under the rush of bodies. Most of us fell into the gap behind the breech mechanism. Two men sustained broken arms and I broke my wrist.

Service discipline was strict – even harsh. I think that the offence of 'dumb insolence' was in the process of being done away with in most branches but I certainly remember being charged with this 'crime' – for looking at an officer in an 'insolent manner'. Result – seven days' pack drill!

Enemy shells bracketed our Nissen hut area one night when we had just come off a twenty-four-hour stint on the guns. Our huts were wrecked and our kit badly damaged by shell bursts.

Although I have the highest regard for the civilians of 'Hellfire Corner', I must admit that we used to get quite a laugh at their expense, especially the salvage men who collected our kitchen waste for the pigs. Every morning two fellows would leave Martin Mill and tour the gun-sites with their lorry. They would race up to Townsend Farm, screech to a halt, get out of the cab in double-quick time to load the pig swill, sweating and swearing all the time. Then off they would go – flat out. They used to say that if they lived for a thousand years they would never get over the nervousness of coming into the danger area.

As an RAF mechanic airframe fitter with Coastal Command, Jim Roberts came home on leave to Sandwich from the remote and stormy regions of Scotland, where there was generally an 80mph wind blowing. Consequently, the ground crews usually wore their greatcoats at work which became stained with engine oil, fabric dope and all manner of things nasty. They all looked rather scruffy:

'Then there was the time some soldiers pinched a long roll of paper music from the pianola at the local pub and spread it out in the road as a sort of trophy.'

I did my best to avoid being spotted by RAF police personnel as they had a reputation for being tougher with improperly dressed 'erks' than the Army Military Police were with defaulting soldiers. Imagine my thoughts when I accidently ran into four service policemen when I arrived in Sandwich. Worse was to come as they were actually billeted at our house. I thought I was in for a really terrible time until I discovered they sympathized with my problem. They related a couple of stories, like the sailors from HMS *Robertson* (the shore establishment at Sandwich) who one day wangled their way into the WAAF quarters and lined up in the cookhouse for supper! Then there was the time some soldiers pinched a long roll of paper music from the pianola at a local pub and spread it out in the road as a sort of trophy. There they were at one end unrolling it while a couple of special constables were trying to roll it back up again from the other end.

No stranger to Dover was the 6-ft tall Major Lord Lovat, the traditional chief of the Clan Fraser, holder of a barony created before 1440, whose family motto was, 'I Am Ready'. As early as 1940 he led the first black-faced commando raid to infiltrate enemy-held territory just west of Boulogne. To test the German defences he repeated the raid in March 1942 and made further clandestine raids right up to D-Day.

'They would race up to Townsend Farm, screech to a halt, get out of the cab in double-quick time to load the pig swill, sweating and swearing all the time.'

Serving with No. 4 Commando under Lord Lovat was Tom Stratford who was trained to a very high degree of efficiency in December 1943:

Every day for several months we would leave and return to Dover in Landing Craft Infantry (LCI). Our HQ ship was the *Maid of Orleans*, a converted cross-Channel ferry. We were usually billeted at Beachborough House just outside Folkestone, also in civilian billets at Sandgate. Then after we had been fully briefed on our operation we were under strict security and moved to Dover Castle.

The operation was aborted three times for various reasons, once when we had almost reached our objective. This extended our stay in the area, including the castle. But because of the strain of these three aborted attempts our leader, Lord Lovat, arranged for us to have a fortnight's leave in civilian billets near Ashford. This was unprecedented considering the secret briefings we had had but was a sign of Lord Lovat's trust in every one of his men.

When Mary Holt (stage name Madam Kusharney) joined the Theatre War Service Council, she was required to wear a uniform with the rank of lieutenant to comply with the Geneva Convention rules:

The forces' entertainment chief Basil Dean called for volunteers to play for the troops, not in the relative safety of some rest and recreation area behind the lines but up at the sharp end, and eventually to follow the liberation army from D-Day through France towards Germany. Showbusiness people filled the seats of the Drury Lane theatre. There was silence because every one realized it was dangerous. Then Jimmy Nervo got up and said that he and his partner Teddy Knox would go. 'What about you, Nelson?' Jimmy asked my husband because they were good pals. Of course, he agreed, and that meant me, too. And so I put on a lieutenant's uniform and went to war.

We spent many weeks entertaining troops in the front line towns or wherever troops were stationed, and often we did not know where we were. Road signs had been removed long ago and no town or county names were ever shown. We travelled in an old camouflaged library van. The driver sometimes used to find his way around using a pack of cards: an ace would mean straight ahead, a club card black would be turn left and a red card meant right. I think we had a map of some sort.

I remember Mary Honri, an accordianist working around Dover. She was the daughter of Percy Honri who was well known for his accordian and mouth-organ playing. The Duncan sisters were dancers and I remember we always had a strip tease artiste on at every show. One in particular, Freda Wyn, used to portray a spider on a web strung from the stage ceiling. She was

'And so I put on a lieutenant's uniform and went to war.' Mary Holt (stage name Madam Kusharney) spent months entertaining troops wherever they were stationed. She has never forgotten Arnhem.

covered with orange and black stripes just like an exotic spider. A lot of the Windmill Theatre strips worked around doing troop shows.

Our act was considered good for the morale of the boys. I always told them everything good to keep their morale up, and after seeing our act they had complete confidence. My partner, Nelson, used to go amongst the audience while I stood on stage blindfolded. Members of the audience were asked to take objects from their pockets and to make it as difficult as they could. But Kusharney would always tell them what the object was, tell them their name, who they were thinking of – nothing was too difficult. The boys loved it – we were known as a good box office draw. Kusharney even knew where all the top stars with the money had vanished to before they suddenly appeared after D-Day. They were the ones who got the OBEs and MBEs at the end of the war. We, who needed the money, went through the horrors just like the civilians and servicemen and women in the battered south-east.

You were really in the thick of it at Dover. I will always remember the woman with her hens and chicks. She would not move out of Dover. I saw her hold up a convoy of army lorries one day while she crossed the road with her brood.

Nervo and Knox, and Flanagan and Allen of the famous Crazy Gang, did a tremendous lot of work with my partner and I for the troops. The latter pair would often do a cod-mind-reading act after we had finished our performance. They went on stage and followed our sequence of events doing everything wrong. It was hilariously funny.

We worked all over the place, at Ashford when the invasion build-up began, on the Romney Marshes, where soldiers suddenly appeared from behind hedges and trees. But I could go on for ever.

But I will never forget going into Arnhem. It had really been blasted apart. The bodies of young soldiers lay at the roadside and they were digging temporary graves in the footpaths for them.

That night the concert party was performing in what remained of a large building, using the headlights of army lorries to spotlight the temporary stage. My husband, who was also a very gifted conjurer, and I operated our mind-reading act. In Nijmegen, we did our show in a church. I had my blindfold on and I thought I heard hailstones. But it was a German fighter machine gunning the church. When I got my blindfold off I could see two men in the audience were dead and a further twenty-seven injured. Nelson, who had been walking among the audience, was lying in the aisle with facial wounds. Although there was an uproar a sergeant jumped on to the stage and shouted, 'On with the show!' As the medics moved in to handle the casualties the audience began to settle down as Mary Honri swung into action to start a singalong going.

'Sir, I was in the Infantry!', said J.W. Ellis when, as a young and inexperienced gunnery instructor, he was pitchforked into South-East Command and attached to 520 Coast Artillery Regiment at Hougham near Dover:

The colonel of the regiment took one look at me and said, 'Good God man, where did you get that greatcoat?' My reply almost sealed my fate before I had even been let loose on one of the hallowed gunfloors. Granted it was a single-breasted greatcoat which had taken some hammering and did look rather unkempt alongside the double-breasted rather smarter greatcoats of his entourage, but therein lies a tale. It begins when as a youth from a small Yorkshire industrial village I enlisted in the Territorial 6th Battalion the Duke of Wellington's Regiment. Having been called up in 1939 at the tender age of seventeen, I served in such far-flung places as Skipton and Keighley; being under eighteen I could not be sent abroad so along with others of a similar status, labelled the 'immatures', I watched my friends depart from our shores leaving me behind. So we came to be stationed in Bradford, then Leeds, to our great mortification as we wanted to visit exotic locations. When we were uprooted even from Leeds when they too moved out abroad, we found ourselves spread over the coastal defences.

And so it came about that in great trepidation the powers that be made me a lance-bombardier, then a bombardier, then a lance-sergeant. I eventually had my own section of two gun teams, a range-finding detachment and a searchlight team, and, being an examination battery, we would scour the sea area night and day looking for something to intercept.

A travelling sergeant-major gunnery instructor would come and look at us occasionally and suggested that I might benefit from a war gunnery course. So I was packed off to Stoke-on-Trent, Bury and Llandudno for nine months and ended up saying, 'Sir, I was in the Infantry!'.

When Colonel McLernon's eyes had unglazed themselves he told me that he did not want a gunnery instructor, he knew more than any of the gunnery staff at Llandudno, he had his own people who could look after things adequately and he resented my being foisted on him like this. After this speech of welcome I tottered off to the sergeants' mess and drowned my sorrows.

My official title was BSM (AIG) which was Battery Sergeant Major, Assistant Instructor of Gunnery. We were not allowed to be 'proper' instructors until we were one more step up the ladder, or an officer, and as we were allowed only one WO1 in the whole command the AIG or a Captain IG were the only two people normally seen. I had Captain Fox and Captain Hanks at Brigade HQ in the castle at Dover and a really good friend, Major Smith, at Command HQ. Being wise people they kept their heads down during this initial period of coolness at 520 Regiment and let me ingratiate myself 'Uriah Heep' fashion by picking the brains of all and sundry and drawing maps and plans and doing bits and pieces of training.

Luckily, I rather liked the guns and my contacts were most rewarding, allowing me to assist in all manner of exercises and shoots. Our armament was two 9.2-inch guns at the Citadel, Dover; two 8-inch guns at Hougham; two 6-inch guns at Lydden Spout, three 8-inch guns at Capel le Ferne; and various Bofors light anti-aircraft guns scattered around. These were supported by battery plotting rooms at Hougham, Lydden Spout and Capel, battery observations posts at all batteries, with depression-type range-finders as the batteries were all well above sea level and could therefore dispense with the less accurate Barr & Stroud sea-level range-finders, and searchlights at Shakespeare Halt, controlled by Lydden Spout Battery. At Hougham we had a Fortress Observation Post and a Fortress Plotting Room, which could control the fire of the whole regiment and which were supported by Fortress OPs at Hythe, Dymchurch and Dungeness (on the lighthouse there).

At a later stage we were supplied with air co-operation and did actually do a shoot using aircraft for spotting fall of shot, and then the ultimate – radar. Beginning from small cabins with a short time base and a hazy image with only a rough idea of range and bearing, we graduated to the sophisticated radar with spiral time bases, twin aerials and plan position indicators, all taken for granted nowadays but enabling us then to man the guns even at night and in fog with a tremendous degree of accuracy.

Battery radars were at Hougham and Capel with an additional radar for general fire control, and these tended to take over from the visual OPs which used the large triangular method of position finding.

As the threat of invasion receded so the role of the coastal artillery became more that of maintaining a watch for small raids and aircraft and to this end a barrage plan was used to enable the 8-inch guns to fire at a specific point in the sky. When this barrage was used it was amazing to see the barrels of the guns at such an elevation and to observe the hole in the sky they made when they fired. I do not know whether they achieved anything but if I had been up there they would certainly have put the wind up me.

During the V1 campaign we had to distribute flash spotting equipment to the observation posts so that they could have a flash spotting role to enable us to see where the V1 launching sites were.

Before long, however, we had to accustom ourselves to the idea that the Home Guard could be used to take over the guns. All too soon the batteries were closed down, one by one, and I departed.

Lila Marshall did her 'square-bashing' at the WRNS HQ at Mill Hill, London, then found herself on a train heading for Hellfire Corner:

I was soon at work, hundreds of feet underground beneath Dover Castle, in the Combined Operations HQ alongside girls in the ATS and WAAF as well as WRNS colleagues. Before long, however, I was transferred to the signals office at the docks and found it was much more interesting working with sailors. We had a powerful telescope to pick up the messages from ships anchored in the harbour. Occasionally, and for relaxation, we would train this on Calais and see sheep grazing on pastures above the French port.

We spent long hours in shelters under the white cliffs just waiting for the 'all clear' to sound. We would then have to sift through everything that had

The German long-range artillery ranged along the Pas de Calais enjoyed superiority in both equipment and instant retaliatory capability. Above: Shells damaged the Southern Railway Marine Station, Folkestone, to such an extent that not one building was unscathed.

come in by teleprinter to make extra copies and telephone through to various places. The shelling warning always seemed to coincide with my nights on duty. I would grab my various bits and bobs and dash like mad for the shelters. The sailors would say, 'Oh, its you again. We might have known you were on watch'.

I will never forget one particular night. The sirens had gone off and I picked up my tin helmet and respirator and tore down the stairs heading for the 'dungeons'. As I was half way across, the entire building rocked on its foundations and the heavy oak doors collapsed into the regulating and the paymaster's offices. The front door seemed to be jammed tight and I began to smell burning material. I thought, 'Well, Lila, this one obviously had your name on it'. I began to resign myself to being either buried alive or burned to death.

But the front door suddenly burst open and some sailors stumbled in from their camp opposite. 'We came to see if you were coming over to the shelters tonight!', one of them quipped. There was a long groove in the door and something sticking out of it. A sailor tried to stop me reaching out for it but it was too late. 'Ow!, it's hot,' I yelled. After the 'all clear', I went back and prised it loose. I still keep that piece of shrapnel in a matchbox to this day.

CHAPTER SIX

'Hey – there's some Jenny Wrens here!'

With a subtle but unconscious irony the civilians in Hellfire Corner had, by and large, settled down to the slow attrition of what most people chose to disregard as, 'What will be will be'.

The majority were perhaps unaware of the carnage that consumed German cities, delivered by Bomber Command and the USAAF, both by day and night. They were more concerned with their own experiences, and the awful uncertainty of the long-range shelling. While familiar buildings were systematically reduced to rubble, buses and trains stopped on the very edge of the danger area until the 'all clear' was sounded. But even then, sometimes within a couple of minutes, the sirens would often wail again their mournful note of warning. Housewives rushed from shop to shop to queue for their meagre rations while nine miles up, above the clouds and out of sight, mindless, iron-clad projectiles hurtled towards them.

Another day, another incident. A mother and child might have been killed, a home completely destroyed, a ship sunk in the harbour, a sailor or soldier stretchered to an ambulance. The people who faced these things were often complacent and few were cast in any heroic mould. They accepted their lot with the totally British habit of self-discipline. There was never any panic or hysterical outburst, even after their homes had collapsed into a heap around them. There was no twilight alert or dawn 'all clear', which had been accepted in London during the 'blitz'.

Instead there existed in the south-east an acceptance of the inevitable. The civilian could elect to stay at home – there was no compulsion to use a cave or shelter – and most of them never even bothered to leave their beds. Those who did had the psychological advantage of the companionship offered by communal sleeping in some of the well equipped cave shelters.

The service personnel, on the other hand, had no option but to do their duty despite the shelling. They had gained invaluable experience when carrying out various exercises. Even the bored coastal gunners had had a foretaste of what was to come later when their places were largely taken over by the Home Guard. Southern and South-East Command gunners were allotted the task of reoccupying the Channel Islands, although few – if any of the rank and file – knew anything about it beforehand.

But the first thing one noticed about Dover in 1944 was the people. They jostled on pavements and in queues, all alive and well and astonishingly fearless. This came as a surprise to many journalists, because they thought by now most of the population would be dead, and the few survivors would be cowering in dread of the bomb and shell.

Evenings off duty for service personnel were motivated by an insatiable urge for conviviality and a good time. Local, smoke-filled bars were jammed to capacity on Saturday nights, where uniforms of umpteen nations rubbed shoulders. But the human race had another urge, even more pressing than waging a war.

It was in November 1943 that a woman appeared at Dover Juvenile Court to answer a summons taken out by the NSPCC in respect of three children, aged seven, six and four years respectively, who were considered in need of proper care and attention.

PC Sutton said the house was the filthiest he had ever seen. It was almost entirely bare of furniture and bedding, and the woman was believed to be using the house for an immoral purpose. PC Grant said that on one occasion he found the children sitting on the doorstep at 11.00 p.m., and he had taken them to the nearest air-raid shelter as the anti-aircraft guns were firing during a raid. PC Sutton said that he had occasion to go to the house and found the children were sleeping on the floor covered with sacking and old clothes. When he appeared nine sailors ran out through the doors and dived through windows to escape.

The war went on. The skilful process of reasoning resulted in Operation 'Overlord' – D-Day – and identified the V1 and V2 rocket sites that had multiplied along the Pas de Calais. These sites were effectively plastered by bombers and fighter-bombers. Doubtless the untenable consequences of a prolonged bombardment of Hitler's secret weapons would have changed the course of history. As it turned out, however, the foundations of an Allied victory had been well and truly laid by the spring of 1944.

Local businesses in Dover and the surrounding district had received plenty of hits and near misses by either bomb or shell. Staff would go to work in the mornings only to find the contents of shelves and display cabinets strewn across the floors. But the managers would soon put up a notice reading 'Business As Usual'. Muriel Sidwell recalls:

The inspector would call and tot up the damaged goods and then we could get on with clearing up the mess and serving our customers with their meagre rations. Sadly, the owner of a fruit and vegetable shop opposite us hanged himself. He and his wife had seemed cheerful folk. It was an awful shock. But I think the effects of the shelling bombardment drove others to suicide in Dover.

I was still working at Peakes Store when I got married in January 1944 at St Andrews church, Buckland. My groom was a soldier stationed far away in

the Orkney Islands. We had met when I was working at the Salvation Army
canteen at the Citadel Barracks. We had a short honeymoon at Rochdale. He
was due back from leave on 13 January which was my nineteenth birthday.
We travelled back to London together then parted. He went off to his unit
and I came back to Dover on my own. I can still remember the feeling of
utter loneliness as I walked up to Buckland late at night carrying my suitcase.
There were no taxis or buses, and in fact very little traffic or pedestrians.

Later that year the shelling increased until we seemed to be getting it every
day. It would start about eleven o'clock in the morning. On a shopping trip
one day I had to take shelter beneath the Co-op and did not come out until
three hours later.

This report, from Surgeon Commander Finsen of the 52nd Norwegian ML
flotilla based at Dover, graphically outlines the traumatic experiences of the crew
of ML 210 when she struck a mine on 15 February 1944:

Just after mine number 6 had been laid on the port side, I heard a terrific
explosion, and was thrown up in the air and out into the water on the starboard side. When I came to the surface I saw several people floating among
the wreckage, about 8 to 10 metres off the starboard quarter of ML 210. She
was still afloat, although her bow was down in the water. I heard screams for
help and people moaning. The boys helped each other and one or two managed to enter the wreck. We swam around the stern and saw the British
ML 104 coming slowly towards the wreck's port side. Another ML also
closed up, and two men were taken on board. The nine remaining survivors
were taken on board ML 104 by means of lines thrown to us. When we had
all been rescued the crew of ML 104 shouted and then listened, to make sure
every one had been taken on board. No sounds were heard and visibility was
good. We could see all the wreckage on the starboard side of ML 104. I was
convinced nobody was floating in the water and nobody answered our calls. I
reckoned the last man to be taken out of the water had been in the sea for
only ten minutes. The crew of ML 104 looked after us in a brilliant way. All
of us were taken below, undressed and wrapped in blankets. They gave us
rum, warm tea and soup.

After I had got my lifebelt off, I helped to dress a bleeding wound, but I
was shivering so much I had to give up. The warm blanket induced sleep and
I dozed until 00.15 hours.

When I awoke I gained a comprehensive view of the wounded. The British
crew of ML 104 had already, in an outstanding way, taken care of the ten
injured, giving morphia to those in great pain, and had dressed every wound.

One of the most severely wounded was Aksel Hansen, the only one I was
really worried about. He was not clear but a grey colour and had a poor, very
weak pulse rate. We gave him warm tea, soup, and massaged his arms and legs
for about two hours. He seemed to recover after that.

I was most impressed by the calmness every one showed, not only in the water, but after we got on board ML 104. There are not enough words of praise one can give for the treatment the crew of ML 104 gave to us.

Dick Whittamore, assistant manager of the Royal Hippodrome in 1943, recalls the following 'incident':

In January 1944 a very large, ornate carpet went missing from the stage of the Hippodrome. Local police were sent for and eventually discovered it cut up into small pieces and tacked to the cabin floors of HSL 186, an ASR launch tied up to the quayside behind the theatre. Mr Armstrong, the theatre manager, declined to prosecute the crew if the carpet was paid for. The RAF lads tried stitching the carpet pieces back together again but this was unacceptable. To raise funds for a new carpet the crew organized a dance to be held at the annexe of HMS *Wasp*. The 'Carpet Baggers Ball' was held on Thursday 17 February 1944 and the crew sent the manager a free ticket!

THE CARPET BAGGERS'
BALL

The Crew of H.S.L. 186

request your company

at the Lord Warden Annexe,

on Thursday, 17th February, 1944

at 7.30 p.m.

By kind permission of the C.O. and Entertainments Officer, H.S.L.'s Dover

The crew of RAF Launch 186, to make amends for their misdemeanour, conceived 'The Carpet Baggers Ball' to raise funds for a new carpet at the Royal Hippodrome.

F. Featherbe wrote this interesting piece:

It was nearing the time of the invasion which was expected at any time and our job was to try to confuse the enemy by towing barges up and down the Channel, knowing full well that he was watching, but not knowing where we were going.

We got to Dover safely and brought the boats into mooring. As I lived in Folkestone just a few miles along the coast, I was ready to go home just as soon as leave was granted. The rest of the crew were in a good mood with the thought of going ashore in Dover but all of a sudden there was a clamour. The skipper sent down to say we were going to France and that everyone must get into working gear. The shock was overpowering, especially as we were now ready to go ashore. We left Dover Harbour and headed for France to look for one of our Motor Torpedo Boats which had broken down on the other side. When we got there we steamed up and down under the German guns wondering why they did not fire at us. It was many hours later that we received a call from base to say that we could return as the missing craft was now making its way home.

We came through the eastern entrance. Just inside we ran straight on to the wreck of a ship that had gone down earlier. We heeled over and that well known call came from the skipper 'Abandon Ship'. The lifeboat was quickly put into the water and the crew were soon aboard. A tug had arrived on the scene and tried to pull our boat off the wreck but that only made things worse – she was holed.

Our lifeboat was being pushed up against the stem of the tug, and this made it impossible to row. At last we got away and drifted out of the western entrance right into the backwash from the pier which we could not stem.

Some time later a motor boat arrived from the harbour skippered by an old friend, Mr Cook of Folkestone. We were towed back into harbour and spent the rest of the night on the tug. We were told the tug would get our boat off as soon as the tide started to flow. Some hours later we were back on our boat, and the tow began. We docked in Wellington Dock and laid up for a couple of weeks and then we were towed to Yarmouth where we knocked a large hole in the jetty on the way in!

Herbert A. Till believed it was a great privilege to belong to the only counter-rocket group in the British Army, a survey regiment of the Royal Artillery. Patiently awaiting the start of the Allied invasion he experienced a state of melancholia:

We are so bored, so utterly bored. When will the invasion start? Silver balloons lie lazily in a hot sky, dummy invasion barges of wood and canvas float tightly packed in the harbour, with MTBs throbbing deeply as they prepare for yet another skirmish with German E-boats.

I am beginning to fret under the daily menial tasks in this army. What is worse I am beginning to resent authority and the power of rank. It's this damned waiting that's the trouble. If only we could get cracking. Discipline through respect is the discipline that counts. How to behave when one feels one is suffering an injustice is a problem that I have never solved in the army. I don't feel very grand about this. What should it be – silence or an attempt at cheerfulness? I think a good way to tackle a fatigue is to do the task in the state of mind of thinking it is not so bad after all. Not half so bad as you darn well know the sergeant had intended it to be. I suppose spud bashing is not so bad, it is having to do it on the very evening that you intended to go up to the YMCA to hear a recital of Beethoven gramophone records that makes it so irksome.

I have such a bleak feeling at this moment. Why doesn't the invasion start? It is the gregariousness of army life that has so changed me. I cannot even walk to a meal without waiting for two or three others, and thus we drift in little flocks towards the cookhouse. I rarely make any plans of my own except to pass my time off duty. I just fit in with a small crowd and we drift from one crowded services' canteen to another. Ten years ago I would tramp through Germany to the Alps, planning, arranging, absorbing. Now I have become merely a 'to the front, salute' piece of mechanism with no freedom of movement, no freedom of thought and an inertia that is just about sending me crackers. Hell, why doesn't something start?

It finally did; the great day arrived on June 6 – the day the Allied armies invaded France. Herbert recalls exactly where he was on that momentous occasion:

This is D-Day. We are all tense with excitement. For me it started dramatic-ally. We were carrying out a survey scheme on the downs behind Dover when a shell exploded in the field where I had set up my theodolite. Immediately the shelling warning could be heard in Dover town, and as I looked seawards I saw three spurts of water rise from the sea and then one of our ships creeping up the Channel was hit. Great bellows of smoke belched forth from her and I saw the ugly red of flames licking her sides. She was on fire but I had no time to think of the fate of those poor wretched creatures who were aboard her, for almost immediately I heard our captain shouting, 'Pack up, pack up quickly, it's started'. 'What's started?' I asked Dai Evans. 'Why, the invasion you bloody fool!', he shouted, as we began to tear down our beacon and gather together our banderoles. I looked again towards the sea – the ship was now well alight, drifting helplessly towards Folkestone, and a destroyer was rapidly laying a smoke screen off the Dover waters.

And so tonight we are at our posts to keep watch. Our OP is quite comfortable, a large room with the usual slit openings. All our instruments for spotting the gun flashes and for taking bearings on objects are securely fixed on a shelf in front of us. In fact, there is very little difference from a peacetime

Coast Guard station. We sit in complete darkness and wait, wondering what the night will bring. We are very quiet.

The night only brought tiredness. For endless hours we peered into the dark towards the French coast, not daring to relax for one minute. What was happening on the other side? How were our boys doing? We were told nothing, we knew nothing. We heard not one sound all night.

On June 7 all through the day long lines of transport ships keep moving up the Channel. Great convoys of merchantmen, tankers and supply ships follow one another and as soon as they reach Hellfire Corner, Jerry begins to shell and now, as I am writing, I can see those great spurts of water showing the fall of shot: sometimes behind the stern of a vessel, sometimes just in front of her bows. Two hospital ships with their red crosses plainly marked have been creeping slowly along towards the corner, but now Jerry has opened fire on them and they have turned about and are pelting full steam back towards the North Foreland. Thick black smoke is pouring from their funnels and they look not unlike the old Clyde pleasure steamers. Maybe they are.

June 8 – still they come – American transport ships, invasion barges, tank landing craft, minesweepers, destroyers, corvettes and the inevitable MTBs making their sorties.

June 12 – the weather up to now has been poor, but today it is brilliantly sunny. The kind of day the vicar always hoped to have for his garden party, but never did. I am sitting at this moment on a stretch of sand entirely alone. There is no sound whatsoever, save for the gentle lapping of the sea, and before me a huge transport convoy silently moves up the Channel to the invasion beaches. It is hard to believe that only a few miles away is taking place what may prove to be the biggest event in our history.

J. Hughes of the Royal Artillery wrote:

I remember being sergeant guard commander on the most forward point of Dover Harbour when the Germans were firing shells across the Channel. Motor torpedo boats had just come back from a patrol and sailors sleeping below deck had been killed. There was a lance-corporal on my guard by the name of Davies, who had been awarded the Military Medal for bravery with the South Wales Borderers in North Africa. But it did not stop him from diving for cover!

Posted to Folkestone in 1944 with the RASC, Brian Best's experiences border on the subservient aspects of an important but subordinate corps:

We lived in civilian houses and slept on double-tiered wooden bunks. No mattresses, just plywood. Three bunks were crowded into one room. We took our meals at a place on the sea front that had once been an amusement arcade. There was a golden dome on top. There were a lot of Canadian soldiers in the town and we would do our best to direct them to various places. We used to mount guard at night, armed only with pickaxe handles. Eventually we were given rifles. There was a roster for beach patrol. We took turns to check the beach at low tide to see if any bodies had been washed up. When the alert went all we could do was don our steel helmets and leg it for the beach. Safer to be in the open, we felt. We used to go down to the pub but more often than not there was no beer. So we played cards in our billet and then went to bed.

Billeted first at Kearsney in a house requisitioned by the Admiralty, Jean Aitchison (now Atkins) recalls her duties with the WRNS Met. Office at Dover Castle:

The meteorological office had been set up to provide information for the clandestine raiding parties and to help with weather forecasts connected with the D-Day invasion plans, such as wind strength, sea conditions and visibility. There was just the one meteorological officer, a Royal Naval Volunteer Reserve (RNVR) instructor, who was also flag lieutenant to the Admiral. There were also two assistant WRNS officers. Our office was the third back from the Admiral's balcony. Sometimes we were allowed on to the balcony to check the visibility, but we were not a full met. station in that we did not actually transmit data. However, we got a full transmission from other met. stations via the teleprinter so 'flags' was able to make the necessary forecasts. These messages were received on the teleprinter down in the depths of the castle, and were supposed to come up in the vacuum tube system. This often broke down so we had to go right down in the bowels of the castle to collect them.

I distinctly remember being shattered when one of my 'cabin' mates did not return. We later heard she was a shell victim. This really brought home to me the reality of being in the front line. After a while I was transferred to the Boys County School where I stayed until leaving Dover. As the met. officer was also the Admiral's personal aide-de-camp (ADC) we were sometimes let in for non-met. duties, like taking the Admiral's pet bull terriers for a walk.

The thing Joyce 'Cherry' Spriggs (née Lancaster) remembers most about her days with the WRNS at Dover was that wonderful whiff of fresh sea air after surfacing from night duty beneath the castle:

The atmosphere down below could be pretty foul, even though air was pumped down to the lower levels. Discipline too was unnecessarily irksome. Our first officer was popularly supposed to have previously been in charge of a home for delinquent girls. But of course this may have been just a wartime rumour.

I worked on the teleprinter switchboard and we did four hours on and four hours off in every forty-eight-hour stretch. Then we had twenty-four hours off duty. We had GPO engineers doing the technical work and one WAAF and one ATS on each shift. At first there was not a lot for us to do although we had to concentrate because we never knew when things might start to hot up. This avoidance of distractions made the hours on duty seem so terribly long. I have always felt there was quite a bit of friendly rivalry between the three services at Dover.

I seem to recall that when I first arrived I was billeted in the town centre, near a church, and when we were shelled out we moved to a school in Folkestone. On our return to Dover we were sent to a house that was reputed to be haunted. After night duty and when the lights had been switched off at the master switch, I used to stumble around in the dark, and this gave some credibility to the haunted story.

For a lot of the time there was a dearth of entertainment from outside the area. Performers seemed reluctant to make the journey into what was, after all, a dangerous spot, although I do recall two gentlemen who played classical music records and enlivened this with amusing repartee. There were the regular 'hops' at the town hall, of course, and the cinemas. I remember the tragedy of two Royal Marine brothers being killed while queuing outside one cinema.

All our mail was supposed to be handed in to the censor but occasionally I would post mine in a public post box as I didn't see why the staff should know all my private business.

Trains to and from Dover were a hit or miss affair. When a list of names was compiled showing WRNS who were to be evacuated from Dover in the event of an invasion I was on the original list. But later my name appeared on the list of those WRNS who were to remain. I have never been quite sure if this was some sort of honour!

When William Martin joined the Royal Marines he found, much to his surprise, that all the instructors were pre-war marines and the cream of the Corps:

There was no shouting and raving, no wringing of hands in despair, no insulting of recruits; just a tap on the shoulder and a quiet order to get your hair cut or an explanation of what you were doing wrong.

In 1944 I found myself at the shore establishment HMS *Robertson*, Sandwich, originally under the Royal Navy. To be honest the place was a tip, with rubbish and equipment littered all over the place. When the Royals started to clean the place up the Navy protested, claiming that this abandoned look led the enemy reconnaissance planes into thinking it really was abandoned and not a target. What an excuse!

I remember the matelots looking on as we scrubbed the cookhouse from top to bottom and changed from overalls to battledress for meals. They thought it was pure bullshine but we regarded it as keeping up the high standards of the Royal Marines.

There were some American Sea-Bees (so named from the initials of the Construction Battalion) who were employed fabricating parts for the Mulberry Harbour sections used in the Normandy invasion. They were a grand crowd and every one of them a tradesman. I made friends with Alvin Friswold from San Francisco.

I think to some extent the huge numbers of landing craft that used Sandwich were part of the bluff to make Hitler think the invasion would hit the Pas de Calais.

Morale had slumped by the time we landed in Normandy. Thousands of us had seemingly missed out on the action. It was frustrating too, not being able to fight back at the doodlebugs.

During 1944 there was one explosion in Dover that was quite unforeseen. It happened at the torpedo workshop in the harbour. Ken Nicholson regarded it as a double miracle:

The workshop was empty of personnel at the time and, although there was high explosive around by the ton, none of it was detonated.

It was a burst compressed-air vessel, and it did considerable damage, wrecking among other things three warheads. Their 'Torpex' contents were scattered liberally all over the workshop and out through the shattered windows. The workshop was a solid stone building next door to the fuel-oil compound at the Eastern Arm. With its huge windows it resembled a chapel.

The Dover Torpedo Department was quite big. The Torpedo Officer had two lieutenants, one a Dutch officer, and the ratings came under a Chief Petty Officer (CPO) who had retired to Dover on full pension before the war and was recalled. He used to cycle to work. In all my naval career I never met a more considerate, helpful and knowledgeable CPO.

My particular job was concerned with deck installations – torpedo tubes, depth-charge and remote firing equipment – on the forty or so boats at Dover. There were several torpedo men, spare ratings helping out when their boats were not going to sea. There were also some marvellous WRNS who undertook most of the loading. Just imagine a two-ton torpedo bobbing about on the water while a team of young ladies were trying to coax it into a tube. It was no mean feat.

The explosives were stored in tunnels beneath the East Cliff, although there were usually several warheads in the workshop waiting to be loaded into torpedoes. A torpedo requires air for the motor, which comes from a compressed-air reservoir driven by an internal diesel combustion engine. An external compressor filled the reservoirs to a pressure of 2000 pounds per square inch (psi), with a permitted error of ten per cent either way. It was normal practice at Dover to charge to almost 2200 pounds psi.

We knocked off work at the end of the forenoon period with officers going to their wardroom, other hands to their respective messes and the CPO cycling home to his lunch. As we all reached the dockyard gate there was one almighty bang. The workshop was a total wreck with the overhead crane, air compressor and several torpedoes in their racks severely damaged.

The work of the torpedo department was badly disrupted. There was an investigation of course, and the cause was traced to the pressure gauge. The compressor had been shut down just as our lunch-time started, and it happened to coincide with the fault known as 'necking' – a stage when metal under pressure begins to crumble like chewing gum before shattering. We were lucky. It could have exploded while we were in the shop!

Vera Selwood (née Boyce) remembers the Shalimar Hotel on the Dover sea front with a little more affection than most. It remained open throughout the war years:

It was kept by two old ladies who had two cats. I stayed there when my husband came on leave. One night we all stayed up late talking. When we eventually went up to our bedroom there was a great chunk of shrapnel embedded in the bedhead. The Shalimar was also a favourite haunt for WRNS who used to enjoy a cup of coffee on Sunday mornings. On reflection so was the Creamery Cafe almost opposite the Shakespeare pub. We used to visit the Shakespeare on pay days usually – they served a good meal there considering there was a war on. And we would sometimes splash out on a night at the Royal Hippodrome.

After Dover College was hit by a shell we were sent up to the Isolation Hospital to live as it was thought to be safer. It was a horrible place with wooden huts, the weather was freezing and it had a ghoulish caretaker. There was nothing to do except go on a three-mile hike to the nearest pub, the Plough. It was so grim I actually used to volunteer to do fire watching duties at the college to get out of going there.

Marrying an airman in December 1944, WAAF Gladys Critchell stood beside her future husband at 11.00 a.m. in the Saxon church of St Mary-in-Castro, within the castle boundary:

Our unit was very small, consisting of eighteen men (mechanics, operators, cooks and admin) and twenty-two women (mostly telephonists or teleprinter operators). We all lived in one barrack block at Connaught Barracks, opposite the Welch Fusiliers. There was an assortment of people at Connaught Barracks, six REME men, and all kinds of other small units. The South Staffords were at the castle and troops from the Second Canadian Division at Old Park Barracks. I was the entertainment 'nut'. The YMCA in Pencester Road arranged a Hallowe'en party: the WRNS decorated the hall, the ATS did the grub, and I did the entertainment.

I must admit that apart from going out with REME lads once or twice I much preferred the Navy or the RAF. The army, of course, was in Dover in abundance: the hunky South Staffords and the whistling Welch Fusiliers. But we did not hold the soldiers in very high regard, I'm afraid. There was often the feeling that the khaki battledress did not attract the girls like Navy or

'The YMCA in Pencester Road, Dover, arranged a Hallowe'en party. The WRNS decorated the hall, the ATS did the grub, and I did the entertainment,' wrote WAAF Gladys Critchell.

Airforce blue! Girls would often complain that resting their cheek against a serge-clad shoulder sometimes gave them a rash.

Another WAAF, Olga Kaye, was a radar operator at the Swingate Radar station, and has many happy memories of Dover:

Going to the Crypt Restaurant on our days off. Going to the public toilets in the town and pulling all the chains, just for the pleasure of flushing them – at our camp we had to make do with Elsan closets.

Serving with the Royal Signals GHQ Liaison Regiment was D. Mann, who remembers his 'hush-hush' unit was normally referred to as the 'Phantom Signals'. Originally it was an RAF unit. Their vital job was transmitting battlefield information back to the War Office without delay, bypassing the normal channels of communication and command. He gives a quite fascinating account of their work:

At Dover initially we departed from our normal role. We were part of the huge deception plan to make the Germans think the invasion of Occupied Europe would start in the Pas de Calais. We were sending and receiving messages in cipher between Richmond and Dover, using remote controlled transmitters from a hill just outside Dover. There were about thirty of us at the castle and nearby barracks.

On 5 June 1944 – the day before D-Day – seven of the senior operators on duty were withdrawn and told to get some rest. They were then told to report to a special room in the castle at seven that evening, bringing everything they would want for the next twelve hours. That evening we were briefed on the Normandy invasion and were kept incommunicado. Wireless silence was to be observed from midnight but we were to maintain listening watch on all frequencies just in case a 'Phantom' patrol came up on the air with something urgent. It was a very long night shift.

As soon as we came off shift the messages started to flood in, giving the locations of our forward troops. This first day was so successful that soon the Americans were asking for 'Phantom' help. We were eventually flown from Amiens to Marseilles to join another 'Phantom' unit operating in support of General Patch's Seventh Army.

Positioned about two miles above Folkestone, Cliff Durbin lived under canvas behind a small wood:

Our job as members of the RAF Regiment was to guard a number of radar trailers – and with what, you may well ask! We had a few motley Storks [tripods] fitted with four .303 electrically operated Brownings taken from bomber aircraft. The only time they fired was when there was an electrical fault – then they fired on their own and it scared the living daylights out of us. The only German shells that landed anywhere near us were those which missed the town. We thanked God that the trees took most of the blast and shrapnel. But when we were in town and the shelling started the cinemas and dances would empty rapidly! Service personnel used to climb into any vehicle, so as to get out of town quickly, without knowing where the vehicle was going. So eventually many of us would have a long walk back to camp.

I remember once having a septic finger and a kindly Salvation Army lady treated me.

I used to drive one of our lorries and would take and fetch the chaps' laundry or fill our water bowser. We used to have a weekly shower at Folkestone fire station. I recall the night when a few lads got back to camp late after visiting the town. They got into the mess marquee but in the gloom knocked over a stove. The tent burned down in a matter of a few minutes. The culprits were never caught.

In April 1944 ATS girl Winifred Lygo (now Crisp) moved into the Dover area with a mixed heavy ack-ack regiment. They had been told they were additional defences just in case the Normandy invasion was followed by a German counter-attack:

To begin with we had only nuisance aircraft to deal with, most of which were Allied aircraft that had failed to switch on their IFF equipment before crossing the English coast.

On 15 June we saw our first real night action. We had been warned a few days earlier that there was a jet-propelled pilotless plane being used by the Germans. We had received a few tips on how to deal with them but in practice none of these actually worked.

When it came the force of the attack was breathtaking. I was on duty one night as radar operator. The action started before midnight and went on until the early afternoon of the following day. By that time we had fired 596 rounds! There was a new feeling in the unit. We were thrilled to be finally doing what we had trained so hard to achieve, and for so long.

The guns hardly ever grew cold during the following weeks and the firework display beat anything we had ever seen during the London blitz. But it was hard work. Although we were supposed to be doing six hours on and six hours off, in fact we often worked twenty out of each twenty-four. It was worse for the men who were actually handling the guns and I distinctly remember one gunner saying he had worked nearly sixty hours non-stop with only about six hours' sleep!

Ack-ack reinforcements started arriving, by which time the RAF fighters had taken over some aspects of the doodlebug defence. We often would stand by and do nothing while these menaces were crashing to the ground all around us. But it was an unforgettable experience.

Built at Tough's Yard at Teddington in 1940 HMML 171, with a crew of around twenty ratings and two RNVR officers, eventually joined the 2nd flotilla. 'She was, like her sister ships,' recalls John Lucas, '. . . a gallant little girl and rather pretty with it.'

She was the 'workhorse' of Coastal Forces but somewhat overshadowed by the more exciting MTBs and MGBs. But MLs nevertheless got into many scrapes between 1939 and 1945.

I joined 171 at Lowestoft in May 1944, just before D-Day, and served on her under the command of Lieutenant R.G. Staddon RNVR. Besides carrying eight depth-charges, she also carried in her 120 foot length and 18 foot beam, a three pounder on the foc's'le and two Oerlikons (later twins) abaft the rakish funnel. On the bridge was a pair of twin Vickers .303. She was not particularly fast, capable of limited period running at 20 knots, cruising happily at about 15 knots and well able to 'fuss around' any convoy.

I had joined her as a telegraphist and shortly afterwards we sailed for Southend where we found the Thames Estuary crammed with shipping. We later did a shuttle service, escorting three or four convoys through the Dover Strait and on to the Normandy Mulberries.

We put into Dover Harbour a couple of times, once seeking calmer waters in a storm which suddenly blew up, and navigating the harbour entrance amidst alarming turbulence beneath us! A run ashore to visit the Dover hostelries was the natural thing to do and I do recall a pub called The Prince

Regent, and a barmaid whose beauty was heightened by the stark and grim surroundings of Dover of those times.

On two occasions we came under shell fire from the German coastal batteries at Cap Gris Nez. The first occasion I would not have known about had I not been on watch on the bridge. It was a grey day, misty, and the convoy was plodding along undisturbed when, in the distance, an American US Patrol Torpedo Boat (USPTB) flashed us on an Aldis lamp. The boat was rolling, a characteristic of MLs, and I had some difficulty reading the Yank's message. I got as far as 'Shell Fell Astern' after which I had a small problem. He seemed to be sending the word 'Bud' which puzzled me and I asked him to repeat it twice before realizing that 'Bud' was short for buddy, a term of friendship not typical of Royal Navy language! Our American friend must have thought me quite thick, which was nothing compared with our officer of the watch who exploded, saying words to the effect that 'Bud' was a quite inappropriate word to use under the circumstances!

The other occasion was when we were escorting a convoy east to west through the Dover Strait. We were stationed on the port side of the convoy in line, with ourselves between the convoy and the German-held French coast. Suddenly, about a thousand yards or so off our port bow, a spout of water was seen to rise from the sea. A sort of pandemonium broke out – it was action stations, although firing back with our armament was pointless. But hastily donning their tin hats, 'The Count', 'Lofty' Hargreaves, 'Tosh' and others manned their guns with purposeful intent. Who knows – E-boats could appear, or the Luftwaffe next, for, as we now know, the Germans at that time still believed that the Normandy landings were a feint and the real invasion would take place in the Pas de Calais.

I vividly remember during this action seeing our escort destroyer racing past us outboard of the convoy placing herself between the enemy and the convoy. She was doing about 20 knots and I heard one of the lads shout, 'Look, she's flying the Battle Ensign!' And sure enough, stiff in the strong breeze, the White Ensign fluttered from the top of the destroyer's mainmast.

The action was short lived, with no damage to any of our ships who sailed serenely to their destination. No doubt the German High Command communiqué for that day made an extravagant claim about damage to ships in a British convoy off Dover!

Harry Fewtrey was a crew member of ML 467 of the 21st Flotilla at Dover:

We were real 'Jacks of all trades', putting up smoke-screens to protect convoys, patrolling at night and so on. I have vivid memories of the time the Canadian Tank Landing Craft *Sambutt* was hit by a German shell. We made tremendous efforts to rescue all the Canucks we could. I was just eighteen at the time and saw some wonderful acts of bravery that day. It is a long time ago but the memory is still there, as clear as can be.

As a sergeant in the Royal Artillery, the Artillery Surveyor John Whitehouse worked frequently in the White Cliffs area:

> I recall clearly one night in the town centre, waiting for the 15 cwt truck to take me on duty to Shakespeare Cliff. Suddenly the shelling warning sounded. The effect was amazing – in seconds the streets emptied. There was an ammunition ship unloading in the harbour at the time and I was somewhat frightened. So I was forced to take cover in a public shelter, although I talked my way out in time to get up to the cliff for my shift. I still have a scar on my right hand but not as a result of the shelling. I caught it on a sharp flint in the chalk entrance to the Shakespeare Cliff observation post!

The resilience of the Salvation Army staff in providing sustenance and good-natured companionship to thousands of service men and women is unquestionably an emotive subject. Mrs G. Wild worked with Captain Louis Aspinall and Major Platt, both of whom were killed by enemy action:

> During the worst times we used to sleep in the Snargate Street caves, walking down from the Red Shield Club every evening about 10.30 p.m. wearing our tin hats and carrying flasks of tea to see us through the night – if not in comfort at least in comparative safety. Every day we went round the town and out to St Margaret's Bay with our mobile van taking tea and cakes to the various units. In the process I made many friends in the forces – sadly, some of them were killed.

For many years J. Whitehouse kept his observation log books but now they are in the Royal Artillery Museum at Larkhill. Among the many items logged were sections of the floating harbour for the invasion of Europe, code-named 'Mulberry'. He put them down as 'bridge sections':

> Also in my log books were panoramic drawings of the French coast, even showing the Hotel de Ville at Calais. We could see this quite clearly when the weather was good. Bearings were accurately shown, including those of the 16-inch guns at Cap Gris Nez, not that they could be hit in their concrete fortresses.
>
> Sometimes the guns at St Margaret's Bay were fired out to sea using sand-filled shells. The object was to draw the fire of German destroyers. If we were not on duty we had to go down the tunnels which, via various passages, connected with those under the castle.

Sergeant Robert Waugh was with 140 Searchlight Battery and had been moved so often since 1941 he considered letter writing to be a luxury:

> It was while we were at the Alkham site that the first doodlebug came over the valley and I think I was the only bloke who didn't see it. There was so

much gunfire in the area that I was trying to lay a beam on to it but I didn't see it – only gunfire. Of course, some wild reports began to come in that parachutists had dropped, and we were getting information from our troop headquarters that they had dropped in my area. We were to take up battle positions at once. I had a chap who was a clerk in civvy street. He panicked and I had to be really nasty with this bloke to knock some sense into him because he was hanging on to my battledress and wouldn't leave me alone. He was crying like a baby, thinking he was going to die, instead of being in his allotted position. This is where discipline really comes in. But things were not as bad as we had been told, although it caused quite a bit of excitement that night.

We had another doodlebug fall quite near us. It was hovering above us, but when we jumped into the slit trenches a gust of wind carried it another 50 or 60 yards further on before it exploded. We went to the point of impact and were amazed to find adders– literally hundreds of them. I had never seen so many at one time. Prior to this we hadn't seen an adder in the area at all.

On the following day another doodlebug landed in Alkham. It moved the village hall off its foundations and the blast just travelled around the hillsides because of their horse-shoe shape. It knocked our huts haywire, so we didn't enjoy our huts for very long.

Life on a searchlight site was very hard indeed as one man was always on sentry duty for a two-hour stint throughout the twenty-four hours, even after an all-night action. Equipment had to be serviced daily and training was constant, so very little time was left for letter writing. When the doodlebug campaign was in full swing I worked a skeleton crew just to take some pressure off the men. They were becoming like zombies. I even did a sentry duty to help out, although orders forbade NCOs to do so – but my men and their welfare came first with me.

A memorable event occurred when Len Hale, a member of an RAF Regiment unit, was guarding the radar site at Kingsdown, Walmer. It was never officially explained:

The gun-site at Kingsdown, overlooking Hawkshill Down, was manned that particular evening by myself and LAC 'Paddy' Brown from Ballymena, Northern Ireland. On the crossroads at the base of the hill on which the camp stood was a rubbish tip that was continually replenished by dust-carts from Walmer, and which quite often caught alight through spontaneous combustion. The local NFS were called out many times because of the blackout regulations. But on this particular night, when the V1s were overhead, the signalling of what I considered to be Morse code was observed.

I immediately reported this to the corporal who decided to make an inspection of the area with myself and 'Paddy'. We crawled down the hillside concealed by the long grass, hoping to surprise whoever was signalling. But the corporal gave the game away by shining a torch on the exact spot, so by the time we arrived on the scene the area was deserted. It was too dark to make a thorough investigation so we returned to camp. But we were surprised when a light appeared from the bedroom of a house which had been unoccupied since the beginning of the war. There were no curtains hanging in the windows. We made our way quietly to the house and entered. A thorough search of the premises drew a blank. The house was empty and revealed nothing of importance to connect with a phantom signaller.

We returned to camp at approximately 01.00 hours to be met by a very irate flight-sergeant who had only known about the incident through the remaining guard on duty. The corporal had not left word before deciding to leave camp. The whole camp had been put on 'stand-by' and were not stood down until dawn. The following day both 'Paddy' and myself were instructed to relate the incident to two civilians (possibly MI5) who pocketed various pieces of paper and other odd items from both sites.

I can only presume that the importance of the 'stand-to' and the civilian interest was due to the forthcoming invasion. Although I never found out what those lights really meant, and I doubt if I ever will, I often ponder on the idea that an enemy agent might have been the culprit.

On board ML 445 21st ML Flotilla was Maurice Gilbraith as it slowly edged through the eastern entrance of Dover Harbour early in 1944:

Our vessel was moored at the Eastern Arm near the submarine pens until we moved to Ramsgate in the autumn to take part in the landings upon Walcheren Island. Our main duties were cross-Channel anti-submarine patrols, mainly at night, and escorting tugs towing unusual objects through the Straits and on to Rye Bay. We learned afterwards that these were sections of the Mulberry Harbour system for Normandy.

On D-Day we laid a smoke-screen through the Dover Strait, with equipment that had been fitted at Dover, to hide the continuous convoy of merchant ships. One of these was hit by a German shell about mid-morning. We went alongside to take soldiers off until it got too dangerous owing to the fire and the exploding ammunition. We then fished both dead and alive out of the sea and landed them into waiting ambulances on the Eastern Arm. The ship stayed afloat for some time but had to be sunk by our MTBs later that evening because it had become a hazard.

Memories of the V1s are quite vivid as we saw one crash into the cliffs. While on patrol between Dover and Folkestone our midship gunner Ken Goodacre, from Hull, hit one with his Oerlikon gun, exploding it in mid-air. On one occasion a British ack-ack shell, aimed at a doodlebug, exploded under our boat and split a fuel tank. We had to put into Rye Harbour for repairs. We were given leave while this was being done and it was really smashing going home to the quiet north east after the shells and V1s in the Dover area.

Eunice Mercer (née Bint) was a WRN cine-operator at HMS *Wasp* and, like others, was on a roster to ensure that someone would be responsible for seeing all those girls off duty went to the cave shelter during shelling:

> There was a girl in a top bunk who refused point blank to move. While remonstrating with her a shell cap flew over my head and embedded itself in the wall just above her bunk. My reluctant bunk companion said, quite briefly, 'OK then, I'll go to the cave'.
>
> One does foolish things in a situation sometimes. Several of us were standing round a table in the galley, enjoying a mug of cocoa, when there was a tremendous whizzing noise going on overhead. We all made a mad dash to get under the table. I was still holding my mug but not a drop had spilled. Unfortunately though, while my head and shoulders were safely under the table, the rest of me was dangerously vulnerable.
>
> In the caves we had a section especially reserved for WRNS. One night we smuggled in my army fiancé, heavily disguised with a blanket round his shoulders and a WRN cap perched on his head. A rather dour-faced WRN officer on her rounds said, 'That doesn't look like a WRN to me'. She couldn't have been as po-faced as she seemed!

Signing 'in' and 'out' did not always go down well with Kathleen Cosgrove (now Higgins) although her living conditions in the WRNS were considered the best at Dover:

> In retrospect, of course, you realize it was for very good reasons, but at eighteen years of age you look upon these things as unnecessary restrictions. I remember one incident when a shell warning necessitated a quick dash to a shelter. To this day I don't know why I picked up a bottle of red ink together with my tin hat. En route I fell over a concrete tank trap and arrived in the shelter covered with red sploshes. An over-zealous medical orderly, thinking I was a casualty, rushed me to the sick bay despite my protestations. It was a long time before I lived that down!
>
> Sailors collecting their mail from the WRNS/RN Fleet Mail Office after D-Day often brought us presents from France – mostly a bottle of perfume in exchange for cocoa powder. On one occasion, however, a large box of grapes arrived and we were delighted, of course. But our enjoyment turned sour next day when a telephone call from headquarters queried the whereabouts of the grapes intended for a senior officer's dinner party. I cannot recall how we explained that one away!
>
> On a sadder note, I remember we watched from the balcony of the Boys' County School, when the German long-range guns scored a direct hit on a clearly marked hospital ship in the Channel.

Trained as a WRNS victualling clerk, Joan Rogers (now Oakley) arrived in Dover to live at 14 East Cliff and work at HMS *Wasp*, where later, a large victualling store was opened:

I was working with a couple of stokers and an able-bodied seaman nicknamed 'butch' who had been a butcher in civilian life. We served a lot of fresh meat to ships' crews and his expert knowledge came in handy. About this time there was a noticeable increase in the number of ships and boats arriving – motor launches, torpedo boats and so on. The late Sir Peter Scott and his flotilla arrived with the steam gun boat *Grey Goose*.

About a month or so before D-Day troops were constantly marching around the countryside. I was going on duty one morning and there was a platoon of soldiers marching by. They were cat-calling and wolf-whistling, as any man in uniform seemed to do in those days, but I was too busy watching out for the seagulls wheeling overhead and praying they would not 'dive-bomb' me. Just as I thought I had got away with it there was a big splosh in front of me, and a gust of wind blew it all over me. You can imagine the huge cheer that went up from the passing soldiers!

On D-Day, 6 June, our captain came to our billet at East Cliff to announce that the Allies had landed in Normandy, and we were to report to our posts at 19.00 hours and work around the clock if necessary. I shall never forget the

HMS *Kingscourt's* gun-turret crew pose for the photographer after laying a smoke-screen around ships heading for the Normandy beach-head. Born during the V1 campaign, 'Doodlebug' the kitten wonders what all the fuss is about.

'Just as I thought I had got away with it there was a big splosh in front of me, and a gust of wind blew it all over me. You can imagine the huge cheer that went up from the passing soldiers.'

sight in the Channel when I went on duty. Huge smoke-screens had been laid, and the Channel seemed to be full of ships with one or two on fire. In the harbour there must have been a dozen or more 'seesaws' being operated by medics who were trying to revive some poor devils brought ashore. There were queues and queues of soldiers who had been rescued, some had mostly just blankets and very little else in the way of clothing. The good old Salvation Army were there dishing out cups of tea. All the time boats were arriving with more survivors, and ambulances were going back and forth, ferrying the wounded. Most of them seemed to be Canadians.

We were rushed off our feet that day with crews dashing in and demanding stores. But time meant nothing to anyone. It was the Spirit of Britain at its best.

A few days later some of the matelots asked me for some soap to take over to France. This was one commodity in short supply in Occupied Europe. In return the crews brought back bunches of grapes, which, of course, we had not seen the like of since war started.

'Butch' and I were working in the store one day when there was the dreaded sound of a doodlebug getting louder each second. The engine stopped and everything went quiet. We both made a dash to get under the trestle table. Then there was an almighty bang and something falling in our store. We had not been hit but the doodlebug had crashed into the cliff face immediately behind us. It had shattered our one and only glass skylight, which promptly landed in a huge block of our precious butter. It was now full of glass fragments and totally unusable. We later had permission to dump it. But the news leaked out to reach nearby sailors who turned up with a stretcher. They placed the butter mound on it and ceremoniously draped some flag bunting across it. With solemn faces the sailors slowly marched out of the store and down the steps to the quay where one of the crew blew his whistle while the mound of butter was respectfully piped into the sea. In those days we had to make our own humour.

We were sometimes invited to dances by the Army. One night the Shorncliffe garrison sent over a 'tilly' (utility truck) to pick up about eight of us. The young lieutenant who met us showed us the 'powder room', which was a tent in a field with a mirror hanging from one pole. The dance was held in a Nissen hut and it was nice and warm and there were plenty of partners. But the funny thing was that in the middle of a dance a whistle would sound and your partner would have to dash outside to man his gun, leaving another soldier to carry on with the dance.

We always seemed to be hungry. I can remember going to the church army canteen for a halfpenny slice of bread and jam, so as to have enough money left over to buy a bar of rationed chocolate.

At one stage there was a mock invasion exercise, the enemy being HMS *Lynx* and the intruders being Royal Marines. The supply branch was put on

'With solemn faces the sailors slowly marched out of the store and down the steps to the quay where one of the crew blew his whistle while the mound of butter was respectfully piped into the sea.'

'mortars' which meant we had to lob potatoes across the viaduct. Not really wasteful because we had to pick them up afterwards.

During one shelling period we were in the cave shelters when some Yanks found their way in. It was at night and they had probably got lost because they were stationed behind the castle to the east of the harbour. Suddenly there was a yell, 'Hey – there's some Jenny Wrens here! Let's have a party!'. Our Petty Officer had other ideas, however, and ever protective, hustled the Yanks out like a mother hen.

I was married whilst serving in Dover, at St Peter and St Paul's church in Maison Dieu Road. The night before there had been some damage to the roof and there was rubble and debris to step over to reach the altar. We had a three-day honeymoon and took the bus to Sandgate. On our wedding night we went to a show in the Folkestone area. On the list of artistes was Betty Driver who was appearing as a singer. She is better known nowadays as Betty Turpin, the barmaid in the television soap-opera Coronation Street.

Office of Flag Officer   To WRN J.R.M. Oakley
Commanding Dover   53850
28 June 1945
It is my pleasure to commend you for the valuable services rendered by you in the Dover Command in connection with the Normandy landings in 1944 and for your devotion to duty during your period of service at Dover.
Signed   H.D. Pridham-Wippel
                      Admiral

To WRN J.R.M. Oakley
6 March 1945
Madam,
I am commanded by my Lords Commissioners of the Admiralty to inform you that they have before them a report of your good services in connection with the operations for the invasion of Normandy, and I am to say that Their Lordships have noted with satisfaction the part you played in this great enter-prise.
I am, Madam,
your obedient servant, H.V. Markham

P. Watling was a member of the RAF Regiment sent to the area to reinforce ack-ack defences against the flying bombs:

We arrived at Folkestone central station in the pitch dark and then heard our first V1. There was no mistaking the burbling sound of a flying bomb, it was like an unsilenced motor cycle. When the engine stopped, signifying that the flying bomb was about to glide earthwards, it was unnerving to say the least, waiting to find out where it was going to explode.

'Suddenly there was a yell, "Hey – there are some Jenny Wrens here! Let's have a party!". Our Petty Officer had other ideas, however, and ever protective, hustled the Yanks out like a mother hen.'

To begin with we manned our guns in an area not far from Hawkinge airfield, right under one of the flight paths used by the doodlebugs. But this was a duplication of effort as we were operating in an area allocated to fighters. One afternoon we saw a Spitfire chasing a doodlebug when suddenly, as the Spitfire opened up, a Mustang crossed the line of fire. The Mustang crashed and set fire to a corn field only a few hundred yards away from our position.

Soon we were moved from Hawkinge to a position on high ground overlooking the Dover–Folkestone road area near West Hougham. We left the Hawkinge area to the fighters. We dug trenches over two foot deep and slept in them with just a tent over the top of us. Directly to our front, on the cliff edge almost, were the 90 mm anti-aircraft guns operated by remote control by the US Army. To our right were Royal Artillery 3.7-inch ack-ack guns near Capel le Ferne. I remember on the few occasions we had time off to go to Folkestone seeing enormous piles of empty shell cases around these guns. Being heavy calibre, they could engage targets well out to sea whilst with our own light Bofors guns we were restricted to the doodlebugs that had already crossed the coast.

When a flying bomb received a near miss, its gyroscope control system would often go haywire, causing it to alter course. Sometimes they flew back over the sea from whence they came until they crashed into the water. One incident caused by a near miss sticks in my mind. It was over Folkestone and the doodlebug soared straight up and then turned over and screamed down towards our guns. We sprinted for our Bofors hell-for-leather and got it into action. The doodlebug blew up about 300 yards above us and we were credited with a 'kill'.

The Germans made sure 'Hellfire Corner' lived up to its name, when one Sunday afternoon they started to shell the Swingate radar masts near Dover Castle. It was hardly a peaceful Sunday. We found out later that one shell had landed near a cinema in the town and badly damaged it. We had been watching a film there the night before!

John P. Dimmer, of the 127 Gun Battalion of the United States Army, first heard the 'putt-putt' of a flying bomb as he travelled through London from Staffordshire to Dover to join his Anti-Aircraft Group and the British AA Brigade that they were assigned to:

A friendly British officer at Brigade HQ invited me to watch 'the night shoot' on one of the doodlebug 'flyways' near Hythe. The British officer led us to an abandoned house leading to the beach near Hythe.

After dark this officer directed my driver, Private First Class Thompson, to a position at the end of the road to the beach. The top of the jeep was taken down and the three of us stood up in the jeep awaiting the arrival of the V1s.

'Sometimes they flew back over the sea . . . until they crashed into the water. . . . the doodlebug soared straight up and then turned over and screamed down towards our guns.'

'Instinctively, we two officers threw up our hands to protect our faces. . . . Shaken, and with our ears ringing from the explosion, we slowly arose. . . . I realized PFC Thompson was not in sight.'

The fantastic show began. Behind us the loud boom of the 3.7-inch guns, the repeated thump of the Bofors guns and the staccato rattle of machine guns of various calibres. Over our heads curved the many coloured streams of tracer. In the distance, and rapidly increasing in size, we saw the flames from the propulsion motors of the buzzbombs.

We soon learned that one on a 'coming' course presented a circular shape of flame, whilst an elongated shape denoted a bomb on a 'crossing' course. Occasionally, when a V1 was hit, there was a deafening explosion as its 2,000 pounds of super high explosive detonated. When the buzzbombs which had not been hit over the sea were still chugging inland, the air all round us was filled with falling fragments from exploding shells, expended machine-gun bullets and the odd 90 mm self-destructing shell after missing its target.

We passed several exciting hours watching the battle of the ack-ack guns versus the V1s. Then my attention was drawn to the rapidly increasing circle of flame indicating a V1 coming almost directly at us. The gunfire aimed at this particular target intensified and the sky to our front was sprinkled with flashes from shells exploding. I said to my two companions, 'I hope they don't hit that bastard' – pointing to the oncoming bomb. But no sooner had I spoken than the sky in front blossomed into a fireball as one shell scored a direct hit only a few hundred yards from us.

Instinctively, we two officers threw up our hands to protect our faces, falling (probably more from excitement than the shock wave) to the floor of the jeep. Shaken, and with our ears ringing from the explosion, we slowly arose. Having discovered that neither of us seemed to have been hurt, I realized PFC Thompson was not in sight. I feared he might have been blown out of the jeep or been hit by shrapnel so I called out, 'You OK, Thompson?' There was no reply. I looked around the vicinity of the jeep, fearing to find a battered body. Then I shouted, 'Thompson, where are you?' This brought a response – a bedraggled, helmetless and be-twigged figure slowly emerged from a nearby hedge. Thompson looked up at us and said in a shaking voice, 'Captain, if you think I'm gonna stand up in this effing jeep while those effing things are blowing up all around me, you're crazy!'.

Paul Alexa, from Mentor, Ohio, was a radar operator with the 127 Gun Battalion of the US Army, who were positioned on top of the cliffs overlooking Dover:

The V1, buzzbomb, flying bomb, doodlebug or Diver (the official name given to the pulse-jet pilotless flying bomb) was launched from France. It was set straight on course for London usually, with a flight time of about fifteen minutes. Early warning radar stations along the Channel coast gave an indication of their approach. These radar stations were originally designed to give warning of low flying aircraft and the V1s usually flew at 2000 feet or lower.

The skill of the AA gunners in downing these doodlebugs forced the Germans to adopt a new tactic of launching in salvoes in the early hours of the morning when they assumed gun crews would be at their lowest efficiency. In this way they hoped to offset the advantage our guns were securing.

Once the range-scope operator had got the target squarely located on his radar, our 90 mm guns were automatically trained on the target by a computer. At 05.00 hours one morning I locked on to a buzzbomb that was part of a salvo. As its range decreased I could see the bursts of our exploding shells shown as tiny stars on my radar screen. Radar continued to track the robot as it passed almost directly over our position with my screen showing an increasing range as it drew away from us. We continued to fire at it. Suddenly the blip on the scope slowed, stopped completely and reversed direction. Through my headphones I could hear the range officer giving coordinates for a new target. I said quickly, 'Sir, the range of the other one is now decreasing', because I had realized we had turned it right around. The range officer acknowledged that this was so, but gave orders to get on to a new target. He knew that the old one would fly out to sea and crash.

Actually, after nearly colliding with one of the radar towers and flying low over our batteries it exploded on the cliff edge. One man yelled, 'Hey, look at that crazy fighter pilot'. But then he recognized it as a buzzbomb and dived for cover. Inside the radar cabin we were tracking a new target and did not know how close we had come to being the unintended target.

Even after almost fifty years Robert W. Fiske, another American with the 127 Gun Battalion, cannot forget the sight and sound of his first V1:

It was something I had never heard before and never since. We got so excited when we shot one down but were dismayed when one got away from us. When that happened I used to pray it would fall harmlessly in a vacant field.

For the first time the new 'proximity' fuse was issued and fitted to all our shells. It did not need to make a direct hit to explode and destroy a buzzbomb. But it was a classified item and could only be used over water, in case fragments should fall into enemy hands. I recall that they had all to be marked with our battery identification so that if they did explode over land they could be traced back to us. I also recall the dire threats made about the future of the battery commander if such fragments should be traced to him.

The funniest episode I remember was the V1 that was shot out of control, looped the loop and spun over our battalion area before falling harmlessly out at sea.

John P. Dimmer, of the same American unit, remembers the occasion when his colonel was discussing the performance of the British Bofors ack-ack guns against the flying bombs with a British sergeant in charge of a Bofors on the breakwater:

'. . . a funny tingling went up and down your spine . . . everyone prayed this nite [sic]. . . . I'll call anyone a liar who wasn't scared.' Above: Four 90-mm ack-ack guns of the 127 AAA Gun Battalion (USA) on Langdon cliff, August 1944.

The colonel asked, in a very informal and friendly way, 'What do you think of our 90 mm guns engaged against the V1s from the cliffs above you?'. 'Sir', said the sergeant, 'We don't like 'em at all.' 'Why not?', queried our CO. The sergeant replied, 'Well Sir, your guns make such an awful crack – every time your chaps fire the bloody seagulls come flying out of the cliffs and s— all over us!'

Alfred Bricker, another American, remembers the range-section tent with shrapnel holes where he monitored a plotting board, appreciating the teamwork of the fighter pilots sending buzzbomb data to the British service girls, who relayed it to the guns:

A recurring memory is of time off at St Margaret's beach where I gave a young woman with a child some oranges. She said it had been a long time since they'd seen oranges. For me they symbolized civilian hardships – bomb harassment, hiding in shelters, meagre food rations and waiting in line for necessities.

Another American, Carl Hiller, recalls a trip to Folkestone on a free pass:

On returning to base camp we came under fire from the German cross-Channel guns so we took shelter in a nearby cave with other personnel. Among them were WRNS from the plotting rooms beneath Dover Castle. To relieve the tension we all started to sing. Naturally the old standby 'Roll me over in the clover' came up. We all enjoyed ourselves so much we forgot about the shelling until the 'all clear' came.

Larry Alcott was on the cliffs with an RAF Regiment armed with 20-mm Hispano guns, helping to combat the V1s:

Against buzzbombs they were not a lot of use – the barrel could not be swung round quick enough. I well remember one particular V1 which struck the cliff face. The ground shook and moments later a blast ring appeared before us just like a rainbow. We were only about a hundred yards away. The funny thing was that only the day before, when we had first arrived on site, we had set up our Hispano right on the cliff edge. Our CO had ordered the gun to be moved – 'Too dangerous' he had said.

No transport was provided for Robert Stamp who had been sent to the RAF radar station at Swingate. So he humped his kitbag up to a grassy bank on the main Deal to Dover road and sat there contemplating how to get to Swingate:

A Royal Navy utility van came along and I thumbed a lift and to my joy they were headed for the same place. They dropped me off at a farm gate. There was nothing there. Not one building. My spirits dropped. A scruffy airman was posted at the gate as sentry so he rang through for the orderly sergeant who directed me to an empty bell tent of 1914–18 vintage. This was September 1944 but there was nothing but mud everywhere, and Dover was being shelled daily.

I was sent in charge of a party of airmen to unload an ammunition train at Dover's Priory station. Unlike the usual lazy working parties, they put their backs into it and emptied the ammo train in record time. Today we would have been mentioned in the *Guinness Book of Records*!

On several occasions we had to unload transport at the local goods station. Flat trucks came to Folkestone Central goods depot for us to remove vehicles. The shelling was continuous. On one occasion we were all round a van about to lift it off the railway truck when a shell exploded nearby. Everyone dived instinctively for cover except 'muggins' who was still holding on to the van!

A GPO Technician at Dover Castle, Charles Hutchings, happened to be on duty when a party of Royal Marines from Deal put in a night attack to test the defences. He remembers the Marines had found a tiny loophole – a small tunnel entrance on the cliffside. They went through the Combined HQ like the proverbial dose of salts:

A 'thunderflash' was tossed into a small cubicle where a GPO colleague was sorting through wired connections. It was a very confined space and naturally the explosion was deafening. He was in no fit state for much during the rest of the shift.

One night, some weeks after D-Day, I was testing the teleprinter circuits. They were connected to the forward element of Supreme HQ Allied Forces. Our 'answer back' automatic code at the time was 'Hellfire Corner' and the operator in France keyed in and got that code automatically. He queried 'R U Dover?'. I typed back in the affirmative and he came back with a brief (and very unofficial) message to say that they were moving up so rapidly that he had not had the time to write home. Would I pass on a message to his parents in Deal that he was OK? I went next day to the address he had given me, a shop on the corner of Duke Street. The shop was full of customers and I was pressed for time so I had to pass the message to his parents in the presence of other people. Naturally they wanted to know how I come to know about their son. When I said I had not actually seen him they assumed I had spoken to him by phone. In those days we were all very security-minded, aware that, as the posters clearly said, 'Careless Talk Costs Lives', so I was only able to mumble that I had not spoken to him by phone. Then I turned and made a bee-line for the door, leaving the parents and customers to make of it what they could.

Basil Carey was a member of a detachment of No. 80 Wing, Bomber Command. His unit was code-named 'King Lear', perhaps because his unit overlooked Shakespeare cliff:

We were right on the top of a steep hill adjacent to an ack-ack battery. It was approached by crossing the cricket ground at Maxton, Dover, and then climbing the hill. We were billeted with various civilian families in the area and they made us very welcome. In one billet the son of the family was a serving sailor and I was looked after as well as I have ever been.

From our site on the cliffs we could see right across the Channel. When we saw the flash of a gun going off on the other side of the water we had about seventy seconds in which to find cover. Yet after a while we became rather blasé about the risks involved and would often go on with what we were doing whenever the shelling warning sounded. That is, until the night when a shell exploded right opposite my billet and blew in all the windows. After that we always went into a shelter.

Our work initially consisted of monitoring and logging various enemy signals. Later on we used transmitters which were on a new frequency, now known as VHF. The signals we transmitted were in code according to the various degrees of 'noise' modulated on them. We had code-words such as 'Rug', 'Mat' and 'Carpet'. I was just the operator and never really understood the technical side of what we were doing. I do recall we used a very primitive device to check whether our aerials were transmitting efficiently enough. This was a long pole with an ordinary electric light bulb at the end, and two metal rods. This was held up in front of the aerial and if it was transmitting correctly the bulb would light up.

We were given a secret code for reporting enemy action but it had to be memorized and could not be written down. But when I contacted our control to inform them that a V1 had exploded near our site, cutting through the interconnecting cables and smashing valves, no one at the other end knew what I was talking about! So much for secret codes.

At one stage sailors worked with us, although I never really understood what their particular job was. This was not unusual in wartime as everyone was supposed to be security-conscious. They were billeted in an empty house on the Folkestone Road, which they referred to as 'their ship'. If we visited them for a game of cards we were invited to 'come aboard' and could be told that so and so was 'in the galley' or perhaps the 'heads' (the loo) or that somebody else was 'ashore'. It was a happy piece of make believe.

Working with sixteen other girl plotters in the Coastal RA Operations Room at Dover Castle was ATS girl Joan Faulkner (now Lidiard):

There was a Combined Services Operations and Signals HQ below us. I was sent down there once on an errand and practically needed a map to get myself back up to our level. The male RA officers used to mess in the Keep, and the ATS girls came under Broadlees for administration. Brigadier Raw (known as 'Daddy') was the Coastal Artillery Commander, Colonel Lindsey, with the curly pipe, was second-in-command, and Captain Owens was the radar officer. The two lieutenants I recall were 'W.G.' Grace and 'Weary Willy' Williams.

Our operations room was next to the naval and anti-aircraft operations rooms. It had a little balcony which looked out over the harbour and across to Calais. But soon after we moved in there was a switch to a brand new operations room for coastal artillery.

I had arrived in Dover with about ten other newly trained girls from Oswestry where we had been taught how to operate predictors. When we arrived and were taken to our billets at Broadlees we had no idea what our duties would be as we were pretty sure we were not sufficiently proficient to be let loose on gunsights. As things turned out we received training as plotters.

We were moved to new living quarters that were used as the CRS at the top of a spiral staircase opposite the Port War Signal Station. Even when off duty we were often on call and expected to descend that spiral staircase like a flash. Half way down there was a steel door with a steel coaming. In my haste, on one occasion, I chose to leap through this in one bound and almost knocked myself unconscious.

After night duty we were supposed to go to bed but I found it hard to sleep and as we were lucky enough to have a little radio we would listen to the American Forces Network (AFN) and hear Glen Miller, Sergeant Ray McKinley or BBC Regimental Sergeant-Major George Melachrino and his band. One morning after night shift we found it too warm and took our bedding out to the top of the billet. The sky was full of aircraft towing gliders going over the Channel. We soon found out they were off to Arnhem.

Our plotting responsibilities covered an area from North Foreland in the east to Dungeness in the west, seven regiments of coastal artillery in all. Brigadier Raw took us on a visit to No. 540 Regiment when the guns were due to fire. We were issued with earplugs, told to bend our knees and open our mouths to help minimize the effects of the shock wave. I remember the brigadier telling me once that I would have a gun crew of my own. He must have been clairvoyant because I did have four sons – not quite enough for a large calibre gun crew!

I can clearly remember one of the characters of the wartime dances at the Dover town hall. Freddy would usually be the compère and master of ceremonies and would also teach dancing. I was dancing there one night when the double warning went, indicating shelling alert. I was tearing up the hill to get to the castle, and in so doing twisted my neck badly when a shell suddenly exploded in the harbour. But I carried on and over the drawbridge, and entered the castle through the tunnel just up from the guardroom. I complained about my neck and somebody, rather brutally I thought, gave it an almighty twist which cured me.

Another time I was caught in the town with a dog-fight going on above. Shrapnel was falling thick and fast all along the roads. My main fear had always been getting injured in the head by shrapnel. I made a bee-line for the nearest WVS canteen where those dear souls served a cup of tea at a penny a time. I distinctly recall posters on the wall showing a drooping chicken being revived after a cup of tea and looking quite perky. One of those ladies made me take her tin hat, then rounded up some soldiers from the castle to make sure I got back safely.

The privates in our billet, the former CRS, lived in what must have been the main wards. The floor was covered with brown lino and this had to be kept polished to a mirror gloss. One of the important visits we had was from HRH The Princess Marina, Duchess of Kent. We were instructed not to complain when asked if everything was all right (even though the food was lousy). So I dutifully answered, 'Yes, Ma'am', to all her enquiries about our welfare. After she had gone we were appalled at the state of our floor upon which her entourage had trodden. But we did appreciate those visits if only for the mysterious improvement in the food on those occasions. Normally I was forever hungry and spent most of my pay on extra food, often borrowing until next pay day. Taking into account my voluntary deductions sent home to my parents, my usual weekly pay came to the present day equivalent of 36p!

When plotting the course of the German ship *Munsterland* we were told to expect prize money if she was sunk. She was sunk – but we never saw any prize money!

Lorna Hawley (now Dawes) regrets never keeping a diary of events when she served at Dover. Recollections fade to some extent and those were historic days in the WRNS:

During the build-up to D-Day and for some time afterwards, travel was restricted to within fifteen miles' radius of Dover. When the ban was finally lifted I was able to snatch quick trips home to Richmond, Surrey, on my days off. It was pretty tight timing but at least it got me home cooking and a night in a bed rather than an upper bunk. But there was still this atmosphere of camaraderie and it was good to come back and find my bunk nicely made up for me.

My duties were typing in the signals distribution office down at the lowest level in the casemates of Dover Castle. Here messages were recieved by many means – teleprinter, W/T (Morse) handed in for transmission, Aldis lamp and telephone and so on. We had to decide their destinations. We had checkers to authorize copies to be made for local distribution and a duplicating machine was used to run these off – if you came across anyone with purple hands you immediately knew what they had been doing. All restricted and confidential messages going out had to be encoded first. We were taken to and from duty in lorries initially, which was not too comfortable. Later we travelled by buses hired from the East Kent Bus Company.

On one occasion when there was thick snow on the ground, the bus driver was sure he could get up Castle Hill and back. He managed to get up the hill, but coming down the bus behaved like a huge sledge. We came to a halt on the very brink of a fresh shell crater. Everyone was shaken rigid but apart from a few broken windows and minor cuts there was no real damage.

Our accommodation at the Dover Boys' County School was in 'cabins', which were, in fact, the classrooms. I was in 'Nelson' which had been the science lab. At the Lord Warden Hotel (HMS *Wasp*) we were up in the attics. There was no time for false modesty as each bathroom had three baths! But at least one could relax after a night watch by resting on the beach almost under Shakespeare Cliff. This had by now been made safe from anti-personnel mines and other hazards.

Pay day was once a fortnight and I used to draw on average £1.50 so it had to be carefully spread over the two weeks, although pay day meant we would lash out and have a cream tea for 8 pence. Another treat was to walk along the hills to Hougham, where Miss Sinclair would feed us with a huge tea, including boiled eggs for 5 pence. After the leathery concoctions made with dried egg powder this was wonderful. It was here that we would see the damage inflicted by the buzzbombs. The sight of a pub completely demolished except for its sign on a post was depressing.

'Still, I clearly recall the Duchess of Kent paying us a visit. At that time we were billeted in the Boys' County School, and we paraded on the school sports field.'

During a shelling alert if we were actually on watch we had to stay put on duty, going in relays to eat or to sleep in the older parts of the tunnels or casemates. It was eerie going through the older tunnels with their dim lighting and I'm glad that these long spells of duty did not happen too often. We saved money whenever we could by walking or hitching a lift on service vehicles. But we tried to avoid being picked up by the American jeeps as these were really terrifying journeys!

Still, I clearly recall the Duchess of Kent paying us a visit. This would have been early 1945. At that time we were billeted in the Boys' County School and we paraded on the school sports field before the Duchess, Dame Vera Laughton-Mathews, and Admiral Pridham-Wippel, who was Vice-Admiral Dover, and the Mayor of Dover, Alderman Cairns.

Later on we had a visit from King George VI and Queen Elizabeth (now the Queen Mother). It was an all-women's Guard of Honour drawn from the WRNS, ATS, WAAF and NFS. This occasion was filmed for the newsreels by Gaumont British News.

Having trained as a naval signalman, Larry Kettley, in all innocence, actually volunteered for the Royal Navy Patrol Service, quite unaware what RNPS stood for!:

'Later on we had a visit from King George VI and Queen Elizabeth (now the Queen Mother). It was an all-women's Guard of Honour drawn from the WRNS, WAAF, ATS and NFS.'

I was drafted to HMS *Willing Boys* at Dover but she had sailed for another base by the time I had arrived at dear old Dover, so I was kept on standby. Then the 'Bunts' on HMS *Alexandrite* was taken sick and I was sent to replace him – a temporary arrangement that became permanent.

Our main task was Orepesa sweeping but we were given other duties such as escort duty through the Straits, escorting Trinity House ships and Dan Buoy laying for the fleet sweepers. One job in particular that nobody liked was 'D' Buoy patrol. This entailed patrolling off Dungeness at night, listening out for E-boats with our hydrophones, and at the same time trying not to get caught up in our east- or west-bound convoys.

Living conditions on board were extremely cramped but just about acceptable and we never went short of grub. All the same I have never been able to look at another tin of pilchards in tomato sauce since those days!

Shore leave was normally a trip to the 'flicks', a cup of tea and a snack at the Snargate Street 'Sally Ann' canteen (wonderful people), and a 'half' at the Mitre Inn before reporting back on board.

Our usual berth in Dover was at the Prince of Wales Pier except during very bad weather when we were either shifted to the Eastern Arm or anchored in mid-harbour. Shelling was quite frequent and, whilst most of them seemed to land in the town, there were some which exploded in the harbour area. During one attack HMS *Lois* had her starboard side blown out.

I got to know two civilians quite well. Sammy and Cliff were both post office operators who manned the telephones in a small hut half way along the pier. They took all messages from the castle and HMS *Lynx* and these were then brought to us by communications ratings.

HMS *Alexandrite* was given the dubious honour of being the only British ship to shell the Dover–Folkestone area. It happened when a convoy was being shelled by the Germans off Folkestone one night and a small coaster was so badly damaged she was abandoned. At daylight she was seen partly submerged off Shakespeare Cliff, and was a danger to shipping. We were ordered to sink her by gunfire but our twelve-pounder shells just ricocheted off her and headed inland!

Towards the end of 1943 John Glover, who was under age, volunteered to serve with the Royal Navy. He eventually joined the Combined Operations section, a tri-service organization devoted to the concept of harassing the enemy in occupied territory by making clandestine raids on coastal installations and so on. It contained in its ranks commandos, army and Marines, the Special Air Service (SAS) the Special Boat Service (SBS) and a variety of other units.

Almost a year later John arrived at Folkestone Central station as an ordinary seaman rating en route to HMS *Allenby*, the monolithic Victorian Royal Pavilion Hotel beside the harbour. HMS *Allenby* was not associated with the exotica of many of the clandestine operations that had taken place previously, but was a mild-mannered component holding landing craft crews in reserve.

But John Glover had already experienced the exotica of a clandestine operation when he landed in France at 02.30 hours on 3 June 1944 – just three days before D-Day! He was quite unaware that he was participating in Operation 'Fortitude', the code-name given to the deception plan to convince the Germans that the Allied invasion would take place in the Pas de Calais.

He had been the junior boy in a two-man beach survey team. Essentially the idea was sneakily to survey the approaches to a particular beach for a potential landing site, west of Boulogne at Berck Plage:

We had been told to contact the French Resistance – how was never explained. We would then make our way back home with their help. I did not know who the genius was who thought up this plan, but I did not like it at all. The outboard engine of our rubber boat was beautiful and would get us home. If not there were the paddles.

My accomplice was a lieutenant-commander RNVR. We were dropped by a motor launch at the appointed location, ran in partly by engine and then by paddles. Then commenced the survey using soundings and a fix from a well oiled astro-bubble sextant, plotting our soundings on a hydrographer's data sheet beneath a canopy.

The lieutenant-commander abruptly stopped his work and said we were going ashore. I protested – there was no valid reason I could think of why I should land in enemy-held territory. I had formed the notion that this man had, in fact, a mission to perform which I was not a part of. After a lengthy whispered argument the lieutenant-commander said, 'We have to go ashore'. So we prepared the boat, getting rid of the excess fuel tanks, and so on. We then moved to shallow water, took our gear off, put it into waterproof bags, sank the boat and landed.

My accomplice knew exactly what he was doing and displayed confidence and extreme competence. There are no words to describe it. He was simply a master practitioner – an expert in the true sense. No one could have penetrated a beach minefield better. He went through barbed wire coils like a dose of salts and, what is more, re-sealed them as he went. It would have been extremely difficult to find our path afterwards – even in daylight.

Forty or so minutes later, either by accident or design, he was gone. I was on my own in enemy-held territory. Not a comforting thought I assure you, least of all to suddenly realize that your accomplice's job was perhaps to deliver you to the enemy! Quite simply, if I had been captured I would merely have confirmed for the Germans that operation 'Fortitude' may have some substance. The Allies were surveying the coast possibly prior to a landing. No one ever told me that a landing would take place in that area. After all, I was only an ordinary seaman. Strange as it may seem, I have never felt acrimonious towards the lieutenant-commander. If he had a job to do and that job was to deliver me to the enemy, that at least left me with the option of choice.

British Intelligence deliberately fed to the enemy several hundred agents. It was supposed to be some kind of nefarious scheme to bamboozle the Germans as a cover for the Normandy landings.

John Glover wandered around northern France for several days. He had no idea the Normandy landings had taken place. He had no terms of reference either, no idea where he was or what he should do: 'I blundered around like a man with no head!'

While John's story exudes fascination, space precludes mention of how he returned to England. However, his arrival back at HMS *Allenby* happened to coincide with the V1 campaign in the late summer of 1944:

In that endless summer there was one incident that stood out above all others. There were about fifteen hundred men on parade, assembled after a visit to the church of their choice. Also present was the base commander, a fallen angel – Vice-Admiral Round Turner, RN Retired, serving as a captain for the duration of the war.

We were lined up in columns of three and just when the order, 'Right Turn – Dismiss!' was about to be given, our obnoxious cross-Channel neighbour chose to intervene. There was an almighty bang as a large projectile exploded nearby. In typical Naval fashion the 'upper deck' stood fast while the 'lower deck' opted for cowardice and all us peasants ducked in unison. The Admiral and his staff remained frozen in time. They never moved a muscle, although some of the RNVR officers definitely looked uncomfortable. Then the old man's face dissolved into a terrifying grimace. He roared, 'How dare you display such cowardice under my command. Get up at once!' Fifteen hundred men snapped to attention with alacrity, albeit rather shamefacedly. Lesson: when you have heard the bang it is too late to duck, therefore stand fast. After having our character read in no uncertain manner we were finally dismissed.

American Joe Miller, HQ Battery 127 Gun Battalion, recalled:

One night we were leaving the gun-site for a meeting in Folkestone but were held up because the jeep driver had not signed the payroll. So we were late leaving our position only to be stopped by the crater from a German shell that had just landed. It would have caught us had we been on time. So you see it does not pay to rush to be on time.

I remember the cut tongue I got just outside Dover Castle. A bottle of Black Velvet was dropped on the cobblestones and I couldn't think of any other way to pick up the contents!

There were four batteries in 173 HAA, RA. Norman Glen was with No. 339 Battery which had the distinction of shooting down four enemy aircraft and

'. . . the phone rings . . . those guns will be manned if a target comes over . . . now who in the hell is he? . . . a guy can get killed standing around.' Above: A German 16-in shell explodes near 127 AAA Gun Battalion.

sharing in the destruction of twelve more. One of them crashed on D7 site within the Citadel Barracks complex where a number of buildings were destroyed:

> We did much experimental work with American and Canadian (SCR584) radar and also had civilian scientists with us at the Citadel for about a year. We also had thirty Polish Army soldiers with us for the whole of our stay in Dover in an effort to retain a nucleus of AA-trained personnel for the post-war Polish Forces.
>
> For three months in the spring of 1944 we had a half-battery of US Army heavy ack-ack attached to us under Lieutenant Rivers. Together we shot down a German plane and much publicity of this event appeared in the national press. During the V1 campaign my battery used the proximity fuse, and by the end of it was credited with or shared in the destruction of, 149 doodlebugs. The Commander-in-Chief AA Command, General Pile, visited us.

With the Royal Navy at the castle, John Cheney was pleased to find he was on a four-watch rota system rather than the two-watch system he had worked at sea. He was further delighted to find he was working with about a dozen WRNS and just three sailors:

There were, I think, a couple of 'Ladies' and an 'Honourable' amongst the girls, daughters or wives of captains or commodores and suchlike. Grand girls who drank pints with us at the Crypt Bar – particularly when we sought refuge there during the heavy shelling which began in Jerry's last days. It was strange to see the flare of the gun across the Channel and to know one had about a minute and a half to select the most attractive shelter.

I enjoyed many 'cuppas' on the little ledge where the NAAFI canteen was situated, and watched the doodlebugs pass close overhead with the unique exhaust-like roar of their ram-jets.

Also based at Dover with the Royal Navy was H. Batty, on the minesweeper HMMS 59, which usually docked at the Prince of Wales Pier:

Fixed in my memory is the smartness, efficiency and cheerfulness of the WRNS when delivering stores to us. Then there was the liberty ship, full of troops, taking a direct hit from a German shell and motor launches going out to pick up survivors. They came back into the submarine pens absolutely loaded to the gunwales with them. I watched a doodlebug hit an ack-ack battery above the harbour, killing, I understand, men and women, and admiring the accurate firing of a Bofors gun on the cliff top and noting with a certain satisfaction the number of doodlebugs shot down. Then we picked up crew members of a Flying Fortress off the Goodwin Sands. We found the wireless operator dead with his parachute wrapped round his neck. Motor minesweepers 56 and 79 both rescued live survivors.

But one particular incident sticks in my mind. We had left harbour in company with motor minesweepers 56 and 79. The latter ship was leading as her skipper (Lieutenant Collier, nicknamed 'Mad Harry') was CO. He was as usual some way ahead of the rest of us. Suddenly he shot even further off at high speed, hove to for a few minutes and then came back towards us at top speed with all flags flying, signalling that he had just picked up a Carley Float full of downed colonial airmen. They had been drifting up and down the coast for days. The signal ended with, '. . . why the bloody hell hadn't they been spotted before?'

On a lighter note I remember a soldier by the name of Sid Flack who was stationed on the breakwater. He was in the habit of missing the last liberty boat that took 'squaddies' back from shore leave. We would let him sleep on the locker cushions, give him breakfast, a fag and a tot of rum and let him get the first boat back to his unit.

Betty Kirby, better known as 'Jackie', was in the ATS at Dover from 1943 to 1945, and lived in several billets around the town:

My first was half way up Castle Hill on the left in a big terrace of houses. Then I went to Kearsney and was billeted with Royal Signals ATS. I was driving the Divisional Commander Royal Engineers about – both civilian and military. I lost a friend when a shell hit Priory railway station. On VE day we joined in the celebrations with the Americans and Canadians. They bought all sorts of receptacles at the shops to put their drinks in. We had enjoyable 'Last Night' parties in notorious Snargate Street on half-pints.

Travelling down to Dover in a train from Chatham, Joan Frost (now Tyson) and her WRNS companions were told by some fishermen they were in for a rough time and they were very sorry for them:

There were about twenty of us in bunk beds in three large rooms, light, clean and airy, and the food was good too. But the Boys' County School was a long walk from town and even longer from our office on the dock-side. We did have pick-up trucks to take us to and fro but it wasn't always convenient. Often we walked back in the dark. I have most vivid memories of tracer bullets flashing across the sky. I think I was more frightened of that than anything else. I had a wonderful 21st birthday party in our 'cabin'. It so disturbed the WRNS officers living above they came down to join us!

The Normandy campaign was a combination of immense strengths and weaknesses. The invasion and subsequent back-up was the result of supreme technical ingenuity. Above: LCTs in Dover Harbour carrying equipment to the recently liberated French ports in 1944.

'. . . shells landed and seemed to follow us. We ran, but the shelter was some way off. Suddenly, and without any warning, we were picked up bodily and thrown over a low wall.'

But then we were moved to the Lord Warden Hotel, a very old building formerly used by the sailors. All the glass had gone from the windows and there was just an opaque material stretched over the frames. Some of the rooms (cabins) were just big enough for six of us. We made some wonderful friends during our two years together. Being near the docks and the railway there was a continuous noise, the trains and the awful rail turntable which seemed to squeal and groan all night long.

I was in the shore station known as HMS *Lynx*, situated in Admiralty House near the docks at the end of Snargate Street. Our office, the signals distributing section, was at the top of the building and we could see clearly from there what shipping was passing through the Straits, the convoys and the Mulberry Harbour sections being towed through for the Normandy beaches. Of course at the time we had no idea what they were. We could see the French coast and often watched our shells landing, and the German guns firing and their shells exploding in the harbour and on the town. Towards the end of the German shelling, which had increased considerably, we spent many hours in the caves and seemed to wear our tin hats most of the time. As the Normandy invasion drew near we became very hush-hush, with leave stopped and all our mail censored. We appeared to be completely cut off from the rest of the country.

There are two shelling incidents which stick in my mind. The first occurred when I was walking back to the office with a friend along Snargate Street. A shell exploded almost in front of us and demolished the Salvation Army canteen. We felt the blast and were completely covered with dust and ran as fast as we could to the nearest shelter.

The second incident happened when we were again walking to the office and a shell exploded in the cliff face alongside the pavement. The double siren warning had sounded while shells landed and seemed to follow us. We ran, but the shelter was some way off. Suddenly, and without any warning, we were picked up bodily and thrown over a low wall. Some quick-thinking men from the docks had seen us running and had come to our rescue. Needless to say we were most grateful.

WAAF Elsie Mawson (now Curtis) BEM served at the Swingate radar station and also at St Margaret's Bay radar from 1943 to 1945:

My job was telecommunications and I worked alongside the radar mechanics. Radar stations were small, compact units with comparatively small numbers of personnel and this made us like a family, working, living and laughing to-gether. Yet there were sometimes tears. Dreadful things were happening around us but we had an important job to get on with.

We lived in Nissen huts high on the white cliffs. There was the usual pot-bellied stove in the centre of each hut and on cold winter nights we would sit around this enjoying the warmth and cracking jokes and telling yarns.

When the V1s came over, they perhaps frightened me but I don't think the shelling ever did. I just seemed to accept it as most people did. I remember we all admired the civilians in the Dover area. They coped with life so cheerfully and when they had to take to the shelters they made their own fun and amusement. A collection of proud, brave people. Their efforts should never be forgotten.

I often wonder what happened to the wonderful Canadian boys who were stationed at Swingate. They contributed to our social life, small dances and so on. Our mess was small but cosy and we always seemed to enjoy good food – the cooks were always keen to produce tasty meals. A good breakfast was my favourite meal after a long spell on night duty. Going off to our night duty we would collect a container of hot cocoa to take to the concrete control centre. We would hop aboard the vans and sit on the wooden slatted seats and off we would go.

I had a collection of 78rpm Frank Sinatra records and a wind-up portable gramophone which I took with me everywhere. The boys had Vera Lynn and the girls had Frankie.

The war in Europe was drawing to a close when the Royal Fusiliers arrived at Shorncliffe Barracks. Alan Styles soon discovered they were to participate in 'Corps Training', which was to be their final training before going to Europe:

The barracks were old, dismal and reminiscent of a medieval prison. We were all in one dormitory-type room and the water supply was cold most of the time. But we were hardly ever in barracks, we were usually out on some exercise: training in street fighting in the ruined parts of Dover, a night forced march and river crossing at Sandwich, using live ammunition on exercises at St Margaret's Bay. Some of the schemes lasted two or three days and involved long marches and mock battles by day and night.

I remember the occasion when we were digging-in on a beach and thought we had cut through some tree roots. When the coastguard came running down the beach we found it was a telephone cable we had chopped through. Come to think of it, there would not have been any trees on a beach!

After February 1945 the training swung over to exercises for the Far Eastern war. We were kitted out with jungle-green uniforms, the short jungle rifle with a rubber butt, even mules! We were out on another big exercise when the news came through that the atomic bomb had been dropped and the war against Japan was virtually over.

We were overjoyed, of course, and a happier period followed. The battalion took part in a victory march at Canterbury and a service in the cathedral. But by the autumn we were on our way to the troubled country of Palestine.

Teleprinter Operator Betty Andrew (née Ash) WRNS received this important signal from France, 'The Citizens of Dover from Brigadier, 9th Canadian Infantry Brigade 302245A/October. Greetings from Brigade and may you enjoy your pint of beer and stroll on the front in peace from now on. We have all of Jerry's Big Berthas.' Now living in Canada, Betty recalls:

Towards the end of the war I made my wedding dress, under the expert tutelage of one of our POs. I think the Admiralty was a bit shaken by the request for so many yards of bridal satin, but they allowed it. Of course, we didn't have any clothing coupons to buy a wedding dress.

Notes from my diary:
June 16 1944: First pilotless planes came over. Watched rocket guns firing at them. Siren for 12 hours.
Aug. 16: Went to Folkestone to see Dennis Noble in 'A Night In Venice'. Doodlebug hit train, came back in truck at 00.30 a.m.
Aug. 20: Went farming stooking oats for four hours. Did so well got paid two shillings [10p] an hour instead of one shilling [5p].
Aug. 29: Went to see 'Gone With The Wind', shelling in middle, went to shelter at 9 p.m. when most shells had fallen. Doodlebugs after that.
May 8 1945: All T/P Ops had lunch in Crypt. After Churchill's speech all ships and trains blew their hooters. Crowds danced in Market Square.

A signal came thru VIC one day
To say we couldn't go away,
They'd stopped our blinking leave once more
To help us win the b. . . .y war.

And on the glorious first of May
They sent us not so far away,
To sunbathe by the deep blue sea,
And treat the WRNS to cakes and tea.

We scrub and scrub our clothes all day
And so we smell like fresh–cut hay,
We wear our tiddly suits on watch
To please the English, Welsh and Scots.

In spite of all those pusser WRNS
And all the other jolly friends,
We sit and drip the whole day thru,
Prefer the old love to the new.

So all you maidens bear in mind
A sailor's heart is hard to find
And if he's victualled down at *Lynx*
His only love is forty winks.

T/P Ops Room, Dover Castle, July 1944

Epilogue

The inevitable change in tempo after the euphoria of the victory celebrations began for both civilian and military as a period of frustration. The civilians in the south-east proudly displayed their scars together with an intimate knowledge of all things warlike. But the military discharge procedure, however, seemed interminably long-winded, and those serving abroad saw even longer delays before they were brought back to 'Blighty'.

To avoid an uncontrollable influx of men and women on to the 'home front' labour market, release from the forces was rigidly enforced. Almost everyone who possessed special skills essential for the new national building programme were given a prompt discharge, while others were considered on an age and length of service basis.

Travelling home direct from the demobilization centres they were about to pick up the bare threads of broken lives, and for many it was a traumatic experience. They arrived home almost strangers after a long absence to find 'civvy street' had altered immeasurably. Few, if any, returning to cities or large towns, found 'their' England anything other than a shabby, scarred and dingy replica of its pre-war existence.

They were to look back not only upon the disruption of family life, the years of separation, the forced conviviality of wartime, rich in emotion and experience, but also upon the vague promises and shared hopes, that would soon fade into public indifference.

Fifty years on, there are still the hidden scars of war, but they are intermingled with happier memories which linger on like a haunting wartime melody. Warren Rodgers, a New Zealander by birth, set his nostalgia in the present idiom:

> The 1990 reunion brought together two groups of delighted ex-navy friends to reminisce and to rediscover, if possible, the haunts frequented more than forty-five years ago. One of their aims was to trace the 'Champagne Cave' which was under the western cliffs. 'Champagne' is something of a misnomer, because pre-war plans to use the cave as a storage area for wines appear never to have materialized. In any event, the name stuck and it was always known as

the 'Champagne Cave' when used by the Royal Navy as a victuallery, and the cash clothing and survival clothing offices of HMS *Lynx* serving the Dover base and Coastal Forces. These offices occupied a smallish area inside the cave's main entrance. The cave itself extended some distance further but there was a barricade at the limit of the navy offices. As with other tunnels under the cliffs, there was apparently an outlet to upper levels as the air was always fresh and the temperature at an even and comfortable level.

The four friends were Doris Carr and Rose Rodgers, two former WRNS who had been on the cash clothing staff, Doris's husband John who had served with Coastal Forces and myself, Rose's husband. We started our sentimental return journey from Dover's Market Square, recalling en route the Crypt Restaurant and went along Snargate Street past the spot where the Salvation Army canteen had sustained a direct hit from a shell in late 1944. There was considerable loss of life although the extent of the casualties was not disclosed at the time. Like the secrecy surrounding ship movements, the castle, East Cliff and the submarine pens – this was the accepted thing.

We went on through Snargate Street and into Limekiln Street, trying to pick out landmarks. We passed the petrol station that also received a direct hit near its forecourt, luckily without too many casualties. From this point on, the four of us thought we must be near the cave entrance but could not recognize the actual spot. We enquired at a nearby workshop but the young man there, though interested in the quest of a quartet of veterans, was unable to help. A little further on we met a middle-aged man who said that with so much demolition and new building having gone on since the war, we had picked a difficult task. The office staff of a fruit and vegetable business just along the road knew nothing of any 'Champagne Cave', but showed us a cave they used for potato storage. This proved to be the old 'Champagne Cave' and it was quite a memorable occasion to line up and be photographed standing at the entrance. Outside once again, we looked seaward and could see the familiar bulk of the Lord Warden Hotel which we knew as HMS *Wasp*. It had been the 'Wrennery' at one stage where Doris and Rose used to sign in after reporting back from a dance at the town hall.

As this anthology of letters has shown, experiences are engraved so indelibly upon the mind that even now, after more than fifty years have elapsed, sometimes the recollections are too poignant to bear with equanimity. Even so, this flicker of emotion in peacetime can sometimes pop up in the most unlikely of places. Stella Barker, who served in the ATS at Dover, was showing her husband where she had been billeted and where she had worked:

When we were walking through a village in Kent there was a gentleman cutting his hedge. He looked up at me quizzically and said, 'I cannot remember your name but you made a smashing cup of tea on night duty!' He was Captain MacCarty, one of our officers.

Index

ACP, 19
Adisham, 42
Admiralty Pier, 5, 19, 73
AFN, 165
Aggressive, HMS, 169, 171
AIG, 40, 131
Alexandrite, HMT, 66, 83, 169
Alkham, 149, 150
Allenby, HMS, 169, 171
American Gun Batt., 158, 160, 161
Archcliffe Fort, 2, 12, 33
Arnhem, 130, 165
Ashford, 11, 48, 64, 100, 128, 130
ASR (RAF No. 27 MCU), 88, 90, 93
Athol Terr., 5, 21
ATS, 16, 61, 64, 72, 94, 96, 99, 106, 107, 110, 115, 116, 132, 141, 144, 164, 168, 173, 180

Balloon Sqn, (No. 961 RAF), 47, 63, 70, 86, 89, 90, 102, 104
Barton Road, Dover, 59
Beachborough House, Folkestone, 128
Beachy Head, 90
BEF, 1, 7
Ben Mycree, 28
Berck Plage, 170
Biarritz (ferry), 26, 27, 28
Biggin Street, Dover, 7, 10
Blanc Nez, 78
Boulogne, 23, 24, 25, 26, 27, 34, 78, 127, 170
Boys County School, 141, 152, 167, 168, 174
Broadlees, 164, 165
Broadstairs, 43, 59, 70
Brock, HMS, 94
Bruce, 122, 123
Buckland, 7, 57, 135, 136
Buffs Regt., 34, 61
Burlington Hotel, 31

Calais, 8, 19, 27, 28, 34, 77, 78, 94, 116, 165
Camber, 67
Canadian Radio Location Unit, 79, 80, 114
Canterbury, 19, 68, 81, 84, 109, 177
Cap Gris Nez, 26, 27, 77, 78, 100, 123, 148, 149
Capel le Ferne, 14, 46, 49, 72, 77, 121, 131, 132, 157
Castle Hill, Dover, 106, 116, 167, 173
Castle Street, Dover, 10, 85, 94, 96
Catterick, 42, 105, 107, 118
Chamberlain, Rt. Hon. Neville, 1, 11
Champagne Caves, 82, 180
Churchill, Rt. Hon. Winston S., 1, 76, 77, 110, 111
Cinque Ports Arms, Dover, 92
Cinque Ports Fortress, (TA), 2, 12
Citadel Battery/Barracks, 7, 40, 42, 56, 82, 83, 94, 131, 136, 172
Civil Defence, 21, 76, 117
CMPs, 19
Coast Artillery, 99, 102, 130
Coastal Force, 85, 100, 147, 180
Coates, Squadron-Leader, 89, 90
Codrington, HMS, 12, 13, 41
Combined Operations, 132, 163, 164, 169
Commando No. 4, 128
Connaught Barracks, 46, 65, 83, 144
Constable Tower, 62, 63, 65
Crabble Avenue, 104, 106, 107, 117
Crabble Hill, 22
Crabble Paper Mill, 119
CRS, 94
Creamery Cafe, 82
Crypt Restaurant, 66, 82, 145, 173, 180

Deal, 60, 72, 83, 84, 86, 97, 106, 109, 112, 163
Devers, General, 102
Dieppe, 90, 101

Dover Castle, 17, 38, 42, 65, 68, 72, 79, 82, 107, 109, 110, 128, 132, 162, 163, 164, 166, 171, 178
Dover College, 74, 82, 144
Dover Civic Restaurant, 76
Dover Harbour Board, 67
Dover Juvenile Court, 135
Dover Torpedo Dept., 143
Dover Town Hall, 94
Dorset Regt., 77, 98
Dungeness, 16, 50, 78, 90, 92, 100, 132, 165, 169
Dunkirk, 12, 13, 19, 21, 27, 28, 29, 30, 31, 33, 34, 35, 40, 41, 45, 56, 63
Duke Street, Deal, 163
Duke of York's School, 35, 61, 97
Duke of Wellington's Regt., 131
Dymchurch, 92, 132

East Cliff, 12, 65, 103, 111, 153
East Kent Bus Co., 5, 166
East Surrey Regt., 60
Eastern Arm, 9, 12, 20, 27, 54, 67, 72, 73, 83, 107, 143, 151, 169
Eastern Docks, 5, 19
Edwards, General Idwal, 102
Eythorne, 60

FANY, 109
Farthingloe, 54, 55, 56, 57, 80
Ferry House, 88, 90, 91
Fervant, HMS, 88
Fleet Mail Office, 152
Flying Fortress (B-17), 92, 114, 173
Flying Fox, 121
Focke-Wulf 190, 66, 81, 86, 90
Folkestone, 49, 51, 52, 68, 71, 84, 86, 94, 95, 109, 128, 133, 146, 156, 157, 162, 163, 169, 177
Folkestone Road, Dover, 22, 56, 110, 164
Frith Farm, Guston, 15, 79
Frith Road, Dover, 47, 65

Gladstone Street, Deal, 106
Gneisenau, 78
Golden Hind Inn, Deal, 106
Goodwin Lightship, 60
Goodwin Sands, 9, 30, 90, 92, 173
Grand Shaft Barracks, 65, 70
Granville Dock, 82
Granville Hotel, 66
Guildford Hotel, 121
Gulfoss, 66

Hampton (ferry), 8
Hare and Hounds, 80
Hawkinge, RAF, 77, 92, 157

Hawkshill Down, 106, 150
Heinkel 111, 99
Heinkel 115, 38
Home Guard, 21, 43, 37, 99, 107, 120, 121, 132
Hotel de Paris 103, 112
Hotel de Ville, 149
Hougham, 55, 130, 131, 132, 167
Hythe, Kent, 42, 92, 102, 132, 158

IFF, 146
Infantry Brigade, 60
Irish Lancers, 63

Junkers 88, 39, 44, 68, 116

Kearsney, Dover, 56, 141, 173
Kearsney Halt, 104
Kearsney Abbey, 44
Kent & Sussex Heavy Brigade, 13
Kent Company, (ATS), 99
Keyes, Admiral of the Fleet Sir Robert, 31, 77
King George V, HMS, 25
King George VI, 168
Kingscourt, HMS, 94
Kingsdown, 60, 150
Knuckle Battery, 12, 158
Knuckle Lighthouse, 73
Kusharney, Madam, 128, 129, 130

Lady Brassey, 67
Lady Duncanon, 67
Lady Man, 30
Langdon Barracks, 12, 46, 99
Langdon Battery, 13
Langdon Hole, 12
Laughton-Mathews, Dame Vera, 168
LDV, 21, 120
Leas Cliff Hall, Folkestone, 94, 112
Lee, General Clifford, 102
Leney's Brewery, 67
Limekiln Street, Dover, 180
Lois, HMT, 53, 169
Lord Warden Hotel, (HMS Wasp), 2, 41, 69, 87, 88, 167, 175, 180
Lovat, Major Lord, 127, 128
Lydden Spout, 34, 35, 77, 109
Lydden Spout Battery 109, 132
Lydden station, 125
Lympne, RAF, 48
Lynx, HMS, 66, 67, 155, 169, 175, 180

Maid of Orleans (ferry), 28, 42, 128
Maison Dieu Road, Dover, 156
Margate, 43, 109
Marina, HRH The Princess, Duchess of Kent, 166, 168

Marine Station, 19
Market Square, Dover, 6, 14, 67, 76, 82, 86, 92, 95, 112, 177, 180
Martin Mill, 53, 122, 124, 126
Maxton, Dover, 40, 164
Messerschmitt Bf 109, 20, 44, 48, 50, 66, 83, 90
Metropole Hotel, Folkestone, 94
Mitre Inn, 169
Monas Queen (ferry), 23, 25, 26, 28
Montgomery, General Bernard, 48, 104
Morgan, Lieutenant-General Frederick, 102
Mulberry Harbour, 142, 147, 149, 151, 175
Munsterland, 166

NAAFI, 35, 63, 65, 83, 106, 109, 173
Newhaven, Sussex, 54, 88, 89, 90, 100, 114
Nijmegen, 130
Normandy, 106, 110, 114, 120, 142, 143, 146, 148, 151, 153, 156, 171, 175
North Foreland, 70, 90, 165
Northampton Street, Dover, 10
Norwegian, 100, 102, 136

Old Park Barracks, Dover, 144
Operation 'Jubilee', 101
Operation 'Overlord' (D-Day), 101, 135
Operation 'Starkey', 102
Ordnance Corps, 77
Oxley Bottom, 99

Paget, General Sir Bernard, 102
Pas de Calais, 40, 101, 135, 143, 145, 148, 170
Pegwell Bay, 36
Pencaster Road, Dover, 144
Pile, General Sir F.A., (C-in-C AA Command), 172
Pioneer Corps, 42, 46, 72
Pooh, 53, 122, 123
Port War Signal Station, Dover, 67, 165
PPI, 56
Pridham-Wippel, Admiral H.D., 82, 156, 168
Prince of Wales Pier, 2, 13, 21, 66, 72, 83, 169, 173
Prince Eugen, 78
Prince Louis Inn, Dover, 100
Priory Street, Dover, 47, 59
Priory station, Dover, 110, 122, 163, 174

Queen Elizabeth, (now Queen Mother), 168
Queen Gull, 121
Queen's Royal Regt., 42, 65

RA, 2, 12, 15, 17, 35, 44, 45, 46, 70, 72, 99, 103, 104, 110, 114, 115, 120, 121, 122, 124, 138, 140, 149, 157, 165
RAF Regt., 146, 150, 156, 162

RAMC, 27, 28, 94, 96
Ramsey, CV, MVO, Vice-Admiral Sir Bertram, 8, 31, 74
Ramsgate, 30, 34, 36, 43, 88, 90, 151
RAOC, 54
RASC, 23, 106, 140
Raw, Brigadier C.W., 72, 165
Reach Court Farm, 113
Red Lion Hotel, Wingham, 43
Red Shield Club, 232
REME, 144
RM Siege Regt., 52, 122
Robertson, HMS, 127, 142
Romney Marsh, 130
Roosevelt, President Franklin D., 76
Royal Corps of Signals, 68, 108, 117, 145, 173
Royal Engineers, 2, 12, 33, 46, 52, 56, 59, 61, 66, 71, 125, 174
Royal Fusiliers, 176
Royal Hippodrome, Dover, 10, 14, 75, 92, 137, 144
Royal Marines, 32, 53, 60, 67, 83, 109, 112, 122, 125, 142, 155, 163
Royal Marine Commandos, 122
Royal Naval Gunnery School, 10
Royal Naval Patrol Service, 53, 168
Royal Pavilion Hotel, Folkestone, 50, 169
Royal Sussex Regt., 61, 86
Rye, Sussex, 115, 151

Salvation Army, 56, 59, 100, 117, 136, 146, 149, 154, 176, 180
Sandgate, 64, 86, 128
Sandwich, 17, 42, 68, 120, 126, 127, 142, 143, 177
Scharnhorst, 78
Searchlight Regt., 79, 149
Sellindge, 48
Shakespeare Cliff, 35, 48, 61, 110, 114, 149, 163, 167, 169
Shakespeare Inn, 144
Shalimar Hotel, 82, 144
Shepperton (ferry), 8, 10
Shorncliffe Barracks, 46, 176
Snargate Street, Dover, 5, 10, 13, 66, 100, 149, 169, 174, 175, 176, 180
Somerset Light Infantry, 86
South Foreland, 73, 90, 100
South Staffordshire Regt., 144
South Wales Borderers Regt., 124, 140
St Margaret's Bay, 17, 19, 21, 42, 46, 53, 60, 61, 63, 66, 68, 70, 81, 74, 81, 86, 106, 113, 122, 149, 162, 176, 177
Stanhope Road, Deal, 72
Stimson, H.L., (US Secretary of State for War), 111
Struma, 121

Stuka, 48, 66
Sulva, 121
Surrey Rifles (1st), 43
Swingate (radar), 35, 76, 145, 158, 162, 176

TA, 1, 4, 33, 46
Temple Ewell, 104, 107
Thanet, 109
Theatre War Service Council, 128
Toland, Dr Gertrude, 85
Tower Hamlets Road, Dover, 20
Townsend Farm, 122, 123, 126
Turner, Vice-Admiral Round, 171

US Army (No. 127 Gun Batt.), 158, 160, 161, 171, 172

VAD (Vice-Admiral Dover), 31, 74, 100
Varne Buoy, 78
Victoria Park, 76
V1, 132, 135, 150, 151, 152, 156, 158, 159, 160, 161, 162, 164, 171, 172, 176
V2, 135

WAAF, 16, 64, 92, 96, 102, 103, 104, 116, 127, 132, 141, 144, 145, 168, 176

Walmer, 99, 106, 113, 150
War Office Signals, 104, 107, 117
War Sepoy, 12, 73
Wasp, HMS, 103, 111, 137, 152, 153
Wedgeport, HMS, 78
Welch Fusiliers Regt., 144
Wellington Barracks, Dover, 71
Wellington Dock, Dover, 90, 92, 138
West Hougham, 157
West Studdal, 79
Western Dock, Dover, 33
Whitefield, 79
Willing Boys, HMS, 67, 169
Wiltshire Regt., 70
Winant, John G., (American Ambassador), 111
Wingham, 43, 44
WLA, 99, 113
Woolwich Arsenal, 37
WRNS, 16, 31, 61, 62, 64, 74, 75, 81, 91, 93, 103, 111, 116, 132, 141, 142, 143, 144, 152, 153, 156, 162, 166, 168, 172, 173, 174, 177, 178, 180
WVS, 59, 76, 166

YMCA Depot, Dover, 97, 117, 139, 144